Away for the WEEKEND™
N E W   Y O R K

by
Eleanor Berman

**Great Getaways
Less Than 200 Miles from
New York City for
Every Season of the Year**

Second Revised Edition

Clarkson N. Potter, Inc./Publishers
DISTRIBUTED BY CROWN PUBLISHERS, INC., NEW YORK

Published by Clarkson N. Potter, Inc., 225 Park Avenue South, New York, New York 10003 and represented in Canada by the Canadian MANDA Group.

CLARKSON N. POTTER, POTTER and colophon, and **AWAY FOR THE WEEKEND** are trademarks of Clarkson N. Potter, Inc.

Manufactured in the United States of America

Library of Congress Cataloging-in-Publication Data

Berman, Eleanor,
    Away for the weekend, New York: great getaways less than 200 miles from New York City for every season of the year / by Eleanor Berman.—2nd updated ed.
    p. cm.
    Includes index.
    1. Middle Atlantic States—Description and travel—
Guide-books. 2. New England—Description and travel—
1981- —Guide-books. 3. New York Region—Description
and travel—Guide-books. I. Title.
F106.B47 1988   87-29189
917.4′0443—dc19   CIP
ISBN 0-517-56802-0 (pbk.)

10 9 8 7 6 5 4 3 2 1

Second Revised Edition

Contents

Acknowledgments

I am grateful to all the state and local tourist offices as well as the innkeepers and local residents who supplied information and guidance during my travels for this second update and revision of *Away for the Weekend*. Thanks also to the innkeepers and readers who have taken time to write, helping me to follow who is in and out of business. Keeping up to date on the attractions, inns, and restaurants included in fifty-two trips in six states would be a daunting task without the help of these many friends.

A special word of appreciation is due to Terry Berman, my diligent research assistant. And a final sincere thank you to my editor, Shirley Wohl, for her encouragement as well as her patience and ability to maintain her good humor while keeping a million details in order.

Before You Begin . . .

WEEKEND GETAWAYS—a change of scene, refreshment for mind and spirit—that's what this book is all about. In the pages ahead you'll find suggestions for trips for every season of the year; jaunts with and without children; visits to country fairs and music festivals, Colonial towns and seaport villages, gardens and galleries . . . with parks, beaches, rivers, lakes, and mountains all along the way.

Some of these destinations may be familiar to you, but I hope that *Away for the Weekend* will prove to be for you, as it was for me in the writing, a source of discoveries and unexpected pleasures even in places you may have visited before.

Human nature being what it is, it is the faraway places that beckon most alluringly, often causing us to overlook attractions nearer at hand. We travel thousands of miles to look at scenery, monuments, mansions, and museums and ignore many equally fine places just a few hours from home. Nature's bounty, 300 years of history, and the many talented residents of our region, past and present, have combined to bless us in the New York area with an abundance of treasures for exploring. I've tried to highlight some of the special places that are easy to miss, particularly the unusual once-private collections that now comprise unique and pleasurable small museums. Wherever possible, I've also provided just a bit of background on the colorful people who have amassed these treasures for us.

All of the trips outlined here are less than 200 miles from New York and its environs, most within three hours of driving time (minus traffic jams), in order to be easily manageable for a weekend sojourn. Their proximity offers still another bonus. Not only are these places easy to get to, but once having found them it's easy to go back!

There are a few things you should know before you start reading. This is, of necessity, a somewhat personal and selective guide to places I have visited and enjoyed. It does not include many large resorts or amusement parks for two reasons: I usually don't like them, and you usually don't need a book to find them.

Nor will you necessarily find every single sightseeing attraction or lodging available in the areas covered. I've tried to stick to places I've either been to myself or have had personally recommended by local sources or frequent visitors to the destination, people whose judgment I consider reliable.

This is a guide to destinations, not to country inns. Sometimes motels are the only accommodations available in a particular area. When inns are mentioned, it is because they are the best in the vicinity, not the pick of all possible inns as you find in books devoted to this subject. Keep that in mind if occasionally you find some place a little disappointing compared to the dream inns you've visited elsewhere. When they are special, however, I've tried to say so.

Basic Information

As for the basic format of the trips, they are laid out assuming you are spending a normal two-day weekend, arriving on Friday night and departing late on Sunday. There usually is a recommended itinerary, with added suggestions to accommodate varying tastes and time schedules. Sometimes there is more than enough to do for a long weekend, and a symbol at the start will indicate trips that fit that category.

If you want to spend more time in any area, check also for trips listed under other seasons for the territory near where you are going. Bucks County, for example, could fill several days if itineraries for both the lower and upper portions were combined. The same is true of the Hudson Valley, much of Connecticut, the Massachusetts Berkshires, and the Brandywine Valley.

The trips are arranged by season not only because activities change around the calendar, but to give you time to read about upcoming special events and reserve rooms before it is too late. Advance notice may also enable you to plan a whole weekend around a special show or open house, rather than see it as a last-minute day trip and miss all the sights and activities in the area nearby.

Since attractions do vary from season to season, you will find some areas mentioned more than once, or, as in the case of Philadelphia, recommended in different ways depending on whether children are along.

Don't, however, feel bound by the calendar. Many of these destinations are equally pleasant and less crowded when nothing special is going on, and they are appealing both in and out of season. Think especially about the seashore in the fall, when you can enjoy the scenery and the best accommodations in the Hamptons or Cape May without the summer crowds—and sometimes at bargain rates.

Symbols will indicate which trips seem most appropriate with children, though you are the best judge of your own family's interest and may find others that sound right for you. There are also symbols for trips that are manageable without a car. Unfortunately, such trips are few. One possibility is to take public transportation to a central point and rent a car for a day for the sights you can't see without one.

The symbols to watch for indicating these varying categories are these:

= recommended for children

= can be done at least in part via public transportation

= recommended for long weekends

As for prices, dollar signs indicate the range, as follows, for a double room:

$ = under $50

$$ = $50 to $75

$$$ = $75 to $100

$$$$ = $100 to $125

$$$$$ = over $125

and for restaurants:

$ = entrées mostly under $10

$$ = entrées averaging $10 to $15

$$$ = entrées mostly over $15

$$$$ = expect to pay $25 or more per person

Some accommodations may also include some meals in their rates, and letter symbols following prices will indicate these. CP (Continental Plan) provides both bed and breakfast; MAP (Modified American Plan) includes breakfast and dinner; and AP (American Plan), all three meals.

Since there is always a lapse of several months between the writing and the publication of a book, I have used general price categories rather than specific figures, knowing that rates change rapidly in these inflationary times. Even so, it is possible that a few of the places listed will raise prices in the future, placing them into the next category. So use the book as a guide—I hope you will find it an accurate one on the whole—but *always* check for specific prices when you plan your trip.

The information here was as accurate as could be determined as of fall 1987. However, innkeepers and chefs change, as do hours and fees for attractions, so do use the telephone numbers that are listed to check for current information.

If you find information that has become seriously inaccurate—that a place has closed or gone way downhill—I hope you will let me know care of the publisher so that it can be corrected in the future. If you discover places that I have missed, I hope you'll share them as well.

As for maps, there was just no way to provide maps detailed enough to take in every attraction or accommodation mentioned. There are basic area maps here to give you your bearings and one map showing ways out of the city, but don't make the mistake of starting off without a really good road map of your destination. One way to get a detailed map free is by writing to the travel or tourism offices in the states included here. These offices offer not only maps but also informative brochures on their states. Note on the list following that many offer toll-free numbers for travelers.

In most cases, there is a source listed for further information at the end of each itinerary. Do write away, for the more you know about your destination ahead of time, the more pleasurable your trip will be.

Anyone who has ever tried to leave the city on a Friday knows that departing as well as returning at peak weekend traffic hours can be a frustrating experience, and can add an hour or more to your driving time. If you can't get away before 4 P.M. on Friday, particularly in the summer, consider having an early dinner in town and depart after 7 P.M., when the roads are more likely to be clear. If your destination is a particularly popular place, such as the Hamptons, you might find it more pleasant to take a train or bus, hop a local cab to your lodgings, and then pick up a car (or maybe a bike) the next day. Just remember to ask about the availability of local car rentals when you make your room reservation and be sure to reserve a car in advance.

Public transportation is subject to its own delays, of course, but sometimes it can be less aggravating to let someone else do the driving and fretting rather than begin or end a relaxing weekend stuck in a traffic jam.

Since the nicest lodgings tend to be expensive, this new edition includes a list of bed-and-breakfast registries, handy whether you are on a budget or just seeking last-minute reservations.

One last word: When it comes to inn reservations, plan ahead if you don't want to be disappointed. If you want to visit popular places at peak summer or fall seasons, three to four months ahead isn't too soon. Most places do offer refunds on deposits with reasonable notice, so remember that old adage and be safe rather than sorry.

With that out of the way, the only thing left to say is read on—and have a wonderful time!

Information

Any of the state offices listed here will provide maps as well as information and literature on attractions throughout their states:

Tourism Division
Connecticut Department of
Economic Development
210 Washington Street
Hartford, CT 06106
Toll free: (800) 243-1685 [in
Connecticut, (800) 842-7492]

Delaware Tourism Office
99 Kings Highway
Dover, DE 19901
Toll free: (800) 441-8846 [in
Delaware (800) 282-8667]

Division of Travel and Tourism
State of New Jersey
PO Box 400
Trenton, NJ 08625
(800) JERSEY-7

Division of Tourism
New York State Department of
Commerce
99 Washington Street
Albany, NY 12245
(518) 474-2121

Massachusetts Division of Tourism
100 Cambridge Street
Boston, MA 02202
Toll free: (800) 343-9072

Bureau of Travel Development
Department of Commerce, State
of Pennsylvania
Forum Building
Harrisburg, PA 17120
Toll free: (800) VISIT-PA

Rhode Island Tourism Division
7 Jackson Walkway
Providence, RI 02903
(401) 277-2601

Bed-and-Breakfast Registry Services

Bed-and-breakfast registries are reservation services with a number of listings in their areas. Rates can range from $35 to $75, depending on the accommodations. Be specific about what you are looking for—extras such as private bath and private entrance, or economy. Most state tourist offices also keep listings for their own states; write for the latest update:

COVERING SEVERAL STATES
Pineapple Hospitality
47 North Second Street
Suite 3A
New Bedford, MA 02740
(617) 990-1696 (area code 508
after July 16, 1988)

Covered Bridge Bed & Breakfast
(Berkshires, Hudson Valley, Rhode
Island shore, southern Vermont)
PO Box 447
Norfolk, CT 06058
(203) 542-5944

The American Country Collection
(Northeast New York, western
Massachusetts, Vermont)
984 Gloucester Place
Schenectady, NY 12309
(518) 370-4948

CONNECTICUT
Nutmeg Bed and Breakfast
222 Girard Avenue
Hartford, CT 06105
(203) 236-6698

Bed and Breakfast Ltd.
PO Box 216
New Haven, CT 06513
(203) 469-3260

*Seacoast Landings Bed and
Breakfast Registry*
(Coast communities, Old Lyme
and above, and Westerly, RI)
133 Neptune Drive
Groton, CT 06340
(203) 442-1940

NEW YORK
Bed & Breakfast of Long Island
(Hamptons and North Fork)
PO Box 392
Old Westbury, NY 11568
(516) 334-6231

A Reasonable Alternative, Inc.
(Long Island)
117 Spring Street
Port Jefferson, NY 11777
(516) 928-4034

Alternate Lodging, Inc.
(Hamptons)
PO Box 1782
East Hampton, NY 11937
(516) 324-9449

*Hampton Bed and Breakfast
Registry*
PO Box 378
East Moriches, NY 11940
(516) 878-8197

Bed and Breakfast USA Ltd.
(Hudson Valley, Rockland,
Catskills, Albany-Saratoga)
PO Box 606
Croton-on-Hudson, NY 10520
(914) 271-6228

*Ulster County Bed and
Breakfast*
(Woodstock, Kingston,
New Paltz)
Ulster County
Public Information Office
607 Broadway
PO Box 1800
Kingston, NY 12401
(914) 331-9300

MASSACHUSETTS
*Berkshire Bed and Breakfast
Homes*
(Western Massachusetts, nearby
New England States)
Main Street
Williamsburg, MA 01096
(413) 268-7244

PENNSYLVANIA
*Bed and Breakfast of
Philadelphia*
PO Box 630
Chester Springs, PA 19425
(215) 827-9650

Bed and Breakfast, Center City
(Philadelphia)
1804 Pine Street
Philadelphia, PA 19103
(215) 735-1137

Guesthouses
(Brandywine Valley and
Philly Main Line)
RD 9
West Chester, PA 19380
(215) 692-4575

*Bed and Breakfast of
Chester County*
610 Ridge Avenue
Kennett Square, PA 19348
(215) 444-1367 or 444-5291

Hershey Bed and Breakfast
PO Box 208
Hershey, PA 17033
(717) 533-2928

*Bed and Breakfast of
Southeast Pennsylvania*
(Reading, Hershey, Lancaster)
Box 278, RD 1
Barto, PA 19504
(215) 845-3526

RHODE ISLAND
Newport Bed and Breakfast
Castle Keep
44 Everett Street

Newport, RI 02840
(401) 846-0362

Bed and Breakfast of Rhode Island
PO Box 3291
Newport, RI 02840
(401) 849-1298

NEW JERSEY
Bed and Breakfast of New Jersey
(Serves the entire state)
103 Godwin Avenue
Suite 132
Midland Park, NJ 07432
(201) 444-7409

DELAWARE
Bed and Breakfast in Delaware
Box 177
3650 Silverside Road
Wilmington, DE 19810
(302) 479-9500

Spring

Arts and Flowers in Pennsylvania

The paintings are overwhelming, floor to ceiling and wall to wall.

There are more than 1,000 of them including nearly 200 Renoirs; masterpieces by Matisse, Picasso, van Gogh, and Rousseau; more Cézannes than you'll find in any one place outside the Louvre; Modiglianis, Klees, and Mirós. And just so the older masters won't feel slighted, there are a smattering of names like El Greco, Daumier, Titian, and Tintoretto.

The Barnes Foundation in Merion, Pennsylvania, just five miles outside Philadelphia, is recognized as the most notable private art collection of this century. But for 24 years almost nobody was allowed to see it.

You'll still need an advance reservation to be sure of admittance— and a pair of field glasses may come in handy for viewing the paintings nearest the ceiling—but if you care about art, this museum is a not-to-be-missed experience. Taken in combination with some nearby pleasures—dogwoods in bloom at Valley Forge, tulips and azaleas at Longwood Gardens, and Wyeth paintings plus the riverside panorama from the glass walls of the Brandywine River Museum—the Barnes can be the starting point for a spectacular spring weekend.

It wasn't that Albert Coombs Barnes didn't intend to share his treasures. A Philadelphian who made a mint developing a medical potion called Argyrol, Barnes became one of the first patrons of modern art, sparked by the encouragement of his childhood friend, William Glackens, who had become one of the painters of the Ashcan School.

Barnes traveled to Europe to study art, then began buying up canvases wholesale—50 Renoirs at a time, the first major purchases of Modigliani's work, 60 Soutines at $50 per canvas.

In 1923 he lent 75 canvases to the Pennsylvania Academy of Art to introduce to Philadelphia the latest in European art. But Barnes's artistic judgment was ahead of his time. The critical reception of his paintings was so vicious that it caused Barnes to withdraw completely from the art establishment. When he built his 24-room museum the next year, only handpicked art students and a few individuals who had nothing to do with musuems or art collectors were allowed to call. Barnes's will saw to it that his foundation remained all but inaccessible to the public until the state of Pennsylvania stepped in in 1961, ten years after his death, to insist that a tax-free educational foundation had to allow people in to be educated.

The hours remain limited, as do the number of visitors allowed. Nor have the curators made it easy to appreciate the paintings fully. There are no titles or dates on the works, just the artists' names, and some believe that Barnes deliberately placed the best paintings highest on the walls. Still, this remains a museum you could visit over and over without exhausting the abundance of fine art to be seen—and it will probably leave you too glutted to be interested in further viewing that day, even though Philadelphia's museums are just a short drive away.

Instead, make this an out-of-the-city weekend. Stay at the perfectly pleasant motel-hotels on Philadelphia's nearby City Line Avenue; enjoy their indoor pools and the shopping malls down the road in Bala-Cynwyd; take a stroll in the arboretum on the campus of Haverford College, not far away on Route 30; or take a 15-minute drive to Valley Forge National Park, off Route 76, where the spring dogwood display across the park's beautiful 2,200 acres brings visitors from miles around between mid-April and mid-May each year.

The park itself is an interesting one, with restorations of Washington's headquarters, the quarters of General Varnum, and the encampments of the enlisted men at this important Revolutionary War site. A marked tour route shows you the historical sights as well as the outstanding scenery on the grounds. You can cover the ground by auto, bus tour, or by bike; bicycle rentals are available in the park. And there are ample accommodations in this area if you want to stay overnight.

Come Sunday, south of Valley Forge, the first stop is Chadds Ford and the Brandywine River Museum, a century-old riverside gristmill that has been beautifully restored and recently enlarged, with a dramatic glass silo tower and brick terraces overlooking the Brandywine. In galleries with hand-hewn beams, pine floors, and plastered walls, you'll find the works of artists who were inspired by this scenic valley. The musuem is a showplace for art by three generations of Wyeths, including the Andrew Wyeth landscapes that have immortalized the area and Jamie Wyeth's famous portrait of a pink pig, as well as work by famous illustrators from the region, including Howard Pyle, Maxfield Parrish, and Frank Schoonover.

Farther west on Route 1 is Kennett Square and one of the most exquisite public gardens in the United States. You don't have to be a flower lover to appreciate Longwood Gardens. The privately endowed former estate of Pierre S. du Pont on 1,200 acres with 12,000 kinds of plants is a visual delight for everyone.

Walk into the conservatory and just breathe in the perfume of early spring and take in the colors of the artfully grouped tulips and lilies and flowering shrubs. The ivy-covered trees stand as straight as the building's marble columns, a counterpoint to the colors of the blooms, and the ferns and orchids are an exotic contrast to the rest of the display. The four-acre conservatory is a pleasure rain or shine, but hope for sun so that you can walk on the magnificent grounds; listen to the fountains at play in the Italian water garden; enjoy the formal patterns of the show gardens, the meandering cherry trees along the lake, and the splashing of the waterfall near the chimes tower. No detail has been overlooked to make the gardens a treat for all the senses.

When you've had your fill of flowers, you can switch to antiquing all along Route 1 between Chadds Ford and Kennett Square. In Kennett Square itself a stop at The Mushroom Place will let you come home with a souvenir, a box of the pearly white giants grown in this mushroom farming center. There's even a little museum to explain the mystique of growing mushrooms.

At dinnertime take your pick of several atmospheric old inns within a few minutes drive, any one a fitting end to a memorable weekend.

Philadelphia Area Code: 215

DRIVING DIRECTIONS Take the New Jersey Turnpike to Route 276 (Pennsylvania Turnpike exit) to I-76 (Schuylkill Expressway). Stay left for exit 33, City Avenue (US 1 South) and continue south past Bala-Cynwyd shops to 54th Street, Old Lancaster Road. Turn right and immediately watch for Latch's Lane on the left. Turn left and continue for about a block and a half to the Barnes foundation.

Total Distance: just over 100 miles.

PUBLIC TRANSPORTATION Amtrak to Philadelphia; Paoli local to Merion Station, short walk to Barnes Foundation. Phone Barnes Foundation for exact directions.

ACCOMMODATIONS *Holiday Inn-City Line,* City Avenue at I-76, Philadelphia, 477-0200, $$–$$$ ● *Dunfey-City Line,* City Line Avenue and Monument Road, Philadelphia, 667-0200, indoor pool and lighted paddle tennis, $$$ ● *Adam's Mark,* City Line Avenue and Monument Road, 581-5000, indoor pool, racquetball, health club, $$$ ● *Sheraton-Valley Forge,* one mile off I-76 at exit 35, Valley Forge, 337-2000, $$$–$$$$ ● *Stouffer's Valley Forge Hotel,* 480 North Gulph Road, Valley Forge, 337-1800, $$–$$$$ ● *Embassy Suite*

Hotel, 888 Chesterbrook Boulevard, Wayne, 647-6700, good value in Valley Forge area, $$$–$$$$. Ask for weekend package rates at all.

DINING   *Dunfey (see above) houses: Café Corianders,* steak and seafood, $$–$$$ ● *General Wayne Inn,* 625 Montgomery Avenue, Merion Station, 667-3330, atmospheric, dates to 1704, best to reserve ahead, $$ ● Near Valley Forge: *Jefferson House,* 2519 De Kalb Turnpike, Norristown, 275-3407, $$–$$$ ● *Vickers,* Welch Pool Road and Gordon Drive, Lionville, 363-7998, highly recommended, $$–$$$ ● *The Terrace Restaurant* at Longwood Gardens and the *Café* at the Brandywine River Museum are both very pleasant for lunch, $ ● *Chadds Ford Inn,* US 1, Chadds Ford, 388-7361. $$–$$$ ● *Mendenhall Inn,* Route 52, Mendenhall, 388-1181, $$–$$$.

SIGHTSEEING   *Barnes Foundation,* 300 North Latch's Lane, Merion, 667-0290; 200 visitors admitted (100 on Sunday), half by appointment, half first-come. Hours: Friday and Saturday 9:30 A.M. to 4:30 P.M., Sunday 1 P.M. to 4:30 P.M. Adults, $1; no children under 12 admitted. Call or write for reservations and explicit driving directions. ● *Brandywine River Museum,* US 1, Chadds Ford, 388-7601. Hours: daily 9:30 A.M. to 4:30 P.M. Adults, $3; senior citizens and children 7–12, $1.50. ● *Longwood Gardens,* US 1, Kennett Square, 388-6741. Hours: April to October, 9 A.M. to 6 P.M., rest of year to 5 P.M. Adults, $5, children 6–12, $1. ● *Valley Forge National Historical Park,* Route 23 at Route 363, Valley Forge, 783-7700. Hours: daily 8:30 A.M. to 5 P.M. Park admission free. Bus tours April to October from visitors' center with narrated 1½-hour circuit of historic sites. Check current rates.

The Other Side of the Delaware: Discoveries in New Jersey

It was bound to happen. With all those tourists heading for Pennsylvania's Bucks County, it was only a matter of time until someone noticed that there were some appealing little towns dozing right across the Delaware in New Jersey.

First, it was a few antiques dealers who made the crossing. Priced out of New Hope, they began to open shops just a footbridge away across the river in Lambertville, New Jersey—and this sleepy side of the Delaware began to wake up. Lambertville's once-neglected Federal row houses and pointy-roofed Victorian homes began to be bought up and spiffed up. More shops followed. Next came several good restaurants to accommodate the shoppers, and then came the inns so that diners could spend the night.

Now the New Jersey side of the Delaware is a delightful destination in its own right, still peaceful but with plenty to offer for a happy weekend of inning and antiquing. As a bonus, you are within easy striking distance of Flemington outlet stores, the many attractions of Princeton, and some lesser known pleasures on the back roads where some of the state's historic past still lives on.

The choicest of the lodgings are in Stockton, a tiny town just a couple of miles upriver from Lambertville. The Woolverton Inn is a very private, mellowed stone country house tucked away high on a hill, surrounded by lawns and meadows populated with the resident sheep. The sheep-fancying owners have a lineup of miniatures on the mantel in the main house as well.

Colligan's Stockton Inn still has the wishing well, said to have been the inspiration for the Rodgers and Hart song "There's a Small Hotel." The long-established restaurant continues to thrive under the new ownership of Todd Drucquer, who made his first culinary mark at the highly regarded Pump House in the Poconos. He hopes to do so again with a gourmet addition to the original inn, calling his new restaurant The Fox.

The Drucquers have also added lodgings, restoring and renovating the upstairs as well as a series of historic adjacent homes and buildings, including the old carriage house and the wagon house. The oversize rooms are luxurious, done in high Federal style with canopy beds and decorator fabrics. Many have working fireplaces, making them cozy to come home to on a chilly spring night.

In Lambertville, the York Street House and Coryell House are small and rather elegant bed-and-breakfast inns, and the Bridgestreet House offers a garden and outdoor Jacuzzi. The largest of the new lodgings, the Inn at Lambertville Station, is adjacent to the old train station that was recently converted into a popular restaurant. The 45-room inn seems large and a bit impersonal for this town, though the riverside location is pleasant enough and many of the suites also offer fireplaces.

There's a choice of fine dining in Lambertville now. Frequent visitors recommend the Bridgestreet House Restaurant, Savoir Fare, Gerard's, Stars and the pub menu at the Swan Hotel, as well as busy Lambertville Station. For a Thai touch and a moderate tab, there's Siam.

You'll need no guide for shopping, since Lambertville's "downtown" totals about four square blocks. Antiques abound here. The Antique Center at The People's Store on North Union is a co-op offering wares from 20 dealers, Bridge Street Antiques holds some 14 shops in one location, and the Porkyard on Coryell, a onetime sausage factory, has been converted to a complex including country furniture, art, and antiques. Other intriguing shops offer imported clothing and tapestries, art and crafts by local artisans, Scandinavian country furniture and gifts, and hand-fashioned gold jewelry. The Lambertville Trading Company is the place for gourmet foods, including raspberry jam that is billed as "the best in the universe."

Stockton's main attraction is Country Tiles, featuring a wide selection of decorative tiles from Mexico, Brazil, Holland, France, and Italy.

You might want to have a look at the restoration of Prallsville Mills just north of Stockton, a National Historic Landmark restoration of an old mill complex that also hosts a variety of exhibits and is a gathering place for Saturday markets in summer. A biking and hiking path has been completed on the old railroad bed running along the canal from the mill past Bull's Island about 15 miles north to Frenchtown.

There are more antiques shops waiting to be explored in Frenchtown, as well as across the river in Bucks County, but you may want to save some time for another kind of shopping—the discount bargains in Flemington.

This major outlet center includes lots of big names, such as Anne Klein, Adidas, Calvin Klein, Corning, Mikasa, and Dansk. You'll find Quoddy Moccasins, Health-Tex clothing for kids, Fieldcrest and Cannon towels and linens, and just about everything else you can think of, from luggage to furs to butcher block tables. The shops are in several locations, clustered in two main complexes known as Liberty Village and Turntable Junction, along Main and Broad streets, at the Flemington Outlet Center, and along Route 202. One easy way to do them is to park and take the Flemington Trolley, which makes a continuous loop connecting the major shopping. A one dollar fare allows you to get on and off all day. On your own, you can write ahead for a map or pick one up in most of the stores when you arrive.

Take time for a stroll on Main Street, for in spite of all the shops, the center of town has managed to retain a quaint look that reflects the town's 1712 origins. The 1828 Greek Revival courthouse, also in the center of town, was the scene of the famous Lindbergh kidnapping trial. The old Union Hotel makes an atmospheric stop for lunch, or you will find light fare at the Bagelsmith or Market Roost.

You can also take a nostalgia break aboard the Black River & Western Railroad, which runs steam trains on hour-long trips to Ringoes from mid-April through November. You'll need advance reservations for a different kind of perspective on the Delaware Valley landscape. Harrison Aire in Ringoes will show you the sights from a hot air balloon, ususally taking off three hours before sunset and sometimes at sunrise as well.

On Sunday, once again you can pick and choose your destinations. Stop off, if you like, at one of two area flea markets held every Saturday and Sunday from 8 A.M. to 5 P.M., on Route 179, 1½ miles north of Lambertville, or on Route 29 about 2 miles south. Then perhaps a stop at Washington Crossing State Park farther south on Route 29, which commemorates the famous river crossing that was a turning point in the Revolutionary War. The park runs on both sides of the Delaware. On the New Jersey side you can visit the Ferry House, a restored Colonial inn where Washington and his men once spent the night, and a Flag Museum showing the evolution of the nation's flag.

Then it's back-roads time, taking 546 to Route 31, then off the main road to Pennington, which has many Federalist and Georgian buildings dating to Revolutionary times. From Pennington go west, then north on 579 to Harbourton, where the historic district is typical of a crossroads farm settlement of the eighteenth and nineteenth centuries.

Continue north to Route 518 and east past Hopewell, then detour south on 206 to Kingston, once an old stagecoach stop and a town where the Delaware and Raritan Canal (now a state park) was a vital transportation link. Near the canal you can still see the mill house used at various times during the last 200 years to produce lumber, flour, and woolen fabrics. Many other old buildings also still stand amid the small shops and antiques stores that dot the village.

Stay on Route 206 south to Princeton, which could fill a weekend on its own with its magnificent campus and historic homes. Sign up for the free one-hour campus walking tours offered by the Orange Key Guide Service in Maclean House to the right of the main campus gate at 1:30 P.M. and 3:30 P.M., or pick up literature in their office for a do-it-yourself tour. At Bainbridge House, the headquarters of the Princeton Historical Society at 158 Nassau Street, you can buy a little map guide to other historic places and interesting architecture in town.

On campus visit Nassau Hall, which was the country's capital back in 1783, the beautiful Gothic University Chapel with its collection of stained glass by American artists, the University Art Museum, and the enormous outdoor sculpture collection that dots the entire idyllic campus with works by Calder, Epstein, Lachaise, Lipchitz, Moore, Nevelson, Noguchi, and many others.

Off campus there are historic sites like Rockingham, Washington's onetime headquarters; Morven, the former official residence of the governor of New Jersey; Thomas Clark House; the Quaker Meeting House; the homes of Woodrow Wilson, Albert Einstein, and Aaron Burr, and hundreds of fine eighteenth- and nineteenth-century homes in either direction on Nassau Street and the side streets around it. Alexander, Mercer, and Stockton are some of the many streets it is a pleasure to drive down or stroll on.

You could easily and happily spend the day in Princeton, and have dinner at the Nassau Inn on Palmer Square or one of the many other restaurants in town. If you decide to make your headquarters here or come back for a longer stay, Scanticon, a conference center/resort with special weekend rates, offers stylish modern accommodations, lots of sports facilities, and fine dining. The Nassau Inn is the traditional spot, and for cozier atmosphere, there's the Peacock Inn, formerly a pre-Revolutionary War home.

But there's yet another choice that may cause you to cut this visit short, and it's one you'll have to make in advance. Duke Gardens on Route 206 in Somerville is right on the way home. Reservations are needed to tour these 11 classic world gardens under glass, and they are worth a visit anytime you are in the area since the blooms change according to the season.

Campus or gardens, route yourself home by way of 287 north and 24 east to Chatham and you can have dinner at The Tarragon Tree, the restaurant one *New Jersey Monthly* dining critic picked as his personal favorite in the whole state. What nicer way to end the weekend?

Princeton, Lambertville, Stockton Area Code: 609
Flemington, Chatham, and Somerville Area Code: 201

DRIVING DIRECTIONS New Jersey Turnpike south to exit 10, then Route 287 north again to exit 10, and Route 22 west for 2½ miles. Exit at Flemington-Princeton, follow Route 202 south for about 25 miles, get off at Lambertville before the Delaware River Bridge, and follow Route 29 north to Lambertville and Stockton.
    Total distance: roughly 75 miles.

PUBLIC TRANSPORTATION Bus service from New York to Flemington and Lambertville via West Hunterdon Transit, trip is under two hours; information from (201) 782-6313 or (201) 782-6057 and from Port Authority Bus Terminal, (212) 564-8484.

ACCOMMODATIONS *Stockton Inn,* Route 29, Stockton, 397-

1250, $$$–$$$$ CP • *Woolverton Inn*, RD 3, Stockton, 397-0802, $$$ CP • *York Street House*, 42 York Street, Lambertville, 397-3007, $$–$$$ CP • *Coryell House*, 44 Coryell Street, Lambertville, 397-2750, $$–$$$ CP • *The Bridgestreet House Guest Lodging*, 67 Bridge Street, Lambertville, 397-2503, $$–$$$ CP • *The Inn at Lambertville Station*, 11 Bridge Street, Lambertville, 397-4400, $$–$$$ CP • *Scanticon-Princeton*, Princeton Forrestal Center, 100 College Road E, Princeton, 452-7800, $$$$$ CP (ask for weekend packages) • *Nassau Inn*, Palmer Square, Princeton, 921-7500, $$–$$$$$ • *Peacock Inn*, 20 Bayard Lane, Princeton, 924-1707, $$–$$$ CP.

DINING *Colligan's Stockton Inn and The Fox* (see above), $$–$$$$ • *Bridgestreet House* (see above), $$–$$$ • *Savoir Fare*, 13–15 Klines Court, Lambertville, 397-2631, $$$$ • *Stars*, 9 Klines Court, Lambertville, 397-8128 $–$$ • *Lambertville Station*, 11 Bridge Street, Lambertville, 397-8300, $$–$$$ • *Gerard's*, 8½ Coryell Street, Lambertville, 397-8035, $$–$$$ • *Swan Hotel*, Swan and Main streets, Lambertville, 397-3552, pub atmosphere and snack menu. Excellent for Sunday Brunch. $ • *Siam*, 61 N. Main Street, Lambertville, 397-3700, $–$$ • *Nassau Inn* (see above), $$–$$$ • *Black Swan*, Scanticon (see above), continental, elegant, $$$–$$$$ • *Tivoli Gardens*, Scanticon (see above), Scandinavian specialties; buffet brunch, $$–$$$$ • *Le Plumet Royal*, Peacock Inn (see above), continental, $$$–$$$$ • *Lahiere's*, 5 Witherspoon Street, Princeton, 921-2798, gourmet's choice, $$$ • *Roberta's*, Princeton Shopping Center, N. Harrison Street, Princeton, 924-9640, nouvelle American, $$$–$$$$ • For lighter fare in Princeton, the locals like *Mexican Village II*, 42–44 Leigh Avenue, 924-5243, $ • *The Tarragon Tree*, 225 Main Street, Chatham, 635-7333, prix fixe, $$$$.

SIGHTSEEING *Harrison Aire Balloon Rides*, Box 330 Wertsville Road, Ringoes, 466-3389, phone for information and rates • *Black River & Western Steam Railroad*, Box 200, Ringoes, (201) 782-9600, Steam Train Excursions from Flemington, phone for current rates and schedules • *Princeton University*, guided tours from Maclean house. Hours: Monday to Saturday 10 and 11 A.M., 1:30 P.M. and 3:30 P.M.; Sunday 1:30 P.M. and 3:30 P.M. Free • *Bainbridge House*, 158 Nassau Street, Princeton, 921-6748. Hours: Tuesday to Sunday noon to 4 P.M. Donation • *Duke Gardens*, US 206 Somerville, 722-3700. Hours: October 1 to June 1, daily noon to 4 P.M. Adults, $5, children 6–12, $2.50; children under 6 free. Reservations required by mail or phone; no high heels allowed.

FOR FURTHER INFORMATION *Lambertville Area Chamber of Commerce,* 4 South Union Street, Lambertville, NJ 08530, 397-0055. For map of Flemington outlets, contact *Flemington Chamber of Commerce,* 76 Main Street, Flemington, NJ 08822, 782-7456 or write to FTA, PO Box 686, Flemington, NJ 08822.

Spring Spectacular: The Dogwoods of Fairfield

Isaac Bronson would hardly believe his eyes.

A retired Revolutionary War surgeon turned farmer, Bronson decided back in 1795 that his Fairfield, Connecticut, property could be enhanced if he transplanted some of the native wild dogwood trees blooming so prodigiously in the nearby woods.

Bronson propagated, and so did his trees. By 1895 the blooms nurtured by the family were so outstanding that the neighborhood Greenfield Hill Village Improvement Society took on care of the dogwoods as an official project, adding many new plantings, including pink varieties that were not native to Connecticut. Today Greenfield Hill boasts 30,000 dogwood trees, and if you drive up early in May, you can enjoy a view of the steepled church, village green, and Colonial homes enveloped in clouds of pink and white blossoms. Bronson's original trees, carefully tagged, are still an integral part of the show.

Thousands turn out each year to revel in this spring spectacular and to attend the annual Dogwood Festival sponsored by the women of the Greenfield Hill Congregational Church. Usually held for seven days the second week in May, the festival offers daily guided walking tours, concerts, an art show, handmade gifts, and homemade food that is legendary. Phone the church for this year's dates.

The town of Fairfield, named literally for the "fair fields" that attracted settlers from Hartford, was founded in 1639, just 19 years after the Pilgrims landed in this country. The 55 families who chose to settle in Greenfield Hill, two miles from the town center, made a lucky move, since it was the only part of town not burned by the British during the Revolutionary War. Now designated a historic district, it was a prime source of food for the American army, and the steeple of the original Congregational Church on the green served as a lookout for the British fleet.

Dogwood Festival concerts are presented in the present church sanctuary, allowing visitors to see its handsome Early American interior, with just 23 pews in a room of white with red velvet cushions and carpet and chandeliers of Colonial blue wood.

The interesting Heritage Walking Tour goes past many surviving Colonial homes as well as later Federal and Greek Revival houses. Down dogwood-festooned Bronson Road, the old windmill that once pumped water for Bronson's farm has been restored in his memory. Also on this road is Ogden House, a saltbox farm restored by the Fairfield Historical Society. Most of its authentic eighteenth-century furnishings have a history of local ownership. The lean-to kitchen and traditional English herb garden here make it well worth a visit, dogwoods or not.

The actual Historical Society headquarters, a red brick building, is near the town center in one of Fairfield's two other historic districts. For a small museum, it offers an unusually large collection of early Americana. Dolls, doll houses, and children's toys fill an entire top floor, and the lower level features an old country store and a country kitchen as well as every conceivable tool for every kind of Colonial craft, from candle- to carriage-making. Many of the wooden tools on the wall are almost works of art in themselves.

The corner of the Historical Society block, Beach and Old Post roads, was the central point of the original "four squares" of the town laid out in 1639. You can while away a pleasant hour exploring these two roads on foot. Though only four of the original homes survived the British fires, there are many beautiful post-Revolutionary homes to see, as well as historic churches and the town hall, whose central section remains as it was when it was rebuilt in 1790. It was on the town hall green that residents refused to submit to a royal proclamation, an act that led to the town's burning.

Save some foot power for Southport, the picturesque harbor area, which also has been named a historic district. Boats laden with onions from the Greenfield Hill farms used to sail out of this harbor. Now it is the home of the Pequot Yacht Club and the Fairfield Country Club; the hilly surrounding residential area, with water views at every turn, is one of the most exclusive and attractive along the Connecticut shore.

Southport's tiny village is an antiques center. There are four shops within about two blocks on Pequot Avenue, as well as the Fairfield Women's Exchange, which combines antiques and gifts with many original articles. You can have a number plaque hand-painted for your front door here, or commission a pen-and-ink drawing of your home, or buy homemade items ranging from booties to braided rugs. Rarebook buffs will want to visit the Museum Gallery Book Shop, 246 Old Post Road.

For a lunchtime snack, try the Firehouse Deli on Reef Road, and for dessert, visit Allinton's Ice Cream Manufactory just down the road. An even nicer lunch suggestion: Pack a picnic and eat on Greenfield Hill's green or by the shore on the sandy Fairfield beaches that stretch for seven miles on and off along the Long Island Sound.

Except for Dogwood Festival days, Fairfield's charms draw surprisingly few visitors, and it remains a peaceful and nontouristy place. The main shopping area on the "new" Post Road, US 1, is typically small-town, and the shopping centers on Black Rock Turnpike are fairly standard. There's an interesting little gallery of limited-edition art prints at the Greenwich Workshop just off the Post Road at 61 Unquowa Road, but for serious shopping, boutiques and the like, follow the Post Road a few miles west into more sophisticated Westport.

It's possible that the beautifully wooded residential sections of Westport boast more celebrity residents than any other single Connecticut town (Paul Newman and Joanne Woodward among the more prominent), but the town itself is hardly a country village. There is a Main Street about two blocks long, with pleasant small shops and a bookstore that is something of a local landmark. The rest of the shopping area stretches along State Street, which is actually busy US 1, and is divided into little modern shopping centers. There's plenty of browsing potential, but by car rather than on foot.

If you continue farther west on US 1 into Norwalk and bear left to West Avenue, you'll come upon two Fairfield County shopping standbys. One is a branch of Loehmanns, well known to bargain-conscious, fashionably dressed women, and down the road a bit is Decker's, a haven for the men. Gant shirts here sell for half the price as at New York stores, there are many other quality labels that vary from visit to visit, and the side wall is stacked with classic Shetland or cashmere sweaters at excellent prices. There are women's sweaters, too, and a few women's shirts, but this is primarily a man's world. On the same block as Decker's are outlet stores for silver and for sheets and towels. If you want to spend a lot of time shopping, better plan it for Saturday and save Sunday for the dogwoods.

While you are in Norwalk, visit SoNo, the revitalized section of South Norwalk that has blossomed into an arty center for interesting shops and restaurants. The local branch of the Brookfield Craft Center, just off busy Washington Street, has a gallery and shop well worth a look.

Due to open in spring 1988 is a Maritime Center at the foot of Washington Street, which will include an aquarium, an Imax Theater, and lots of hands-on exhibits.

If you're more interested in the out-of-doors, back in Fairfield the Connecticut Audubon Society and its Larsen Sanctuary have more than six miles of trails along 168 wooded acres. The sanctuary is a managed wildlife area where you will find not only woods but also meadows, streams, marshes, and ponds. The Birdcraft Museum of the society is a refuge for songbirds, the first of its kind in New England.

The closest lodgings to the dogwoods are motels, but there are more interesting places to stay a short drive away. The Inn at Longshore, a former estate on Long Island Sound, was acquired by the town of Westport as a recreational facility for its residents. The renovation included 14 guest rooms, done in attractive prints with period reproduction furniture. Some of the rooms have water views. The surroundings here are super—golf course, beach, beautiful grounds.

The intimate Cotswold Inn is exquisite but expensive. Save it for a splurge.

On the more traditional New England side is Silvermine Tavern, a 200-year-old inn on a millpond with ten simple Colonial rooms upstairs. The food here is average, but the low-ceilinged dining room filled with old tools and the deck overlooking the ducks and geese on the pond are so pleasant that you may want to eat here anyway, at least for the generous Sunday brunch buffet.

The Silvermine Guild of Artists is just across the way (though the official address is New Canaan). It's an art school housed in barns that has changing exhibits and a gift shop of paintings and handcrafts.

For dinner, Fairfield's best bet is an unpretentious (though not inexpensive) café called Gregory's. Westport selections are far wider, though the offerings do seem to change with the seasons. Some old standbys that have stood the test of time are Le Chambord and Chez Pierre for French cuisine, and Allen's for seafood. Among the new favorites are the airy and pretty Pompano Grill, the warm and elegant La Clé d'Or and Dameon, which is also a popular watering hole. If these have vanished by the time you read this, don't say I didn't warn you.

Another good bet for interesting places to dine these days is South Norwalk's Washington Street. And if you want to end your weekend with a Sunday dinner that makes the most of the Connecticut countryside, head home on the Merritt Parkway and detour at exit 42, go about four miles north on Route 57 to Cobb's Mill Inn. It's the perfect country hideaway, full of antiques and with a view of trees, waterfall, and stream that is picture perfect.

Fairfield Area Code: 203

DRIVING DIRECTIONS Via I-95 to exit 21 to Fairfield, go left on Mill Plain Road, left on Sturgess, right on Bronson to Congregational

Church and the Dogwood Festival. Via the Merritt Parkway, take exit 44, make immediate right on Congress Street to Hillside, left on Hillside to Old Academy Road and the church.

Total Distance: 52 miles.

ACCOMMODATIONS   *The Inn at Longshore,* 260 Campo Road South, Westport, 226-3316, $$$$ ● *Cotswold Inn,* 76 Myrtle Avenue, Westport, 226-3766, $$$$ ● *Silvermine Tavern,* Silvermine and Perry avenues, Norwalk, 847-4558, $$ ● *Fairfield Motor Inn,* 417 Post Road, Fairfield, 255-0491. $$ ● *Westport Motor Inn,* 1595 Post Road East, Westport, 255-1256, $$–$$$$.

DINING   *Gregory's Restaurant,* 1599 Post Road, Fairfield, 259-7417, $$$ ● *La Clé d'Or,* 8 Sconset Square, Westport, 222-0770, $$$ ● *Dameon,* 30–32 Railroad Place, Westport, 226-6580, $–$$$ ● *Chez Pierre,* 146 Main Street, Westport, 227-5295, $$$ ● *Allen's Clam & Lobster House,* 191 Hills Point Road, Westport, 226-4411, $$–$$$$ ● *Le Chambord,* 1572 Post Road East, Westport, 255-2654, $$$–$$$$ ● *Cobb's Mill Inn,* Weston Road, Weston, 227-7221, $$–$$$ ● *Silvermine Tavern* (see above), $$–$$$ ● Some lively and popular places in trendy South Norwalk: *Pasta Nostra,* 116 Washington Street, 854-9700, $–$$ ● *Water Street,* 50 Water Street, 838-9044, $$ ● *Jasper's Oyster Bar and Restaurant,* 204 South Main Street, 852-1716, $$.

SIGHTSEEING   *The Dogwood Festival,* Greenfield Hill Congregational Church, 1045 Old Academy Road, Fairfield, 259-5596. Write or phone for information and brochure giving current dates and schedule, rates for walking tours and sit-down luncheon, and reservations ● *Silvermine Guild of Artists,* 1073 Silvermine Road, New Canaan, 966-5617. Hours: Tuesday to Sunday 12:30 P.M. to 5 P.M. Free ● *Connecticut Audubon Society,* 2325 Burr Street, Fairfield, 259-6305. Hours: Tuesday to Saturday 9 A.M. to 4:30 P.M. Free; Sanctuary daily, dawn to dusk. Trail fee: adults, $1; children $.50 ● *Birdcraft Museum and Sanctuary,* 314 Unquowa Road, Fairfield, 259-0416, Thursday, Saturday, Sunday, noon to 5 P.M. Admission, $1 ● *Brookfield/SoNo Craft Center,* Brookfield Alley off Washington Street, Norwalk, 853-6155, Tuesday to Saturday 10 A.M. to 6 P.M.; Sunday noon to 5 P.M. Free.

FOR FURTHER INFORMATION   Fairfield Chamber of Commerce, 1597 Post Road, Fairfield, 255-1011.

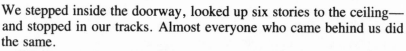

"The Mercer Mile" and Other Bucks County Byways

We stepped inside the doorway, looked up six stories to the ceiling— and stopped in our tracks. Almost everyone who came behind us did the same.

Hanging above us, suspended at various levels from a vast central core, were Early American objects of every conceivable size and shape—chairs, barrels, cradles, whaleboats, baskets, bellows, sleds, cigar store Indians, a full-size buckboard, even a Conestoga wagon.

Circling the room on a spiral ramp were display cubbies jammed and crammed with the hand tools that made these items and scores of others—tools used by butchers, dairymen, cooks and coopers, carpenters, weavers, leathermakers, and printers; tools for doctors, clockmakers, surveyors, and seamstresses—130 crafts represented in all and a total of almost 60,000 objects.

It is an eye-boggling display that greets visitors to the Mercer Museum, the largest collection of early hand tools and their finished products ever assembled. But the museum, located in Doylestown, the county seat of scenic Bucks County, Pennsylvania, is only the first of three extravaganzas in an area that has come to be called the Mercer Mile.

And the Mercer Mile is just the start of the many attractions in this county along the Delaware River, a setting of rolling hills, covered bridges, and distinctive stone houses that serve as country retreats for some of the nation's best-known authors and entertainers. Shopping and shunpiking are two major activities here, and though there's history galore, it comes in lively form—riding on a steam train, gliding downstream on a mule-drawn canal barge, watching an antique printing press or a water-powered gristmill in action, or seeing Mr. Mercer's dream houses, monuments to a man who was an authentic American genius—and eccentric.

Henry Chapman Mercer was one of the nation's leading archaeologists when his personal passion for collecting Early American tools led to a surprising midlife career change. Mercer became so intrigued with the tools used by the old Pennsylvania German pottery and tile makers that he determined to perpetuate the dying craft. He apprenticed himself to an old German potter, rented a decrepit kiln, and by 1898 exhibited a talent that brought him a new kind of fame. Mercer tiles can be seen today from the casino at Monto Carlo to the Gardner Museum in Boston, from a high school in Havana to the King Ranch in

Texas. His largest work is the tile floor in the Pennsylvania state capitol at Harrisburg.

Mercer called his enterprise the Moravian Pottery and Tile Works. The factory is now a living museum, part of the Mercer Mile, still turning out his original patterns according to his formulas and methods. You can pick up a few as souvenirs in the museum gift shop, which also has a fine selection of early Pennsylvania crafts—boxes of Pennsylvania Dutch designs, tinware, unusual weathervanes, and the like. If you are searching for books on early American art or antiques, you'll find 400 titles here.

The most incredible display of tiles, however, awaits in Mercer's own home, Fonthill, a castlelike concrete fantasy that took 106 men more than two years to build. Mercer's mansion is a fantastic mélange of columns, balconies, beams, towers and arches, and winding stairs. Tiles are everywhere—on columns and beams, serving as headboards, tabletops, and ceilings, even lining the stairs. There is a copy of an English tapestry in tile, the story of the discovery of the New World told in tile, and, in addition to Mercer's own creations, fine specimens of historic tiles he gathered from every part of the world.

Fonthill and the museum that Mercer built in 1913 to house his enormous collection of tools and artifacts established Mercer as an eccentric prophet of modern architecture. The October 1960 issue of *Progressive Architecture* says: "Though the effect is often weird and theatrical . . . [Fonthill] with its unique spatial plan and its frank and bold techniques . . . [is] one of the important forerunners of the modern movement." The museum's ramp arrangement is believed to be the inspiration for New York's Guggenheim Museum.

The Mercer Mile can take a good half day, but there should be enough time left to enjoy some of the many other pleasures of Bucks County.

You might start with a short walking tour of Doylestown center, reached by driving west from the Mercer Mile on Court Street. Main Street, State Street (Route 202), and Oakland Avenue are the main streets in town and are lined with interesting homes dating from early to late nineteenth century.

Heading back east on 202 you'll come to Buckingham, a tiny village that maintains the early flavor of Bucks County and that is also the site of Buckingham Farmer's Market on 202 held on Saturdays from 9 A.M. until the farm produce is sold. (Bountiful Acres, a little farther east on 202, also has fresh-picked produce in season.)

Another famous Saturday event in Buckingham is Brown Brothers auction on Route 413 just south of 263. It begins at 9 A.M. with box lots and moves on to bigger and better things as the day progresses, including all kinds of antiques, furniture, and accessories that change by the week.

Lahaska, a little farther east on 202, is for shoppers. Peddlers Village, a nicely landscaped Colonial-style complex (so nice it has been designated as one of the few "All-American Selections") has dozens of shops crammed with clothes, crafts, jewelry, and gifts. More shops adjoin in The Yard, a Victorian mélange of boutiques. The café in The Yard is a good place for lunch.

Afterward, cross the street to an antiquer's haven, the Lahaska Antique Courte, with 14 shops featuring all kinds of collectibles.

All of Bucks County is an antiquer's paradise. The last printed guide listed 60 stores. There are three big annual shows in and around Doylestown, the last usually held in mid-October. Write to the Bucks County Antique Dealers Association for this year's dates and locations.

Finally, follow Route 202 north to where all roads in Bucks County lead eventually—New Hope, the picturesque artists' colony on the banks of the Delaware. Take a nostalgic river ride here on the last operating mule-drawn canal barge in the country. Beginning in May, you can also hop a huffing, puffing steam train for an 8½-mile loop through the countryside that includes the famous trestle from the rescue scene in *Perils of Pauline*.

New Hope's labyrinth of paths and alleyways offers lovely old homes, almost 100 shops, and lots and lots of shoppers, a good reason to avoid the busiest summer months.

Two favorite attractions in town are the Parry Mansion, which displays in ten rooms the furnishings and decor that might have been used by the one family who lived here for 182 years from the late eighteenth to early twentieth centuries, and the Bucks County Playhouse, the famous old summer theater in a restored gristmill that now has a season almost year-round.

Take time to mingle with that mass of shoppers in New Hope. The shops have interesting wares, particularly the Old Franklin Print Shop, which not only sells reproductions of rare documents but demonstrates the techniques of early hand printing.

Save a good chunk of your Sunday for a back-roads tour to see the rural countryside and the stone farms and barns that are the special trademark of Bucks County. Part of the fascination is that no two of the houses are alike. Even the color and texture of the homes varies according to the native stones that were used for construction. You'll see mostly limestone and shale in central Bucks and craggier granite in the upper regions. Notice the double houses with twin doors, the big tri-level barns, and the "bride and groom" trees that flank many doorways. The trees were planted long ago for good luck by newlyweds who hoped their love would flourish along with the saplings.

The main roads are the River Road (Route 32), 611, and 413, and you can't go wrong making your own way back and forth. One possible route is to follow the River Road north. The thin strip of land running alongside the canal is officially called Theodore Roosevelt Park but is generally just referred to as the tow path, named for its historical use as a path for the mules that pulled barges down the canal. Now you'll see hikers and bikers using it.

The drive takes you through the sleepy town of Lumberville and to Point Pleasant, where you may be tempted to take an hour out to see the river from one of its nicest perspectives—by canoe. Point Pleasant Canoe can provide all the necessary equipment, and even novices need not worry about this placid stretch of water. Rubber rafts and tubes are also for rent, or you can opt for a "pedal and paddle" tour allowing you to bike one way beside the river and return via canoe.

In Ralph Stover State Park near Point Pleasant you can see the Big Red Bridge, and there are other covered bridges farther north in Erwinna and Uhlerstown. Stover Mill in Erwinna still has its old machinery intact but is used now by the Tinicum Civic Association as a gallery for local art. There's also a restored Federal-style home in Tinicum Park on River Road, as well as picnic facilities if you want to take a break.

Two and a half miles west of River Road in Upper Black Eddy is a strange 3½ acres of huge boulders known as Ringing Rocks because many of the rocks, when struck, do actually ring.

From Upper Black Eddy continue west on 32 to the connection with 611 and proceed south once again through more charming towns such as Pipersville (site of Cabin Run and Loux covered bridges and another restored mill) and Plumsteadville. Not far away in Dublin is a home with a special kind of history. It is Green Hills Farm, where Pulitzer and Nobel prizewinning author Pearl Buck lived and worked for 40 years. Mrs. Buck's 1835 stone house is filled with Oriental antiques in a rustic setting of Pennsylvania beams, wideboard oak floors, and big stone fireplaces. It is open on Sundays, May through September, and on weekdays the rest of the year.

There are winery tours at the Bucks County Vineyards near New Hope. And there are more covered bridges (12 in all) and more historic sights all over the place. For a more comprehensive listing, write for the Bucks County folder before you make your trip.

The final bonus is from the large number of historic houses that have been converted to atmospheric inns and restaurants.

For romance, try the Inn at Phillips Mill; for country charm, Barley

Sheaf Farm. Evermay is a Victorian beauty with a fine dining room, 1740 House offers river views, Innisfree is a picturesque gristmill turned inn, and Pineapple Hill is simple and beautifully accented with folk art. The list is long—and you can hardly go wrong.

Bucks County Area Code: 215

DRIVING DIRECTIONS Take the New Jersey Turnpike south to exit 10, then go north on US 287 15 miles to another exit 10 (287 widens to five lanes just before the exit, so stay left). Drive west on Route 22 for about 3½ miles, then turn right at the sign marked Flemington-Princeton for Route 202 south to Doyleston.
Total Distance: about 85 miles.

ACCOMMODATIONS *Barley Sheaf Farm,* Box 10, Route 202, Holicong, 794-5104, $$$–$$$$ CP • *Innisfree,* Cafferty Road (off Route 32), Point Pleasant, 297-8329, $$–$$$ CP • *Pineapple Hill,* 1234 River Road, New Hope, 862-2984, $$–$$$ CP • *1740 House,* River Road (Route 32), Lumberville, 297-5661, $$ with private bath and buffet breakfast; dinner $$$ (bring your own wine) • *Centre Bridge Inn,* River Road, New Hope, 862–2048, $$$–$$$$ CP with bath • *Inn at Phillips Mill,* North River Road, New Hope, 862-9919, $$$ CP • *Evermay,* Delaware River Road, Erwinna, 294-9100, $$–$$$ with breakfast and afternoon tea; five-course prix-fixe dinner, $35.

DINING *Inn at Phillips Mill* (see above), romantic, $$$ • *Centre Bridge Inn* (see above), nice location, $$$ • *Pear and Partridge Inn,* Old Easton Road, Doylestown, highly rated "new American cuisine," 345-7800, $$$ • *La Bonne Auberge,* Village II, New Hope, 862-2461, classic French, $$$$ • *Jean Pierres,* 101 S. State Street, Newtown, 968-6201, former Le Bec Fin chef, $$$ • For a light lunch try the *Marketway Café,* 52 East State Street in Doylestown or *Mothers,* 34 North Main Street in New Hope; for a scenic brunch, *Cuttalossa Inn,* River Road (Route 32), Lumberville, 297-5082.

SIGHTSEEING *Mercer Mile,* open March 1 to December 31. *Mercer Museum,* Pine Street, Doylestown, 345-0210. Hours: Monday to Saturday 10 A.M. to 5 P.M.; Sunday 1 P.M. to 5 P.M. Adults, $3; students and children, $1.50 • *Fonthill,* East Court Street, Doylestown, 348-9461. Hours: daily 10 A.M. to 5 P.M. Adults, $3; students $1.50. Reservations advisable • *Moravian Pottery and Tile Works,* Swamp Road (Route 313), Doylestown, 345-6722. Hours:

daily 10 A.M. to 5 P.M. Adults, $2; children, $1; families, $4 ● *Green Hill Farm,* 520 Dublin Road, Dublin, 249-0100, guided tours. Hours: March to mid-January, weekdays 10:30 A.M. and 2 P.M.; May to September and also on Sunday 1:30 P.M.and 2:30 P.M. Adults, $4; senior citizens, $3; students and children, $2 ● *Peddler's Village,* Route 222, Lahaska, 794-7438. Hours: Friday 10 A.M. to 9 P.M.; Saturday 10 A.M. to 5 P.M. ● *Mule-Drawn Barge Rides,* New Street at southern end of New Hope, 862-2842. Hours: May to mid-October, daily 11:30 A.M. and 1, 2, 3, 4:30, and 6 P.M. Adults, $5.50; children 2–11, $3 ● *New Hope Steam Railway,* Bridge Street (Route 179) near the center of New Hope, 345-0292. Hours: May to October, Saturday and holidays 1 P.M. and 3:30 P.M.; Sunday 11:30 A.M., 1:30 P.M., and 3:30 P.M. Adults, $5; children, $3 ● *Point Pleasant Canoe Rental and Sales,* Point Pleasant, 297-8181. Check for current canoe, raft, and tube rental rates.

FOR FURTHER INFORMATION For New Hope information, contact Chamber of Commerce, South Main and Mechanic streets, New Hope, PA 18938, 862-5880. For antiques show information, Bucks County Antique Dealers Association, Inc., PO Box 573, Lahaska, PA 18931. For Bucks County guides, write to Bucks County Tourist Commission, 152 Swamp Road, Doylestown, PA 18901, 345-4552.

 # Stony Brook and the North Shore: A Springtime Ramble

A set designer couldn't have done better. Old white Colonial homes, a peaceful harbor, tiny tots toddling down the sloping green to feed the ducks on the pond. Even the shopping center of Stony Brook is built in Federal style so as not to spoil the picture.

This little North Shore village, so atypical of most people's visions of Long Island, is one of the island's most historic enclaves—and it provides the perfect inn to suit the atmosphere.

Three Village Inn, a 1785 Colonial home at the end of the village green, where even the desk clerks wear Early American garb, is a must for its dining room as well as its old-fashioned accommodations. Start planning your trip by making your reservation here for dinner as well as for one of the seven Colonial rooms upstairs. There are more motel rooms in cottages around back, but the main building is much more atmospheric.

Early June is the best time for a visit, after the attractions are open but before the summer crowds descend.

After filling yourself on Friday night with New England clam cakes or Long Island bay scallops or roast turkey with chestnut stuffing, get a good night's sleep and after breakfast head straight for the Stony Brook museums, a sampler of the past.

The clang of blacksmith hammers and the ring of a nineteenth-century recess bell greet you at a complex of buildings that includes a nineteenth-century schoolhouse complete with potbellied stove; a museum of more than 100 horse-drawn carriages from farm wagons to European stagecoaches; costumes, textiles, decoys, toys, and 15 exquisite miniature rooms in a history museum; a working blacksmith shop; and an art museum featuring the works of ''the foremost nineteenth-century American genre painter,'' William Sidney Mount. Mount's paintings, appropriately, focus on everyday life on rural Long Island.

After a stop at the Victorian-style Dark House Museum Shop for pamphlets to guide your way, you're ready for further exploring of the real historic settlement known as the Three Villages. Setauket, East Setauket, and Stony Brook were among Long Island's earliest settlements, and their historical society brochure is accurate when it states that the years have been kind to them.

You might want to head for the farthest point, the village of East Setauket, where Dining Car 1890 with its old nickelodeon makes a perfect spot for a lunch. Follow Old Post Road, Coach Road, and Dyers Neck and a few of the back roads of East Setauket, where the shingled farmhouses in their wooded settings probably reflect better than any other part of the area the original rural character of these communities. The oldest house in the villages is the 1655 Brewster House here.

On to Setauket and the Thompson House, the interesting headquarters of the Three Village Historical Society. Built in 1720, it is unique for its high ceilings and the decorative details on the exposed beams. Guides will take you through the house and answer your questions about the original inhabitants and the early Long Island furnishings inside.

An herb garden and the Thompson family cemetery are on the grounds of the house, as are the 1800s headquarters building for the Society for the Preservation of Long Island Antiquities, a barn, an icehouse, and a corncrib.

Not far away is Gallery North, a showplace for contemporary art housed in an 1870s structure, and the Tucker-Jones House, a former ship captain's residence, which has a working blacksmith shop open to the public.

If you want to take a shopping break, there are plenty of temptations in nearby Port Jefferson, near the lively dock area where the ferry to Connecticut is berthed. If there is no room at the inn in Stony Brook, Danford's Inn here is the closest alternative, pleasant though pricey. The other choices are also well over $100 for ordinary motel accommodations.

Back in Stony Brook, the Three Village Garden Club Exchange near the inn is worth a look for china, glassware, and antiques. If you want to try another dining place in town, the Country House restaurant, a 1710 farmhouse, is a good bet.

On Sunday, after a final walk through the village and a look at the old gristmill, you can spend a pleasant afternoon winding your way back home with a choice of attractions along the North Shore.

Route 25A will bring you to Northport and, just past the town, the Vanderbilt Museum, or Eagle's Nest, a natural science museum and planetarium in a 24-room mansion on 43 wooded acres.

Go along 25A until you come to Cold Spring Harbor, just south of Huntington, a perfectly delightful old whaling village that has been declared a National Historic District. There are several appealing shops here, as well as a small whaling museum that is one of the best of its kind, filled with harpoons, scrimshaw, paintings, ship models, and an old Long Island whaling boat.

A little farther on, in Oyster Bay, follow the signs in town to Theodore Roosevelt's "bully" home at Sagamore Hill, a huge Victorian affair with a big shaded porch where Teddy used to sit and rock and look at the sunset.

There's no mistaking whose home this is. Teddy's huge hunting trophies—buffalo heads, elephant tusks, bearskins, and the like—are all over the place. Even the inkwell is made from a rhinoceros foot.

The great north room where the President entertained foreign dignitaries contains some of their gifts—samurai swords, ivory, paintings, and photographs. Roosevelt's masculine touch dominates all of the home's three stories and 22 rooms except for Mrs. Roosevelt's parlor, where the First Lady was allowed her own patterned brocade armchairs and flowered lampshades.

Aside from bringing the spirit of the late President to life, Sagamore Hill offers a glorious view of Oyster Bay and Long Island Sound.

If the weather is warm and you haven't eaten by now, you can walk down past the windmill to the cafeteria and enjoy your snack at a picnic table with a view. Or if you prefer to end your weekend with a proper fresh seafood dinner with a view, Steve's Pier One on the water in nearby Bayville is just the spot.

Long Island Area Code: 516

DRIVING DIRECTIONS   Long Island Expressway (Route 495) to exit 62. Proceed north on Nicolls Road and turn left on Route 25A into Stony Brook.
   Total Distance: about 58 miles.

PUBLIC TRANSPORTATION   Long Island Railroad service is available from New York's Penn Station to Stony Brook. You can walk around the village sights, take a cab or a ¼-mile walk from the station to the museums, then taxi or walk to the inn.

ACCOMMODATIONS   *Three Village Inn,* 150 Main Street, Stony Brook, NY 11790, 751-0555, $$$ ● *Danford's Inn,* Bayles Dock, 25 East Broadway, Port Jefferson, NY 928-5200, $$$$ ● Two other possiblities are *Holiday Inn,* 1740 Express Drive, South Happauge, 234-3030, $$$$ ● *Burt Bacharach's East Norwich Inn,* Routes 25A and 106 (near Oyster Bay), 922-1500, somewhat motelish but plush with gardens, heated pool, sauna, and game room. $$$$.

DINING   *Three Village Inn* (see above), complete dinner $$$; lunch, $–$$$ ● *Country House,* Route 25A, Stony Brook, 751-3332; dinner, $$$–$$$$; lunch, $$ ● *Dining Car 1890,* Route 25A at Nicolls Road, East Setauket, 751-1890, dinner, $$–$$$; lunch, $ ● *Steve's Pier One,* 33 Bayville Avenue, Bayville, 628-2431, complete dinner, $$–$$$.

SIGHTSEEING   *Museums of Stony Brook,* Route 25A, 751-0066. Hours: Wednesday to Saturday 10 A.M. to 5 P.M., Sunday from noon. Adults, $4; students and senior citizens, $2.75; children over 6, $2; family rate, $10 ● *Thompson House,* North Country Road, Setauket, 941-9444. Hours: late May to mid-October, Saturday and Sunday 1 P.M. to 5 P.M. Adults, $2; children 7–14, $.50 ● *Vanderbilt Museum,* Little Neck Road, Centerport (watch for signs on 25A), 261-5656. Hours: May to October, Tuesday to Saturday 10 A.M. to 4 P.M.; Sunday noon to 5 P.M. Adults, $2.50; senior citizens and children under 9, $2; planetarium fees extra ● *Cold Spring Whaling Museum,* Main

Street (Route 25A), Cold Spring Harbor, 367-3418. Hours: Memorial Day to September, daily 11 A.M. to 5 P.M.; rest of year, Saturday and Sunday only. Adults, $1; children 6–14, $.50 ● *Sagamore Hill*, Cove Neck Road, Oyster Bay, 922-4447. Hours: April to October daily 9:30 A.M. to 5 P.M.; rest of year, closed Monday. Adults, $1; under 12 and over 62 free.

Down to the Sea at Mystic Seaport

Wait for the weather forecast. Make sure it's going to be the kind of perfect spring day when breezes billow the square sails, masts and rigging stand out against the blue sky, and the sun warms you while you listen to sea chanteys being sung on the green.

That's the kind of day to save for Mystic Seaport Museum, not only a place for ships but a 17-acre total re-creation of a nineteenth-century maritime village. You can only pick your weekend at the last minute if you go to visit the Northeast's major maritime attraction before summer tourists fill the local motels. And you'll enjoy your visit even more without summer humidity and crowds.

Mystic's shipbuilding history dates back to the 1700s. When wooden shipbuilding was at its peak in the 1800s, Mystic yards produced some of the fastest clippers on the seas, many built at the George Greenman and Company Shipyard, the site of the present Seaport Museum. Three town residents formed a Marine Historical Association back in 1929 to preserve some of the objects of the town's maritime past, and sea-minded friends from all over soon became involved, helping the museum grow to more than 60 historic buildings, four major vessels and more than 300 smaller boats, important collections of maritime artifacts and paintings, and a planetarium to teach the secrets of celestial navigation.

No question that for most visitors the most exciting part of Mystic is the ships, especially the big three: the *Charles W. Morgan,* America's last surviving wooden whaling ship; the full-rigged training ship *Joseph Conrad,* and the fishing schooner *L. A. Dunton.*

You can come right aboard, pace the decks, examine the intricate rigging and enormous masts, go below to see the crew's cramped quarters and the officers' cabins, even take a imaginary turn at the wheel. On the *Morgan,* the whaleboats, tryworks, sails, and rigging are all in place. Aboard the *Dunton,* crew members show another kind of fishing expertise in action—the cleaning, splitting, and salting of cod for dry-ing. Fishermen's skills like trawling, net weaving, and lobster-pot building are also demonstrated.

Smaller boats once used for oystering, lobstering, salmon fishing, clamming, and other kinds of fishing are moored near the *Dunton,* and you can see the fishing gear used by three generations of one family at the Robie Ames Fishing Shack nearby.

Almost as interesting as seeing the boats is learning how they were built. Mystic's Henry B. du Pont preservation shipyard is a unique facility with the equipment and craftsmen to perform almost any task in the restoration and preservation of wooden boats. A visitor's gallery overlooks the carpenter's shops, rigging loft, and other areas where older vessels are maintained and new ones are built.

In the Small Boat Shop, boat builders are at work crafting small wooden sailboats or rowboats. Some are sold to finance the seaport's boat-building apprenticeship program, which keeps the old craft alive. Others are part of a fleet of nineteenth-century dories, wherries, canoes, split-sail boats, and catboats that are sailed and rowed on the river, enlivening the waterfront.

All of this goes on against the backdrop of a nineteenth-century seafaring village with more than 20 authentic structures—grocery store, printer's shop, school, chapel, ship chandlery, sail loft, ship-smith, cooperage, and other necessary services. Some of these shops and houses are on their original sites; others were moved here from the town of Mystic or from other New England communities. All are fur-nished with authentic period items, and in many, craftsmen are on hand to explain and demonstrate their trades.

There are several galleries on the grounds displaying maritime art and artifacts, ship models, paintings, and scrimshaw. One exhibit traces the development of the maritime industry from the seventeenth to nineteenth centuries; another tells the story of fishing, America's oldest industry. One of the most delightful displays for adults is the collection of ships' figureheads and wood carvings in the Wendell Building. Children are invariably charmed by the Children's Museum, done up like the interior of the ship's quarters for a captain's family. Young visitors can climb up in the bunks to peer out of portholes at a mock sea and play with reproductions of toys that might have been used to amuse children on a sea voyage long ago.

It's all educational, but they also keep things lively here with dem-onstrations, sail setting and furling, whaleboat rowing and sailing, a breeches buoy rescue drill. And there are "sailors" all around the grounds ready to break into a sea chantey at the drop of a sea breeze. It's almost impossible to absorb it all in a single visit. You can opt for a two-day ticket that allows you to rest up and come back for more. At least take a long break for a clamburger at the Galley snack bar and a cruise down the river on the jaunty little steamboat *Sabino* to rest between bouts of seeing the sights.

And don't think the sights of Mystic are finished when you leave the seaport. The Mystic Marinelife Aquarium is almost as popular with youngsters as the museum itself for its dolphins and seals; the Memory Lane Doll and Toy Museum has more than 1,500 dolls from all over the world; and there's the Denison Nature Center if you want to take a spring walk in the woods.

The town of Mystic is also appealing, with many fine old homes (ask for the walking tour at the information center in Olde Mistick Village). A nautical flavor remains downtown with the river running through; check out the riverside art gallery and the railroad station that was the model for millions of toy train sets for years.

There are shops galore—Olde Mistick Village, a pseudo-Colonial shopping mall, and the Clockworks Factory Outlet nearby, plus all manner of stores in town selling everything, including antiques. One of the most interesting complexes is Factory Square, a century-old brick mill transformed into stores, a crafts workshop, a bakery, restaurants, and apartments. And don't overlook the Seaport Store, headquarters for nautical paraphernalia and memorabilia and also an old-time country store and bakeshop.

Just outside Mystic you can visit Whitehall, a 1770 country mansion that has been restored and authentically furnished by the Historical Society of neighboring Stonington.

As if all that isn't enough, there is Stonington village just four miles away. This is one of the most picturesque towns on the Connecticut shore, filled with eighteenth- and nineteenth-century homes that belonged to sea captains of another age, a Greek Revival town center, village green with requisite white churches, and a lighthouse that dates to 1823. Should you be here in summer, don't miss the little museum in that lighthouse or the view of the sound from its tower.

If you are totally taken with Stonington (and lots of people are), ask at Whitehall for a walking tour pamphlet and while away some time getting a closer look at the town's charming homes. There are a couple of excellent antiques shops for browsing on Main Street and a few good places to eat, informal Noah's or the Skipper's Deck, or the very elegant Harbor View. J. P. Daniels, back toward Mystic, is another good choice.

Dining in Mystic is also varied and good. Visit the Seaport's Seamen's Inne or try the Steamboat Café in town, or the Moorings at the Hilton. For lobster, Abbott's in nearby Noank, a no-frills establishment with outdoor picnic tables, has been famous for years, and Noank has two other fairly priced seafood restaurants on the water, the Sea Horse and The Yankee Fisherman.

And there are a lot of little places for less formal meals. Two Sisters Deli and Kitchen Little in Mystic are among those liked by local residents.

Where to stay? There are scads of motels and a new Hilton and a couple of country inns, and more possibilities farther up the shoreline. And surprisingly, tucked on a hilltop behind one of the motels, the Mystic Inn, is a true inn that is one of the most elegant to be found. It's a former private estate with beautiful gardens, the place where legend says Humphrey Bogart and Lauren Bacall spent their honeymoon. It has recently been renovated in exquisite taste. The unbeatable views of the harbor needed no improvement. If you want to forget about the children and make Mystic a romantic nautical getaway for two, this is definitely the place.

Connecticut Area Code: 203

DRIVING DIRECTIONS Take I-95 to exit 90. Mystic Seaport is about one mile south of the exit on Route 27.

Total distance: about 127 miles.

PUBLIC TRANSPORTATION Amtrack trains and Greyhound buses serve Mystic daily.

ACCOMMODATIONS *Mystic Motor Inn* (motel and real inn), Route 1 at Route 27, 536–9604, $$$ ● *Howard Johnson,* Route 27 at I-95, 536–2654, $$ ● *Days Inn,* off I-95, 572–0574, $$–$$$ ● *The Mystic Hilton,* Coogan Boulevard, Mystic, 572–0731, $$–$$$ ● *Red Brook Inn,* 10 Welles Road, Old Mystic, 572–0349, pleasant bed-and-breakfast accommodations in two historic houses, $$$–$$$$ ● More possibilities a few miles up the coast: *Palmer Inn,* 25 Church Street, Noank, 572–9000, gracious old columned mansion near the water, $$$–$$$$ CP; *Shore Inne,* 54 East Shore Road, Groton Long Point, 536–1180, modest home with an incredible water view, $ CP ● Two modest Stonington B&B homes: *Lasbury's Guest House,* 24 Orchard Street, Stonington, 535–2681, $$ CP; *The Farnan House,* 10 McGrath Court, Stonington, 535–0634, $$ CP.

DINING *Seamen's Inne,* Greenmanville Avenue, 536–9649, seafood specialties, lunch, $; dinner, $$ ● *Steamboat Café,* 73 Steamboat

Wharf, 536–1975, $ • *J. P. Daniels,* Route 184, 572–9564, $$–$$$ • *Captain Daniel Packer Inne,* 32 Water Street, 536–3555, $–$$ • *Harbor View,* 60 Water Street, Stonington, 535–2720, $$ • *The Mooring,* Mystic Hilton (see above), $$–$$$ • *Skipper's Deck,* 60 Water Street (behind Harbor View), Stonington, 535–2000, $–$$ • *Noah's,* 113 Water Street, Stonington, 535–3925, $–$$ • *Abbott's Lobster in the Rough,* Route 215, Noank, 536–7719, $–$$$ • *Sea Horse,* Marsh Road, Noank, 536–1670, $ • *Yankee Fisherman,* Groton Long Point Road, Noank, 536–1717, $$.

SIGHTSEEING *Mystic Seaport Museum,* Route 27, Mystic, 572–0711. Hours: April to October, daily 9 A.M. to 5 P.M.; rest of year to 4 P.M. Adults, $10; children, $5. Two-day tickets: adults, $12.; children, $6.; children under 5 free. Steamboat *Sabino* rides: adults, $2.50; children, $1.75. (Many special weekends are scheduled: photography, a sea music festival, and lobster festival. Phone for specific dates.) • *Mystic Marinelife Aquarium,* Route 27, Mystic, 536–3323. Hours: daily 9 A.M. to 4:45 P.M.; to 6 in summer; hourly dolphin, sea lion, and whale demonstrations from 10 A.M. Adults, $6.25; children, $3.25 • *Memory Lane Doll and Toy Museum,* Route 27, Mystic, 536–3450. Hours: Monday to Saturday 10 A.M. to 6 P.M.; Sunday noon to 6 P.M. Adults, $.75; children, $.25; children under 5 free • *Denison Pequotsepos Nature Center,* Pequotsepos Road, Mystic, 536–1216. Hours: April to October, Monday to Saturday 8 A.M. to 4 P.M., Sunday from 1 P.M.; rest of year 10 A.M. to 4 P.M. Audlts, $1; children, $.50, under 6 free.

Winterthur and Other Delaware Delights

Who could have foreseen what lay ahead in 1923 when Henry Francis du Pont acquired his first American-made antique, a simple Pennsylvania chest dated 1737?

A man of extraordinary taste as well as wealth, du Pont recognized the distinctive work of Early American craftsmen before collecting native antiques had become fashionable. He saw the nation's early culture reflected in its decorative arts and was soon amassing not only the finest furniture from the period between 1640 and 1840, but also curtains, bed hangings, rugs, lighting fixtures, silver pieces, and ceramics.

Even that wasn't enough to satisfy him. It wasn't long before du Pont was combing the eastern seaboard for paneling, fireplace walls, doors, and ceilings from the finest homes of the period, dismantling and reinstalling them at Winterthur as proper background for his collections.

Eventually there were almost 200 room settings, and after living pleasurably with his antiques for almost 30 years, du Pont turned his home into a museum and educational facility in 1951 so that the rest of the world could appreciate it with him.

Winterthur is now one of the outstanding attractions in the Northeast. There is no better place to see the very best of America's early arts. Nor is there a pleasanter place to visit in spring during the annual open house from mid-April to early June, since the du Pont gardens are also a showplace, a 64-acre woodland wonderland of rare azaleas, rhododendrons, and other prize plants.

During most of the year visitors without special appointments see only 16 rooms, the "Two Centuries Tour" showing the chronological development of American crafts. During the spring open house another 16 rooms are open. All along the way there are elaborate spring bouquets and specially trained guides to point out the treasures in each setting.

If anything stands out after touring so many rooms, it is the variety of the settings and the progression of styles. Among the memorable recreations are a simple seventeenth-century dining room with tables and benches before an open hearth; the Readbourne Parlor with woodwork and appropriate accompanying furnishings from a 1733 Maryland home; a drawing room with New England Queen Anne furniture and an equally elegant parlor from Port Royal, with yellow carved sofas and wing chairs, Chippendale side chairs and highboy, Oriental rugs, marble fireplace, and crystal chandeliers.

The gardens, like the rooms, were created under du Pont's personal direction, with meticulous care to make them appear as natural growth among the native trees and shrubs that have been preserved around them.

Tanbark and turf paths wind through shaded woodland and over rolling hillsides, bringing spectacular vistas into view at every turn. The Azalea Woods for which the gardens are most noted reach their peak in the first half of May, a mist of white, pink, and salmon as far as the eye can see, under a canopy of flowering dogwood and tall tulip trees. Be sure to see the quarry area as well, in full bloom in May with Asiatic primroses in jewel colors.

There is no nicer way to welcome spring than to visit Winterthur, and one pleasant way to do it is to arrive late morning, spend about two hours in the house, have lunch in the cafeteria-style Garden Pavilion, and then wander the gardens in the afternoon. You can take a tram tour or make your own path or follow the arrows posted to give you the best route for seeing the peak of the blooms. The two and a half miles of paths can be covered in a leisurely hour and a half.

Although Wilmington isn't thought of as a tourist city, it is an interesting one. If you want to live like a du Pont, choose the Hotel du Pont with its carved ceilings, marble stairs, and antiques. The Christina Room has a million dollars' worth of Wyeths on its walls. The Hotel Radisson is contemporary in decor but is also quite attractive and offers an indoor pool, and the Christina is an all suite hotel. Fairville Inn is an attractive country inn near Winterthur, just across the Pennsylvania border.

Take a walk from your hotel down the Market Street Mall to see the Grand Opera House, a cast-iron, highly decorative neoclassical building recently restored to become Delaware's Center for the Performing Arts. Willingtown Square, the 500 block on the mall, is a historic complex of six eighteenth-century houses. The Old Town Hall, dating to 1798, has displays of decorative arts and a restored jail inside.

At dinnertime, try to sample some of the crabmeat dishes that are local specialties at places like the Columbus Inn or Leoune's at the Mansion.

On Sunday there are many more diversions to choose from. The recently expanded Delaware Art Museum in Wilmington is dedicated to Howard Pyle, whose Brandywine School turned out illustrators like N. C. Wyeth and Frank Schoonover, whose distinct works of art enlivened countless magazines and books early in this century. Pyle's own works are generously included in the exhibits. The museum's other speciality is Pre-Raphaelite art, a London school of the mid-1800s represented here by Rossetti, Millais, and Ford Madox Brown, the gift of a Wilmington industrialist and art collector, Samuel Bancroft, Jr. A new wing features changing exhibits.

The evolution of industry in the Brandywine Valley and in the nation as a whole is shown at the Hagley Museum on Route 141 in Greenville. The history of the du Pont Company, which dominates the valley, is prominent. The buildings include the original du Pont "black powder" mills, an 1814 cotton spinning mill, an operating waterwheel, and a water turbine. The first office of the du Pont company is also part of the exhibits, as is the company founder E. I. du Pont's first home, Eleutherian Mills. Not the least of the attractions of the Hagley is its lush setting along the banks of the Brandywine River, which powered these and many other mills.

If you want to appreciate the fruits of the first Mr. du Pont's labors, pay a visit to Nemours, the Louis XVI chateau built by descendant Alfred I. du Pont in the early 1900s. The 77-room house and formal gardens do full credit to the French chateau country that inspired them.

A more down-to-earth way to pass the time is to take a ride on the old steam train at the Wilmington and Western Railroad in Greenbank, a huffing, puffing hour's excursion into the countryside.

An even more delightful visit to the past is the easy six-mile drive south along I-95 to New Castle, where you walk cobbled streets into Colonial times. Historic New Castle was Delaware's first capital and a meeting place for the Colonial assemblies. Later overshadowed by Wilmington and Philadelphia, it fell out of the mainstream of commerce, and its lack of prosperity kept architectural changes to a minimum. Today the old town, with its mellow red brick townhouses and public green, seems hardly changed by the passing of time. Many of the old homes are exquisitely furnished and open to the public, as is the Old Court House that once housed the state assembly. The handsome cupola atop the Court House is distinguished by being the center of the 12-mile circle surveyed by Mason and Dixon, which formed Delaware's northern boundary with Pennsylvania.

The tiny William Penn Guest House just across from the Court House and the David Finney Inn are perfect historic hostelries for the town, and there's even an appropriately atmospheric dining place, the New Castle Inn, in an old arsenal behind Delaware Street.

The third Saturday in May each year is designated as "A Day in Old New Castle," and many of the private homes and gardens in town are open to the public. If you can time your trip to coincide, set aside the day and save Sunday for Winterthur.

Also note that the first Saturday in May each year is Wilmingon Garden Day, a once-a-year opportunity to visit some of the city's finest houses and gardens, and another reason to postpone Winterthur until the next day.

Either event, plus Winterthur in the spring, makes for an unbeatable combination.

Delaware Area Code: 302

DRIVING DIRECTIONS Take the New Jersey Turnpike to the end, cross the Delaware Memorial Bridge to Route 295, and turn north on I-95 into Wilmington. From Wilmington to Winterthur, take Route 52; the entrance is on the right about two miles past the railroad tracks at Greenville Shopping Center. From Wilmington to New Castle, follow I-95 south to Route 141 east.

Total distance: about 125 miles.

PUBLIC TRANSPORTATION Amtrak serves Wilmington. Bus
No. 14 (Kennett Pike line) goes from the train station to Winterthur
daily. Check for current schedule at station.

ACCOMMODATIONS *Hotel du Pont,* 11th and Market streets,
Wilmington, 656–8121, $$–$$$$; ask about special weekend package
plans ● *Radisson Wilmington,* 700 King Street, Wilmington, 655–
0400, $$$–$$$$; lower weekend rates—check for current packages ●
Holiday Inn–North, 4000 Concord Pike, Wilmington, 478–2222, $$ ●
Christina House, 707 King Street, Wilmington, 656–9300, all suites,
$$$–$$$$ ● *William Penn Guest House,* 206 Delaware Street, New
Castle, 328–7736, $ (no private baths) ● *David Finney Inn,* 216 Dela-
ware Street, New Castle, 322–6367, $$–$$$ ● *Fairville Inn,* Route
52, Mendenhall, PA (215) 388–5900, $$$–$$$$ CP.

DINING *Hotel du Pont* (see above). Brandywine Room and Green
Room, both elegant, lunches, $–$$$; dinners, $$–$$$$ ● *Columbus
Inn,* 2216 Pennsylvania Avenue (Route 52), 571–1492; regional sea-
food specialties, especially crab, $$–$$$ ● *Leoune's at the Mansion,*
Bancroft Estate Road, 658–5266, atmospheric old home near Dela-
ware Art Museum, $$–$$$ ● *Bellevue In the Park,* 911 Philadelphia
Pike, 798–7666, $$–$$$ ● *Tiffin,* 1208 North Market Street, 571–
1133, a local favorite, $$–$$$ ● *Ristorante Amalfi,* 3801 Greenville
Center, Greenville, 658–0852, $$–$$$. ● *New Castle Inn,* behind the
Court House, New Castle, 328–1798; historic arsenal buildings with
specialty chicken and oyster pot pie, dinner $$–$$$; Sunday brunch,
served 11 A.M. to 2 P.M., $ ● *Greenery Too,* Route 52, Greenville
Center, 655–8000, lunch $; dinner $$; brunch $ ● *David Finney Inn*
(see above), $$.

SIGHTSEEING *Winterthur Museum,* Winterthur, 654–1548.
"Winterthur in Spring" Two Centuries Tour of 16 rooms plus "Port
Royal Tour," 16 additional rooms usually seen by reservation only,
and self-guided garden tour, mid-April through May, Tuesday to Sat-
urday, 10 A.M. to 4 P.M.; Sunday noon to 4 P.M. Adults, $8; children
12–18, $6.50; under 12 free. Rest of year, general admission is for
"Two Centuries Tour" only, Montmorenci or Readbourne Tours, by
reservation only, adults, $12.50, children 12–18, $6.50 ● *Delaware
Art Museum,* 2301 Kentmere Parkway, Wilmington, 571–9590.
Hours: Tuesday to Saturday 10 A.M. to 5 P.M., until 9 P.M. on Tues-
day; Sunday noon to 5 P.M. Free ● *Hagley Museum,* Route 141,

Greenville, 658–2400. Hours: daily 9:30 A.M. to 4:30 P.M. Adults, $5; children 6–14, $2.50; children under 6 free ● *Wilmington and Western Railroad,* Routes 2 and 41, Greenbank Station, one-hour steam train ride from Greenbank to Mt. Cuba Picnic Grove. Hours: May to October, Sundays only 12:30, 2, and 3:30 P.M. Adults, $5; children, $3; children under 2 free ● *Wilmington Old Town Hall,* 512 Market Street Mall, Wilmington, 655–7161. Hours: Tuesday to Friday noon to 4 P.M.; Saturday 10 A.M. to 4 P.M. Free ● *Nemours Mansion,* Rockland Road, Wilmington, 651–6912. Tours from May to November. Hours: Tuesday to Saturday 9 A.M., 11 A.M., 1 P.M., and 3 P.M.; Sunday 11 A.M., 1 P.M., and 3 P.M. Over 16 only, $7 ● *Amstel House Museum,* 2 East 4th at Delaware Street, New Castle, 322–2794. Hours: Tuesday to Saturday, 11 A.M. to 4 P.M.; Sunday 1 P.M. to 4 P.M. Adults, $4.50; children 5–12, $.50, under 5 free ● *Old Court House,* 2nd and Delaware, New Castle, 571–3059. Hours: Tuesday to Saturday, 10 A.M. to 4:30 P.M.; Sunday 1:30 P.M. to 4:30 P.M. Free ● *Old Dutch House,* 32 East 3rd Street, New Castle, 322–9168. Oldest dwelling in state, early eighteenth-century furnishings. Hours: April to October, Wednesday to Saturday, 11 A.M. to 4 P.M.; Sunday 1 P.M. to 5 P.M. Adults, $1, children 5–12, $.50 ● *George Read II House,* 42 The Strand, New Castle, 655–7161. Georgian home with period antiques, formal garden. March to December, Tuesday to Saturday 10 A.M. to 4 P.M.; Sunday noon to 4 P.M. Adults, $3; children, $1.50.

FOR FURTHER INFORMATION Wilmington Convention and Visitors Bureau, 1300 Market Street, Wilmington, DE 19801, 652–4088, or (800) 422–1181.

On the Back Roads in Connecticut Laurel Country

All of Connecticut may be known as the Laurel State, but it is the northwest corner that seems to have cornered the most magnificent displays of the state flower—and a little known spot near Torrington that has the most spectacular show of all.

Known as Indian Lookout, it's actually the private property of the Paul Freedmans, who some 35 years ago began clearing their 6 acres of mountainside to allow the wild laurels to spread and gradually landscaped the area to provide a balanced natural setting. The 6 acres grew to 100 and the pale pink clouds of laurel enveloping the mountain grew more beautiful with the seasons until, in 1958, the owners decided it was too beautiful to keep to themselves.

So visitors are now welcome to come to Indian Lookout for laurel season only, from mid to late June. Come dressed for the occasion—you'll have to climb the hill on foot unless you are one of the senior citizens who are allowed to drive through on weekdays from 5:30 to 6 P.M. But the view is worth every step of the climb.

Having literally scaled the heights when it comes to laurel watching, you're now all set for further excursions into the countryside, a rural ramble through little towns where the residents still patronize the general store, past historic homes and unexpected museums, in and out of antiques stores. You'll have plenty of opportunity to get back to nature, to hike, or possibly even to paddle your way down the Housatonic River.

All along the way, the laurels lend a pastel glow to the scenery.

Just a few miles north of Torrington along Route 8 is Winsted, a tiny town that calls itself the Laurel City. Until the late 1960s, Winsted celebrated the appearance of its bountiful blossoms every year with a weekend festival. Recently town residents have revived the custom, staging a true bit of small-town Americana with bands and a home-made float parade, the crowning of a Laurel Queen, booths of home-made goodies set around the village green, and an old-fashioned square dance on Saturday night.

Festival or no, Winsted usually posts markers to send visitors on self-guided auto tours of the most scenic laurel views. While you're in town stop at the corner of Lake and Prospect streets to see the Solomon Rockwell House, an antebellum mansion that is a national historic landmark, furnished with Hitchcock chairs, Thomas and Whiting clocks, and memorabilia dating to the Revolutionary War.

Take Route 20 north from Winsted to Riverton for a closer look at Mr. Hitchcock's famous chairs in a museum building that was once an old church meetinghouse. The Hitchcock Museum has an extensive collection of the originals; the modern factory nearby makes reproductions, using some of the traditional hand procedures, and you can visit a showroom and a gift shop there.

Also in the village is a Seth Thomas factory outlet where you can get good buys on mantel, wall, and grandfather clocks from America's oldest clockmaker.

There are a couple of antiques shops in Riverton, an herb shop, a contemporary crafts gallery that specializes in pewter, and a gift shop that has many Appalachian and Blue Ridge Mountain craftwares. For lunch, the Catnip Mouse Tearoom will serve your sandwich on homemade bread, and the Village Sweet Shoppe has tempting chocolates and ice cream for dessert.

From Riverton, plot your course according to your inclinations. If you want to get out and hike, there are two possibilities. The People's State Forest on Route 44 in Barkhamsted offers miles of well-marked trails. Or, since it's laurel season, you might want to go back toward Winsted and follow Route 44 northwest to Haystack Mountain State Park or Dennis Hill State Park, both in Norfolk. Eack park has summit buildings with magnificent views, but Dennis Hill is a particularly good choice if you are looking for laurel vistas.

If you prefer to continue traveling the back roads by car there are two possible routes. Head south to the junction of Route 44 and Route 219, then north to the Lake McDonough Recreation Area for a scenic ride and perhaps a pause for a picnic or a rowboat ride. At the junction of 219 and 318, drive west to the Saville Dam and Spillway, a picture-perfect scene of rolling hills and lakes with rushing white water cascading down the spillway in spring. Don't forget the camera.

Or you might take Route 183 out of Winsted to Colebrook, where you'll find a genuine one-room schoolhouse and a general store that has been in operation since 1812. The town hall dates to 1816. You couldn't have found a more authentic, nontouristy New England village. And there's also a haven for book buffs, the Book Barn, with more than 5,000 selections, some rare, some just secondhand.

Catching up with the hikers in Norfolk, you'll find a drive through the local parks an enjoyable outing. Beginning in late June, this is also the site of the Yale Summer School of Music and some excellent summer concerts. It may be a bit early, but check locally to see if the season has begun. Music Mountain, not too far away in Falls Village, also begins its season in mid-June, running through early September, with mostly chamber groups, but a bit of Gilbert and Sullivan and jazz mixed in for spice.

There's a happy choice of country inn headquarters for this weekend. Norfolk offers three winners. Mountain View is homey Victorian, while Manor House is just what the name implies—a grand and spacious manor with handsome paneling, Tiffany windows, and oversize rooms. Greenwoods Gate is Colonial and decorated with high style and taste. The Old Riverton Inn is a different type of Colonial charmer, a wayside inn that has been welcoming travelers since 1796, and the little town of New Hartford offers two delightful bed-and-breakfast homes. Highland Farm is another gracious old Victorian, while Cobble Hill Farm is a dream Colonial home tucked away on 40 magnificent acres with a pond.

On Sunday you can continue shunpiking on Route 44 to Canaan, where you may well want to hop aboard the Housatonic Railroad for an hour and a half scenic jaunt through the wooded countryside along the picturesque Housatonic River. The restored 1872 station here is the oldest in continuous use in the United States. If you don't take the ride, you may still want to stop at the Depot Restaurant for lunch.

If more motoring is your aim, keep on Route 44 west to Salisbury, Lakeville, and Sharon and you'll be passing through three of the loveliest northwest Connecticut towns. In Sharon the Northeast Audubon Center on Route 4 offers self-guided nature trails over 684 acres of sanctuary.

If your timing is right and a race is scheduled, you may also decide to take in the speeding autos at Lime Rock Park, just a few miles east of Lakeville.

In your own car, don't be afraid to venture off onto the side roads. One of the real pleasures of this kind of weekend is discovering your own memories—a white steepled church, a picture-book Colonial farmhouse, or a babbling brook.

But really to make the most of the Connecticut springtime, there's nothing to compare with the quiet and the country scenery on a cruise down the Housatonic River by canoe. Follow Route 7 south out of Canaan to Falls Village, and a place called Riverrunning Expeditions will provide everything you need. Don't be frightened by the name—the portion of the river from Falls Village to West Cornwall is almost all placid flatwater, and if you remember your strokes from those long-gone days at summer camp, you'll have no trouble at all. They'll give you a quick refresher or a whole day of instruction if you really want to prepare for running a river, even the whitewater. And if you don't trust yourself at all, you can splurge and hire a guide who'll lead you safely down the river, filling you in on the history and the wildlife and vegetation of the area as you float by.

If you debark at Cornwall Bridge, you're in just the right place for a last bit of picturesque scenery—the covered bridge that gives the town its name. Proceed across the bridge into town to Freshfields, and you can have a drink or a meal with a waterfall view, the perfect end to a country ramble, whether by land or by canoe.

Connecticut Area Code: 203

DRIVING DIRECTIONS Hutchinson River Parkway to Merritt Parkway. Follow the Merritt past Bridgeport, then take Route 8 north to Torrington. Follow Route 4 through Torrington and past town to Mountain Road and Indian Lookout.

Total distance: about 109 miles to Torrington.

ACCOMMODATIONS *Mountain View Inn,* Route 272, Norfolk, 542–5595, $$–$$$ CP. ● *Manor House,* P.O. Box 701, Maple Avenue, Norfolk, 542–5690 $$–$$$ CP ● *Greenwoods Gate,* Greenwoods Road East, Norfolk, 542–5439, $$$$ CP ● *Highland Farm,* Highland Avenue, New Hartford, 379–6029, $$–$$$ CP ● *Cobble Hill Farm Inn,* Steele Road, New Hartford, 379–0057, $$$ CP (with a big farm breakfast) ● *Old Riverton Inn,* Route 20, Riverton, 378–8678, $$ CP.

DINING *Mountain View Inn* (see above) $$–$$$ ● *Old Riverton Inn* (see above), $$ ● *Yankee Pedlar Inn,* 93 Main Street, Torrington, 489–9226, $$–$$$ (rooms also available, $$) ● *Freshfields,* Route 128, West Cornwall, 672–6601, $$–$$$ ● *The Tributary,* 19 Rowley Street, Winsted, 379–7679, pleasant and unpretentious, $$.

SIGHTSEEING *Indian Lookout,* Mountain Road, Torrington. Hours: weekdays 1:30 P.M. to 6 P.M., weekends 11 A.M. to 6 P.M. Free, but donations accepted ● *Solomon Rockwell House,* Lake and Prospect streets, Winsted, 379–8433. Hours, June 15 to September 15, Thursday to Sunday 2 P.M. to 4 P.M. (Hours are extended for the Laurel Festival weekend.) Donation ● *Hitchcock Museum,* Route 20, Riverton, 379–1003. Hours: June to October, Wednesday to Saturday 11 A.M. to 4 P.M., Sunday 1 P.M. to 4 P.M.; April and May, Saturday only 11 A.M. to 4 P.M. Free ● *Northeast Audubon Center,* Route 4, Sharon, 364–0520. Hours: Monday to Saturday 9 A.M. to 5 P.M.; Sunday 1 P.M. to 5 P.M. Adults, $2; children, $1 ● *Riverrunning Expeditions Ltd.,* Main Street, Falls Village, CT 06031, 824–5579. Write or call for brochure and current rates. Canoe rentals are also available at *Clarke Outdoors,* Route 7, West Cornwall, 672–6365. ● *Norfolk Music Festival,* Route 44, Norfolk, box office (in season) 542–5537, information (off season) 436–0336 ● *Music Mountain Chamber Series,* off Route 7, Falls Village, 496–1222 ● *Lime Rock Park Auto Races,* Box 111, Lakeville, 435–2814.

Big Bird to Ben Franklin:
Family Fun near Philadelphia

There goes little Susan, diving and paddling her way through a spongy-bottom "pool" filled with 80,000 little plastic balls. And there's brother Mark, pushing through a forest of giant punching bags. And who's that coming right behind them? None other than Mom and Dad, both with grins every bit as wide as the kids'.

Sesame Place, a "family play park," in Langhorne, Pennsylvania, just south of Trenton and north of Philadelphia, is a place where 3- to 13-year-olds can exercise mind and muscle cavorting on one of the nation's most innovative playgrounds, trying out do-it-yourself science experiments, and having a go at dozens of specially designed educational computer games.

This is a totally "kid-powered" park, run on the energy of the eager youngsters who come to play. Indeed, there's enough energy flying around to light a small city. The kids gliding, tumbling, climbing, sliding, and bouncing around the playground never stop to miss the passive roller coasters and rides that have no place in this park. Nor do they realize all that fun is teaching them things. The idea here is to encourage children to try new activities and master new skills.

And then there are all those computer games. This is the first real encounter with computer games for many of the children (not to mention their parents), and the games are designed to be appealing rather than intimidating.

There are other goings on as well—do-it-yourself science experiments, storytelling, the "Sesame Players" who invite youngsters to participate in their plays—even classes for those who are serious about learning to conquer the computer.

Sesame Place gets crowded, so it is a good idea to make it your first destination in the morning, enjoying a few hours of fun and then lunching in the restaurant where the see-through kitchen and a two-way microphone to the cooks make even food preparation a learning experience for the kids.

When you can convince the family to leave, go back through Big Bird's Beak (the park entrance) and you're ready to proceed to Philadelphia. Families love Philly because it offers not only the perennial historic pleasures, but also a host of innovative attractions for kids.

Everyone seems to get a special kick from seeing the real Liberty Bell, crack and all. The bell is just one of the sights in a complex called Independence National Historical Park, which is billed rightly as

America's most historic square mile. Start at the visitors center at 3rd and Chestnut streets to see a 30-minute film to put it all in perspective, then take the walking tour map and see the sights. These include Independence Hall, where the Declaration of Independence was adopted; Congress Hall, the home of the legislature in the late eighteenth century; Franklin Court, the site of Benjamin Franklin's home and of a lively underground museum; Old City Hall; Carpenter's Hall, where the first Continental Congress met; the First and Second U.S. Banks (literally); City Tavern; and any number of other historic homes, churches, and businesses. It's all free, and you can take in as much or as little as your family can absorb, a neat little American history lesson to close out the day.

Get a good night's rest because Sunday offers a delightful choice of directions. The Treehouse at the Philadelphia Zoo, for example, was specially designed for 4- to 11-year-olds. It is unique, letting youngsters experience for themselves what it might feel like to climb through a 35-foot-high honeycomb for a bee's-eye view of the world, or to hatch out of a giant egg in the Everglades Swamp. They can scramble to the top of a four-story fiberglass tree then take a slide down between the roots for a look underground, or use a magic ring to unlock nature's secrets, such as who might be found living inside a rock or underneath the ground. The zoo is a quick and easy ride from downtown on the Fairmount Park trolley.

Even the youngest won't get restless at the "Please Touch" Museum, the first in the nation to be designed especially for children under 7. They are enthralled here, dressing up as firefighters or ballerinas, ringing up sales in their own grocery store or running a doctor's office. This is also one of the few museums offering an attended "Tot Spot" for children under 3. Big brothers and sisters will find computer games and other things to keep them happy, too.

"Discovering Dinosaurs," the $2.5 million exhibition that opened recently at the Academy of Natural Sciences, is an eye-opener for all ages, changing old perceptions about these fascinating prehistoric giants. The dozen or so specimens on display are not lumbering slowpokes, but graceful and quick-footed animals, fitting the latest picture that scientific research has revealed. The interactive exhibits allow kids to dig for fossils, step into a dinosaur's footprints, play archaeologist at the "build-a-dino" station, work a dinosaur jaw, or call up pictures, facts, and figures on a sophisticated video-disk system. A favorite corner is the one where film clips give a hilarious review of how dinosaurs have been treated in the movies.

One of the best of Philadelphia's many museums—and one of the best science museums in the nation—is the imaginative Franklin Institute, a place where visitors find out about science by sitting in the cockpit of a real Boeing 707, climbing aboard a 350-ton steam locomotive, observing the solar system in action, or taking a walk through the chambers of a giant walk-through heart. Even physics is far from boring here, when you discover that by finding the right distance, you can use a rope and pulley to lift a giant weight by yourself.

The fun continues down at Penn's Landing on the Delaware River waterfront, where there are tall ships as well as battleships and a real live submarine ready for boarding. If you are inspired to set off on a cruise of your own, the sleek *Spirit of Philadelphia* will be glad to oblige with regular luncheon and dinner cruises on the river, and special rates for small fry.

Even eating can be a new adventure in the City of Brotherly Love. Kids invariably love soft pretzels from the ever-present street vendors, and cheese steaks like those at Jim's at 4th and South streets. You can dine at Penn's Landing on the four-masted barque *Moshulu,* the largest all-steel sailing ship in the world, now converted to a seaworthy restaurant. Or you can head for the colorful stalls and the reasonably priced Italian restaurants in South Philly or have lunch amid the bustling action at Reading Terminal Market, where generations of Philadelphians have shopped for fresh produce and meat. Knowing locals descend here at lunch for freshly carved turkey sandwiches—or Peking duck, gyros, or enchiladas.

However you slice it, Philly is a feast of fun for families.

Philadelphia Area Code: 215

DRIVING DIRECTIONS Take I-95 into Lower Bucks County, Pennsylvania, to the Levittown exit (25-E). Follow signs for the Oxford Valley Mall on the US 1 bypass and you'll see signs for Sesame Place. To get to Philadelphia, continue on I-95 south.

Total distance: 80 miles to Sesame Place, about 100 miles to Philadelphia.

ACCOMMODATIONS Most convenient when driving in from Sesame Place are lodgings northeast of the city, such as ● *Holiday Inn Northeast,* 3499 Street Road, Bensalem (near US 1), 638–1500, $–$$ (children under 18 free in same room) ● *Sheraton Inn Northeast,* 9461 Roosevelt Boulevard, Philadelphia, 691–9700, $$–$$$ (under 18 free in same room) ● *Holiday Inn Independence Mall,* 4th and Arch streets, 923–8660, $$–$$$ (under 18 free in same room) ● *Quality Inn–Center City,* 22nd Street and Benjamin Franklin Parkway, Philadelphia,

568–8300, $$ • Don't overlook special weekend family packages in many hotels. For current available packages, contact Philadelphia Convention and Visitors' Bureau, 15 Market Street, Philadelphia, PA 19102.

DINING   See Philadelphia Dining, page 212.

SIGHTSEEING   *Sesame Place,* Oxford Valley Mall off US 1 bypass, Langhorne, 752–7070. Hours: 10 A.M. to 5 P.M. daily May through early September; weekends only September to mid-October; until 8 P.M. from mid-June to Labor Day. Adults, $13.95; children, $10.95, less in spring and fall • *Independence National Historical Park,* 3rd and Chestnut streets, Philadelphia, 597–8974. Hours: daily 9 A.M. to 5 P.M. Free • *Penn's Landing,* Delaware and Spruce streets, Philadelphia, 923–8181. *USS Olympia,* hours: daily 10 A.M. to 4:30 P.M., summer till 6 P.M. Adults, $3; children under 12, $1.50. *Gazela,* hours: Saturday and Sunday 12:30 P.M. to 5 P.M. Adults, $1; children, $.50. • *Franklin Institute Science Museum,* 20th Street and Franklin Parkway, Philadelphia, 564–3375. Hours: Monday to Saturday 10 A.M. to 5 P.M.; Sunday noon to 5 P.M. Adults, $4.50; children 4–12, $2.50; children under 4 free • *Philadelphia Zoological Garden,* 34th Street and Girard Avenue, Fairmount Park, 243-1100. Hours: 9:30 A.M. to 5 P.M. weekdays, to 6 P.M. weekends and holidays. Adults, $4; children, $3. • *Please Touch Museum for Children,* 210 North 21st Street, 963–0666. Hours: Tuesday to Saturday 10 A.M. to 4:30 P.M., Sunday from 12:30 P.M. Admission, $3 • *Academy of Natural Sciences Museum,* 19th and Benjamin Franklin Parkway, 299–1000. Hours: Monday to Friday 10 A.M. to 4 P.M., Saturday and Sunday to 5 P.M. Adults, $4; students, $3.50; children 3–12, $3.

FOR FURTHER INFORMATION   Contact Philadelphia Convention and Visitors' Bureau, 1515 Market Street, Philadelphia, PA 19102, 636–1666. For free information packet, phone toll free (800) 523–2004.

Mansion-Hopping Along the Hudson

For years the spectacular views of the Hudson River Valley and the gentle juxtaposition of the river and mountains seen from the river's east bank have fascinated artists—and millionaires. The area's beauty inspired the first cohesive group of American artists, aptly known as the "Hudson River School," and also attracted people like the Vanderbilts, Roosevelts, and Livingstons, who built their mansions on sites overlooking the majestic river.

Today, many of those magnificent estates are open to the public, offering both a living lesson in American history and a firsthand look at the life-style of a more opulent era. A weekend of mansion-hopping also provides an ample helping of scenery, with special towns, antiques, and unexpected pleasures to be found all along the way.

Ideal headquarters for a Hudson River ramble is the pretty town of Rhinebeck, home of the hotel that proudly calls itself the oldest in America. The Beekman Arms, a stagecoach stop dating to 1700, fascinates modern visitors with its venerable guest books. Washington, Lafayette, and Aaron Burr stayed here, along with later notables like Horace Greeley, William Jennings Bryan, and many of our presidents. Franklin Roosevelt, who lived nearby at Hyde Park, wound up every campaign with an informal talk on the inn's front porch.

Recently the inn has bought up the 1844 Delamater House and other vintage village houses and added look-alike new structures to form a little complex around a court that is even nicer than staying in the main building. Many of the rooms have working fireplaces. And pleasant bed-and-breakfast inns are opening in the area, as well.

Once settled into Rhinebeck, you can plan a first day of touring to the north and your second day making mansion stops downriver, on the way home. In between, there are lovely old homes and shops to explore in Rhinebeck (be forewarned that most shops close on Sunday), plus the Old Rhinebeck Aerodrome, a one-of-a-kind place with antique airplanes both on display and in the air for shows held every weekend. Everything's in the spirit of the old glory days, including the pilots who wear uniforms dating to World War I.

Rhinebeck is also the site of an excellent crafts fair in late June and the old-fashioned Dutchess County Fair in August, both held at the fairgrounds.

Start your mansion tour driving north on scenic route 9G to Hudson. Make a stop along the way at Clermont, the former estate of the Livingston family and now a museum home and state park with grounds that are among the most beautiful of any along the river. They're open free for picnicking or just looking.

About four miles below Hudson you'll come to Olana, the Persian castle built by painter Frederic Lewis Church, well-known member of the Hudson River School.

Whether your interest is art, gardens, decorating, or architecture, you'll find much to see in the domain of the well-traveled Mr. Church. The unusual structure and decor of the house and the meticulously planned grounds are strongly personal expressions of his taste, and outside the windows there is virtually a finished Hudson River School painting, with sweeping views of the river and the mountains beyond.

The city of Hudson offers its own perspective of the river from the Parade Walk, and its restored and revitalized Warren Street is almost a miniature Georgetown. The American Museum of Fire Fighting in Hudson tells its own special history from bucket brigade to horse-drawn pumps to contemporary gear. There are also some fancy antique fire engines used by volunteer brigades, more for show than fighting fires, and they are fun to see.

There are still more mansions awaiting to the south. One of the lesser known is the Mills Mansion in Staatsburg, an 1895 neoclassical 65-room affair designed by Stanford White and furnished in fancy Louis XV and Louis XVI styles.

Far less elaborate and more famous is Franklin Roosevelt's home and library in Hyde Park. This is not so much a showplace as a warm testament to an exceptional family who left the home stamped with their own personalities. Franklin Roosevelt grew up here, and he and his wife, Eleanor, spent a great deal of time in Hyde Park with his mother, Sara.

The family memorabilia ranges from FDR's boyhood pony cart to papers that shaped world history. The collection is arranged chronologically, and seeing it is a wonderful way to learn or remember what happened here and abroad between the years 1932 and 1945. There are also records of Eleanor's humanitarian activities extending to 1962. In 1984, Eleanor's own modest home, Val-Kill, was opened to the public. Situated just two miles from the big house, it was her private retreat while her husband was alive, and the place where she chose to spend her last years.

A marked contrast to Hyde Park is the opulent mansion down the road built by Frederick Vanderbilt, grandson of "The Commodore." Designed by the famous firm of McKim, Mead, and White in the late 1890s, it is a lavish Beaux Arts structure where hundreds of guests could be, and were, entertained. The landscaping of the grounds and the views of the Hudson and the Catskills are magnificent.

If the Rhinebeck lodgings are filled, you can drive over to Amenia to Troutbeck, a lovely estate that is a conference center during the week and a wonderful retreat on weekends. Otherwise, there are motels in Hyde Park and in Poughkeepsie, a few miles south.

There is a bounty of good restaurants in the area. Across the Rip Van Winkle Bridge from Hudson in Catskill is La Rive, the kind of

French country restaurant you would be pleased to find in France. The Beekman Arms serves good traditional American fare, and in Hyde Park you can sample haute cuisine produced by the soon-to-be-greats at the nation's top school for chefs, the Culinary Institute of America. If you want dinner or luncheon in the American Bounty or Escoffier rooms, you'll have to make reservations as much as three months ahead for weekends. From Monday to Friday, there's a less formal choice, St. Andrews Café, which takes no reservations.

Continuing south, the Treasure Chest in Poughkeepsie dates to 1741 and still maintains a bit of Colonial ambience, while Dutchess Manor in Beacon gets high marks for food and its Hudson River view. Farther west in Patterson, there is another classic French inn, L'Auberge Bretonne, and if you are in the mood to splurge, Harralds in Stormville is a five-star winner.

Better get explicit driving directions for country retreats like La Rive when you make your absolutely essential reservation for dinner.

But you'll need no help finding the antiques shops in the area. They're plentiful on Route 9 and on the main street of Rhinebeck and almost anywhere you go in the Hudson Valley.

Rhinebeck, Hyde Park, Poughkeepsie, Patterson Area Code: 914

Catskill Area Code: 518

DRIVING DIRECTIONS New York Thruway to exit 19, across the Rhinecliff Bridge to Route 9G south, then a right turn onto Route 9 south. Or take the Saw Mill onto the Taconic Parkway and get off at Route 199, following 308 left to Route 9 Rhinebeck.

Total distance: about 100 miles.

PUBLIC TRANSPORTATION Amtrak service to Rhinebeck; Metro North Service to Rhinecliff, three miles away (the Beekman Arms will meet guests).

ACCOMMODATIONS *Beekman Arms,* Route 9, Rhinebeck, 876–7077. Main House, $$; Delamater House, $$ CP; Carriage House, $$$ CP; Delamater Courtyard, $$$ CP ● *Montgomery Inn,* 67 Montgomery Street (Route 9) Rhinebeck, 876–3311, $$ CP ● *Fala House,* 46 E. Market Street, Hyde Park, 229–5937, small pleasant B&B, $$ CP ● Some motel possibilities: *The Roosevelt Inn,* Route 9, Hyde Park, 229–2443, $–$$. *Super 8 Motel,* Route 9, Hyde Park, 229–0088, $. *Inn at the Falls,* Route 376, Poughkeepsie, 462–5770, $$$$.

DINING   *Beekman Arms* (see above), $$ • *La Rive,* Catskill, 943–
4888, $$$ • *Culinary Institute of America,* Route 9, Hyde Park, 471–
6608. Escoffier Room, complete dinner $36, complete lunch $18;
American Bounty, $$$; St. Andrews Café, $$ • *Treasure Chest,* 568
South Road, Poughkeepsie, 462–4545. Lunch $–$$; dinner $$–$$$ •
L'Auberge Bretonne, Route 22, Patterson, 878–7882, $$$ • *Dutchess
Manor,* Route 9D, Beacon, 831–3650, $$–$$$ • *Harralds,* Route 52,
Stormville, 878–6595, prix fixe, $50. • For lunch in Rhinebeck, try
Harvest on Market Street, $.

SIGHTSEEING   *Old Rhinebeck Aerodrome,* Stone Church Road, off
Route 9, Rhinebeck, 758–8610. Display hours: mid-May to October,
daily 10 A.M. to 5 P.M. Adults, $1.50; children 6–10, $1. Air show
hours: Sunday 2:30 P.M.; July and August, Saturday and Sunday 2:30
P.M. Adults, $6; children, $3 • *Clermont State Historic Park,* Route 6
(off Route 9G), Hudson, 537–4240. Hours: late May to October,
Wednesday to Sunday 9 A.M. to 5 P.M. Free • *Olana State Historic
Site,* Route 9G, Hudson, 828–0135. Hours: late May to October,
Wednesday to Saturday 10 A.M. to 4 P.M.; Sunday from 1 P.M. Adults,
$1; children, $.50 • *American Museum of Fire Fighting,* Harry How-
ard Avenue, Hudson, 828–7695. Hours: April to October daily except
Monday 9 A.M. to 4:30 P.M. Free • *Mills Mansion and State Park,* US
9, Staatsburg, 889–4100. Hours: Memorial Day to Labor Day,
Wednesday to Saturday noon to 5 P.M.; Sunday from 1 P.M. to 5 P.M.
last tour, 4:30 P.M. Free • *Franklin D. Roosevelt National Historic
Site,* US 9, Hyde Park, 229–9115. Hours: April to October, daily 9
A.M. to 5 P.M.; rest of year closed Tuesday and Wednesday. Adults,
$3.50; under 16 and over 62 free • *Eleanor Roosevelt National His-
toric Site,* access by shuttle bus from F.D.R. site, buses April to October, daily 9:30 A.M. to 5 P.M., November, December, March, 10
A.M. to 4 P.M., closed January and February. Adults, $2.50; children
4–15, $1.65 • *Vanderbilt Mansion National Historic Site,* Route 9,
Hyde Park, 229–7770. Hours: April to October daily 10 A.M. to 5:30
P.M., rest of year, 9 A.M. to 4:30 P.M. Adults, $2; under 12 and over
62 free.

Horsing Around in New Jersey

"We raise 'em, we ride 'em, we race 'em."

Way out west in New Jersey, the subject was horses and a gentleman was explaining to us that in this state, which is better known for turnpike traffic than green pastures, there probably are more cowboys to be found than anywhere else east of Texas. The reason is that raising horses is one of the state's principal industries, particularly in Monmouth County, not far from the Jersey shore.

The horse farms are in full view along the roads, concentrated in a triangle between Holmdel, Freehold, and Colt's Neck—a particularly pleasant sight in spring when the colts are in the fields grazing beside their mothers. The trotters run at Freehold and the thoroughbreds at Monmouth Park. With all of that within easy reach of some interesting historic sights and prime antiquing territory, and just a breeze from the shore, what better plan for a late May to early June weekend than a sampling of horse country?

The best base is the Molly Pitcher Inn in Red Bank, not your cozy country inn by any means, but an imposing red Colonial structure with a beautiful view of the Navesink River out the dining room windows. There are rooms in the inn as well as a motel unit in back and an outdoor pool in season. An alternative might be the Sheraton Gardens in Freehold or Hilton Inn in Tinton Falls.

Since you are only heading about 45 miles out of the city, it should be easy to make it for Friday night dinner. A highly recommended restaurant for French food is the Fromagerie in nearby Rumson. In Red Bank itself there is the Olde Union House on the river, a good bet for seafood, steak, or chops; Little Kraut for German; Everybody's Café for light fare; and the Left Bank Café for creative cuisine.

Save Saturday morning for a look around Red Bank. Masted schooners once plied the river here, carrying shellfish, farm produce, and other goods from the area to the world markets in New York. Later on romantic paddlewheel steamers brought vacationers from the city to this quaint Victorian town perched on the red soil banks for which it was named. Carriages in Red Bank would take them to the races or the shore or out into the gentle countryside, much the same kinds of things that attract visitors today. Red Bank grew as a shopping hub as well as a racing and boating center, but it never completely lost its Victorian feel. The shops along Front, Broad, Monmouth, and Maple have kept their old facades, making for a pleasant stroll on a spring morning.

But the real shopping attraction in Red Bank is its Antiques Center, a complex along West Front Street and Shrewsbury Avenue that just keeps growing. There are some 100 dealers congregated here, spread over several buildings, and there isn't much in the way of antiques that is not for sale.

Marine Park at the foot of Wharf Avenue is the most popular recreation spot in town, and for history there is the Allen House in neighboring Shrewsbury. Its lower floor has been restored as a tavern and upstairs is a small museum.

On the way into Shrewsbury on Route 35, the Outlet Center has some interesting tenants, including Anne Klein.

There is more interesting history to be found farther along Route 35 in Middletown. The Spy House complex overlooking Raritan Bay once harbored spies who watched British shipping. It is now the home of the Middletown Historical Society as well as the Shoals Harbor Marine Museum, with exhibits on area fishing and shipping history, and the Penelope Stout Museum of Man, featuring examples of crafts from 1663 to the 1900s. Marlpit House in Middletown is another interesting stop, an old Dutch cottage enlarged in English style in 1740 and furnished with fine period pieces.

If you're going to the races, you will have to schedule it for Saturday afternoon, since neither track operates on Sunday. Freehold runs all other days of the week January through May at 1 P.M., resuming again in August. Monmouth goes into action in late May and continues to early September with races starting at 1:30 P.M.

Afterward, try Freehold's historic American Hotel for an atmospheric dinner. The 1824 landmark has an impressive collection of Currier and Ives prints as well as all kinds of harness-racing memorabilia.

Sunday, it's time for your horse farm tour. You needn't go far looking for farms in that Holmdel–Colt's Neck–Freehold triangle. Some of the roads to follow are Routes 537, 520, 34, and 516. But feel free to turn off onto smaller lanes. You're not likely to get lost, and even if you do for a bit, you'll have fine scenery as compensation.

You'll find a couple of interesting stops in Freehold, site of the Revolutionary War Battle of Monmouth, where Molly Hays took over for her wounded husband and brought water to the parched troops, earning her place in the history books as Molly Pitcher.

Monmouth Battlefield State Park commemorates the site with an audio-visual display and an electric relief map tracing the battle. Craig House is a restored 1710 home that the British used as a hospital; Owl Haven is a nature center with live animals. The Monmouth County Historical Museum has many exhibits from Revolutionary to Civil War memorabilia, and rooms furnished in period furniture from the seventeenth to early nineteenth centuries. The kids love the attic, filled with toys, dolls, and dollhouses played with by children of another age.

From Freehold you can pick your destination. One of the biggest flea markets around takes place every weekend to the west in Englishtown—five buildings with everything from antiques to live chickens. To the south is the Deserted Village, a restored ironworking town in Allaire State Park. The site of a historic iron and brass foundry, Allaire was once a self-sustaining community, and it retains some of the furnaces, forges, and casting houses that used to turn out pots, kettles, stoves, and screws used by residents. The old town bakery, a barn and carriage house, and a general store and post office also remain, giving an interesting and vivid picture of an industrial community of the past. The Pink Creek Railroad here offers steam train rides.

If the weather is fine you may prefer to forget about sightseeing and just head for Route 33 east to the shore and the boardwalk. Spring Lake is the prettiest nearby shore town. Even Asbury Park, which can seem pretty shabby in season, has a nostalgic charm when you see the amusement area without summer crowds. Ocean Grove, a religious colony by the sea right next door, has a fascinating collection of Victorian houses.

Drive north along the shore parallel to the water on Ocean Avenue to see the gracious old vacation homes in Deal. If you've worked up an appetite for a seafood dinner, Riverhouse on the Quay in Sea Bright should fill the bill. Then cut over to River Road and follow the scenic Navesink to Front Street, and back to the parkway home.

Red Bank Area Code: 201

DRIVING DIRECTIONS Garden State Parkway southbound to Route 109, Red Bank. Route 34 runs into Rumson. Take Route 109 west and Route 50 south to Route 537 east to Freehold.
Total distance: about 50 miles.

ACCOMMODATIONS _Molly Pitcher Inn,_ State Highway 35, Red Bank, 747–2500, $$–$$$ ● _Hilton Inn,_ Hope Road at Garden State exit 105, Tinton Falls, 544–9300, $$$$ ● _Sheraton Gardens,_ Route 537 and Gibson Place, Freehold, 780–3870, $$$.

DINING _Fromagerie,_ 26 Ridge Road, Rumson, 842–8088, $$$ ● _Shadowbrook,_ off Route 35, Shrewsbury, 747–0200, Georgian mansion with gardens, $$$ ● _Olde Union House,_ 11 Wharf Avenue, Red

Bank, 842–7575, $$–$$$ • *Little Kraut,* 115 Oakland Street, 842–4380, $–$$$ • *Everybody's Café,* 79A Monmouth Street, 842–4755, $ • *Left Bank Café,* 8 Linden Place, Red Bank, 530–5930, $$–$$$ • *American Hotel,* 18–26 Main Street, Freehold, 462–0189, $$–$$$ • *Riverhouse on the Quay,* Ocean Avenue, Sea Bright, 842–1994, $–$$$.

SIGHTSEEING *Freehold Raceway,* Park Avenue at US 9 and Route 33, Freehold, 462–3800. Hours: January to May, August to December, daily except Sunday 1 P.M. $2 • *Monmouth Park,* Oceanport Avenue (Garden State exit 105), 222–5100. Hours: late May to early September, daily except Sunday 1:30 P.M. except Friday, 3 P.M. Grandstand, $1.50; clubhouse, $4. • *Allaire Village,* 938–5524. Hours: May to Labor Day 10 A.M. to 5 P.M., weekends only September and October. Parking fee, $2.50 weekends, $1.50 weekdays; train rides, $.75 • *Monmouth Battlefield State Park,* Route 33, Freehold, 462–9616, Visitor Center hours: Memorial Day to Labor Day 10 A.M. to 6 P.M., rest of year to 4 P.M. Free • *Monmouth County Historical Museum,* 70 Court Street, Freehold, 462–1466. Hours: Tuesday to Saturday 10 A.M. to 4 P.M.; Sunday 1 P.M. to 4 P.M. Adults, $2; senior citizens and children 6–18, $1 • *Englishtown Auction Sales,* 90 Wilson Avenue (Route 527), Englishtown, 446–9644. Hours: Saturday 7 A.M. to 5 P.M.; Sunday 9 A.M. to 5 P.M. • *Allen House,* Route 35 at Sycamore Avenue, Shrewsbury, 462–1466. Hours: April to December, Tuesday, Thursday, and Sunday, 1 P.M. to 4 P.M.; Saturday 10 A.M. to 4 P.M. Adults, $2; children 6–18, $1.

Chocolate and Roses in Hershey, Pennsylvania

The streetlights are Hershey kisses, the signs are chocolate color with candy-bar lettering, the main intersection of town is at Chocolate and Cocoa streets, and they give you a Hershey bar when you check into the hotel.

There's no mistaking the main attraction in Hershey, Pennsylvania, where even the grand hotel is placed to include the chocolate factory in its hilltop view. And there are few better places for a family weekend than this "company town," where chocolate really is only the beginning of the fun.

Magnificent gardens, a major theme park, a zoo, a museum of

American life, and sports facilities that include five golf courses are all waiting after the chocolate tour is over.

It's all a bit ironic since Milton Hershey, who made a fortune satisfying America's sweet tooth, probably never expected further profits from tourists. When the former farmboy came back to his hometown of Derry Township to build a chocolate factory in 1904, his main aim was to make the town a pleasant place for his workers to live. The first parks, gardens, museum, and zoo were strictly for their benefit.

But from the very start people wanted to see how this new confection called milk chocolate was made, and the factory began offering tours to meet the demand. Savoring the sweet smells, the free samples, and the pleasant atmosphere of this unusual small town, visitors told their friends to come. In 1928 the count was 10,000; by 1970 it was pushing a million and the factory could no longer accommodate the crowds. Chocolate World was built to take the place of the old tour, and it is now almost everyone's first stop in Hershey.

The free 10-minute trip in a Disney-like automated car whisks you off to the cacao plantations of Ghana. You watch the story of chocolate unfold from bean to candy bar, from picking and shipping the beans, grinding and blending them with milk in a simulated factory, to the wrapping of the bars. There's no more chocolate smell or free samples—but well over a million and a half took the ride last year, anyway.

You exit from the tour into a tropical garden containing some 99 varieties of trees, including cacao, and hundreds of flowering plants and shrubs. You're also facing stands stacked high with Hershey bars and dozens of other souvenirs, chocolate and otherwise. And there's a refreshment pavilion specializing in you-know-what.

Opposite Chocolate World is Hersheypark, once a place where factory employees came to picnic, play ball, go boating, and be entertained at the pavilion. Mr. Hershey kept improving the facilities, adding a swimming pool and a convention hall that doubled as an ice-skating rink. Hershey Zoo was actually Hershey's own private animal collection, one of the country's largest, housed at the park for all to see. And for the kids he bought a carousel and, as a twentieth birthday present to the town, a roller coaster.

As the growds grew the notion of an actual amusement park seemed a natural one, and in 1971 redevelopment began. Unless you have a total aversion to theme parks, it's hard not to like this clean and pretty one, where you stroll through a mock English town called Tudor Square, a Pennsylvania Dutch community known as Der Deitschplatz, and an eighteenth-century German village labeled Rhine Land. All come complete with appropriate costumes, music, shops, and restaurants. It's undeniably commercial, but the happy crowds don't seem to care.

The original 1919 carousel at the park now has a lot of company, including three roller coasters (scariest is the sooperdooperlooper that literally turns you upside down), a flume ride, and a couple of dozen others, from "scream machines" to rides for tots. You can get a view of the whole 87-acre park from the kiss-shaped windows of the 330-foot Kissing Tower or take the Monorail for a scenic ride with an audio accompaniment. The Monorail will even take you into town.

There is also continuous live entertainment at four theaters scattered through the park, and the adjoining arena hosts not only the Ice Capades and hockey games, but also name entertainers such as Johnny Cash and John Denver.

Almost everyone's favorite souvenir of the park is a photo taken with the life-size candy-bar characters that greet visitors. Don't forget your camera.

The zoo, too, has come a long way. It now represents the major natural regions of North America—waters, desert, woodlands, plains, and forest, with native plants and animals of each zone in their native habitat. You'll see alligators in the swamps; pumas, bison, and eagles in Big Sky Country; black bear and timber wolves in the forest; wild turkeys, bobcats, otters, and raccoons at home in the woodlands.

There's more than enough to fill a Saturday here—but more still to fill your Sunday. All ages can appreciate the beauty of the Hershey Gardens, which have grown in 40 years from an old-fashioned rose garden into 23 acres featuring 700 varieties of roses, as well as six classic gardens—English, Oriental, Colonial, and Italian, a rock garden, and a fountain garden.

Even the Hershey Museum proves to be more than you might expect. In addition to some fascinating collections of Indian artifacts, Pennsylvania Dutch crafts, and early clocks, you get a compact tour through the changing life-styles of America in terms of decorative styles and fashion, including the effect of inventions like the sewing machine. It's less overwhelming than a lot of museums and for that very reason makes its point unusually well. Try to time your visit to coincide with the performance of the Apostolic Clock, 15 minutes before each hour, with moving carved figurines depicting the Last Supper.

One other unique sight in Hershey has nothing to do with tourists. The Milton Hershey School was founded in 1909 by childless Milton and Catherine Hershey to provide a free home as well as an education for orphan boys. Now co-ed, the school tries to re-create the feel of family living for its residents with 92 campus homes spread across

10,000 acres of campus. Each house shelters 12 to 16 children with house parents. The schooling, which extends through high school, is unusual in many ways. It includes time working on community farms and the opportunity to learn a trade or prepare for college, according to each student's talents and inclinations.

Founders Hall, a striking domed marble building that is a tribute to the Hersheys, is awesome architecturally, yet it serves well as church, theater, and concert hall for 1,300 very energetic orphaned children. Some of the profits from Hershey's current commercial ventures are used to supplement the endowment Milton Hershey left for his school. Founders Hall is well worth a visit—if you can only find the time with everything else there is to do.

Where to stay in Hershey? The natural choices are the excellent Hershey-run accommodations, not cheap but not as expensive as you might think when you figure all the admissions included in weekend packages. Hotel Hershey does seem a bit steep and elegant for a family jaunt, but it is a grand hotel in every sense, Mediterranean in style, with a lobby that looks a little like a small Spanish town with its tiled fountain and arcaded stucco walls. The circular dining room has windows all around that look out at gardens and grounds, and the food is a match for the setting. There are pools indoors and out, four tennis courts, and a golf course. You could happily spend a weekend here without ever venturing off the grounds.

The Lodge is motel-style and obviously more family-oriented, as you can tell when you drive up and spot the children feeding the ducks on the pond out front. There are pools here, too, a playground, tennis and paddle tennis, a golf course and a par-3 pitch and putt, a game room for the kids, and movies at night.

June is the perfect time for Hershey, when the roses are in evidence but the summer crowds are not. The only problem may be how to see it all in one weekend. You may decide to take it in parts. That way you can see the gardens with tulips or mums as well as roses in bloom.

Hershey Area Code: 717

DRIVING DIRECTIONS   Take I-80 or 78 to the I-81 west exit at Route 743 and follow signs to Hershey.
Total distance: about 183 miles.

PUBLIC TRANSPORTATION   Amtrak service to Harrisburg. Hotel Hershey and Hershey Lodge limousine service for guests; free shuttle service to all attractions from June 13 to September 7. Bus service to Hershey via Capitol Trailways.

ACCOMMODATIONS *Hershey Resorts,* Hershey, 533–3131, or toll-free (800) 223–1588: *Hotel Hershey,* $$$$ MAP; *Hershey Lodge,* $$$ (children under 18 free in same room). Both hotels offer summer package plans including meals, lodging, and admissions. Call for information and brochure ● For less expensive lodgings, try *Best Western Inn,* 533–5665, $$$, including movies in room and continental breakfast; *Hershey Colonial,* 533–7054, $$; *Milton Motel,* 533–4533, $$; *Spinner's Motor Inn,* 533–9157, $$.

DINING Unless you want to settle for *Friendly's,* $, just opposite the Hershey Lodge, or *Spinner's Restaurant,* at that motor inn, $$, it's a Hershey world once again: *Hotel Hershey* (see above), $$$–$$$$; *Hershey Lodge* (see above), choice of three dining rooms, $$–$$$. (Lots of restaurants at the park, all prices.)

SIGHTSEEING *Hersheypark,* 534–3900. Hours: late May to Labor Day, daily 10:30 A.M. to 10 P.M.; usually weekends only early May and late September 10:30 A.M. to 8 P.M. Phone to check dates and hours. Age 8 to adult, $15.75; children 4–8, $12.75 ● *Hershey Museum of American Life.* Hours: Memorial Day to Labor Day, daily 10 A.M. to 6 P.M.; rest of year, 10 A.M. to 5 P.M. Adults, $3; children 5–18, $1.25 ● *ZooAmerica.* Hours: daily 10 A.M.; closing varies with season. Adults, $3; children 5–18, $1.75 ● *Hershey Gardens.* Hours: Memorial Day to Labor Day, daily 9 A.M. to 6 P.M.; April, May, September, and October, daily 9 A.M. to 5 P.M. Adults, $3; children 4–18, $1; families, $7.50 ● *Hershey Chocolate World.* Hours: April 1 to early June, daily 9 A.M. to 4:45 P.M.; early June to Labor Day, daily 9 A.M. to 6:45 P.M.; September to March, Monday to Saturday 9 A.M. to 4:45 P.M.; Sunday noon to 4:45 P.M. Free ● *Founders Hall.* Hours: May through October, weekdays, 9 A.M. to 4 P.M., weekends, 10 A.M. to 4 P.M.; November to April, weekdays, 9 A.M. to 4 P.M., weekends, 10 A.M. to 3 P.M. A film on the Milton Hershey School is shown hourly. Free.

FOR FURTHER INFORMATION Contact Hershey Information, Hershey, PA 17003. 534–3005, or Central Reservations, (800) 533–3131.

Summer

Summering with the Arts in Saratoga Springs

Horses and Health. The nation's oldest racetrack and the mineral-water baths were the drawing cards that brought the elite to Saratoga Springs in its 1870s heyday.

Both still entice visitors, but they share billing these days with music and dance, performed in an amphitheater in the middle of a 2,200-acre park. Since Saratoga Spa State Park expanded in 1962 with swimming, tennis, golf, and hiking facilities in addition to the bathhouses, and since the addition of the Saratoga Performing Arts Center in 1966, only real racing aficionados need wait for the August racing season, when the rates in town almost double. Saratoga now is a super destination for almost any summer weekend, particularly for ballet fans during the three-week residence of the New York City Ballet in July, and for jazz lovers during the annual big weekend when the Newport Festival takes over. The New York City Opera has also recently become a regular, and for those willing to pay the price for rooms, the Philadelphia Orchestra is the main attraction in August.

If you want to experience the flavor of old Saratoga, make your reservations early for the Adelphi Hotel, the only one of the grand hotels remaining in town. It was built in 1877, when Saratoga was undisputed queen of the spas, and it still boasts a piazza overlooking Broadway, once a spot to see who was out taking a morning stroll. Breakfast is served on the piazza on sunny days. The grand staircase, tall windows, and lofty ceilings of the lobby have been restored, and each of the 21 rooms has been done with period wall coverings and bedspreads and Victorian curlicue sofas and chairs. Some have fireplaces; all have their original woodwork and high ceilings.

The Inn at Saratoga is also in an elegant restored Victorian building, but is closer to the look of an English country house, with an English garden to match. Other alternatives include the Gideon Putnam Hotel, which is gracious and Old World inside as well as out and has the advantage of being right in the park, and the big Ramada Renaissance Hotel, with an indoor pool and exercise room. And there are scads of motels in town.

Once you've set your accommodations, there is one other absolutely necessary reservation to be made: for a mineral bath and massage at the spa that made Saratoga famous. The brochure says to call 24 hours in advance, but on a recent Fourth of July weekend there wasn't one free hour for four straight days.

The state of New York acquired the rights to the mineral waters in 1910 to conserve this natural resource, and then began purchasing the land that has been gradually developed into the present park. The waters geyser up and are available for drinking in six locations in the park, and the "treatments," which have remained reasonable in price, are a real treat.

First you are shown to a private room, where a tub is filled with naturally carbonated water at body temperature. After you've sat back and let the tiny bubbles bathe you into a relaxed state, you proceed to the massage table, where a masseur takes away any tension the mineral water hasn't already dissolved. Then you're wrapped in hot sheets and put to bed to relax—most probably to fall into a divinely restful sleep. No wonder people used to flock here.

Also available in the park are both an 18- and a 9-hole golf course, 4 swimming pools, tennis courts, 12 picnic areas, and the Ferndell Nature Trail—most everything you might need in the way of summer recreation.

At the Saratoga Performing Arts Center, known locally by its initials SPAC, something happens almost every night from June through Labor Day. The attractions are of uniformly top quality. The amphitheater, done in browns and greens to blend with its park setting, seats 5,100, and its outdoor "mezzanine" of sloping grounds has accommodated as many as 30,000.

The stage was designed to George Balanchine's specifications for the New York City Ballet, and it is also used by other dance companies such as the Nikolais Dance Theater and the Alvin Ailey dancers over the summer. In addition to dance companies, the New York City Opera, and the Philadelphia Orchestra, there are top-name popular performers on the schedule.

The jazz greats usually play on a late June weekend from noon until night. Theater and modern dance are presented in the park's Little Theater, a 500-seat indoor arena. New York's Circle Repertory is frequently featured here, along with such groups as José Limon Dance Theater and the Acting Company. Write to SPAC for schedules and order blanks, but remember you'll never be shut out of a concert if you're willing to sit on the lawn.

To see the sights of Saratoga, go into town and stop at the Information Center in front of Congress Park on Broadway for free maps and a walking-driving tour. Then stroll into Congress Park, a green oasis of fountains and gardens, and get some sense of Saratoga history at the Casino, a mid-Victorian structure with a ballroom and reception room that were once part of a flourishing gambling establishment during the town's grander days. Upstairs here the Historical Society of Saratoga Springs shows Saratoga's development from a frontier village to flamboyant resort town with some of the country's grandest hotels. There is an elaborate re-created Victorian parlor taken from a town mansion and a period bedroom with a four-poster bed and a rocker in front of the fireplace.

Upstairs on the third floor the Walworth Museum is a sampling of the rooms from the home of Reuben Hyde Walworth, the last chancellor of the state of New York, whose family lived in Saratoga for 125 years.

Saratoga had gone downhill, but it is obviously on the way back up. With walking tour in hand, go back to Broadway to see the section of downtown shops being brought back to their charming original Victorian appearance, and the sidewalk cafés and boutiques that are beginning to flourish. On North Broadway, Circular Street, and Union Avenue, you can tour the architecture of the mansions that have survived since the 1800s, and at Franklin Square, examine the Doric columns and pediments of 1830s Greek Revival houses currently being restored.

Wherever you go you'll see natural springs of mineral water bubbling up—in Congress Park, and even at the race track. Many of the spring sites offer samples of the none-too-tasty waters.

Saratoga's very attractive National Museum of Racing, a Colonial brick structure across from the track, is the only one of its kind in the world. You don't have to be a racing fan to appreciate the colorful silks of the sport's top stables, the magnificent silver trophies that have gone to prizewinners like Man O'War, and the really fine collection of equestrian paintings on display here.

Saratoga also boasts the nation's only museum devoted to dance, which opened in 1986 in the renovated Washington Bathhouse, a national historic landmark on the edge of the state park. The exhibit includes a Dance Hall of Fame, named in honor of Mr. and Mrs. Cornelius Vanderbilt Whitney, whose support made the museum a reality.

Outside Saratoga proper you can visit the campus of Skidmore College and the grounds and garden at Yaddo, the gray stone mansion that has been an inspirational refuge for writers and musicians such as Aaron Copland, Carson McCullers, and Saul Bellow.

On US 4 in Schuylerville, Saratoga National Historic Park marks the Battle of Saratoga, one of the critical encounters of the Revolutionary War. The Visitor Center offers a 20-minute film and the route for a nine-mile self-guided driving tour of the battlefield. Among the sights is the residence of General Phillip Schuyler, who commanded the troops before the battle.

If kids are along, you might want to head for Saratoga Lake, three miles west on Route 9P, which has two amusement parks on its shores, or the Petrified Gardens, three miles west on Route 29, to see reefs and other relics of the days when the area was covered by the ancient Cambrian Sea. The prehistoric specimens have been declared a national landmark by the U.S. Department of the Interior.

If you are looking for further evening amusement, a festival of baroque music goes on in town, and there is harness racing every summer night except Sunday, regardless of whether the thoroughbreds are running.

If you decide to come for the August activity at this beautiful track dating to 1863, save a morning for one of its traditions, a buffet breakfast followed by a tour of the paddocks behind the scenes. The running of the big Travers Stake Race in the middle of the month touches off a whole week of festivities in town, including antiques and art shows, a parade, and polo matches at the Saratoga Polo Grounds.

If you're after antiques stores, you'll find them on Route 29 east and west of town and in two major centers, the Farmstead on Route 9 south and Museum Antiques and Art in town at 153 Regent Street. Each of the centers represents 25 to 30 dealers.

Finally, there are more than enough restaurants in the area to provide good eating for a weekend, many in atmospheric locations such as antique farmhouses or the local old firehouse. Fine cuisine is just one more of the arts that make Saratoga a special summer destination.

Saratoga Area Code: 518

DRIVING DIRECTIONS   New York State Thruway to exit 24 at Albany-Northway (Route 87) to exit 13N, Saratoga.
Total distance: 175 miles.

PUBLIC TRANSPORTATION   Amtrak or Greyhound to Saratoga. It's easy to get around town via minibus (schedules at visitors' center), or you can rent a bike from Springwater Bike Rentals at the Gideon Putnam Hotel.

ACCOMMODATIONS   (Expect minimum stays in season) *Adelphi Hotel,* 365 Broadway, Saratoga, 587–4688, $$$–$$$$ ● *Gideon Putnam Hotel,* Saratoga Spa, 584–3000, $$$$ AP; inquire for EP rates ● *Carriage House Motel,* 178 Broadway, Saratoga, 584–4220, $$ ● *The*

Inn at Saratoga, 231 Broadway, Saratoga, 583–1890, $$$ ● *Ramada Renaissance Hotel*, 534 Broadway, 584–4000, $$–$$$$ ● *Holiday Inn*, Broadway and Circular Street, Saratoga, 584–4550, $$–$$$. (All are higher in August.)

DINING *Chez Pierre*, US 9, Wilton, 793–3350, French fare, $$–$$$ ● *Ye Olde Wishing Well*, Route 9 North, Gansevoort, 584–7640, 1823 farmhouse, $$–$$$ ● *Gideon Putnam* (see above), $–$$$ ● *The Charles' Restaurant*, Washington Street, 548–4111, $$–$$$ ● *Canterbury Restaurant*, Union Avenue and Route 9P, 587-9653, converted barn, $$–$$$ ● *Old Firehouse Restaurant*, 543 Broadway, 587–0047, $–$$ ● Three best bets are on one street: *Mrs. London's Bake Shop and Café*, 33 Phila Street, local landmark patisserie serving all three meals, $–$$$; *Hattie's Chicken Shack*, 45 Phila Street, 584–4790, chicken and ribs, $; *Eartha's Kitchen*, 47 Phila Street, 583–0602, grill specialties, $$–$$$ ● *The Elms*, Route 9, Ballston Springs, 587–2277, worth the drive for good homemade pasta and other Italian fare, $$–$$$. For after-dinner entertainment, the place is *Caffe Lena*, upstairs at 47 Phila, 583–0022.

SIGHTSEEING *Saratoga Performing Arts Center*, Saratoga Springs, 587–3330. Phone or write for schedule of performances. Prices vary with attractions, running from $8 to $25; lawn tickets $6.50 to $13. Tickets are also available at Ticketron ● *Saratoga Spa State Park Recreation Center*, South Broadway (Route 9), 584–0200. Pool, tennis, golf, par-3 golf course. Call for fees and hours ● *Saratoga Spa Mineral Bathhouses*, Saratoga Spa State Park, 584–2011. Phone for mineral-bath reservations. Bath with massage: $13 ● *National Museum of Racing*, Union Avenue and Ludlow Street, 584–0400. Hours: June 15 to September 15, Monday to Friday 9:30 A.M. to 5 P.M., Saturday and Sunday noon to 5 P.M.; August, daily 9:30 A.M. to 7 P.M. Free ● *The Casino, Walworth Museum, and Historical Society of Saratoga Springs*, Congress Park, 584–6920. Hours: July to August, daily 9:30 A.M. to 4:30 P.M.; June, September, and October, Monday to Saturday 10 A.M. to 4 P.M., Sunday 1 P.M. to 4 P.M. Adults, $1.50; students and senior citizens, $1.25; children under 12 free with adults ● *Saratoga Race Track*, Union Avenue, 584–6200, August, daily except Tuesday, 1:30 P.M. Call for this season's exact dates. Grandstand seats, $4; general admission, $2; clubhouse admission, $5. Breakfast is first-come first-served on clubhouse patio, $4 to $12 ● *National Museum of Dance*, South Broadway, 584–9330. Hours: summer, Tuesday to Saturday 10 A.M. to 5 P.M., Sunday noon to 4 P.M.; rest of year, Thursday to Sunday, same hours. Adults, $2;

students, $1; under 12, $.50 ● *Saratoga Harness Track,* off Route 9, 584–2110. Hours: May to November, Monday to Saturday 7:45 P.M. Call for off-season schedules January to March. Grandstand, $1.75; clubhouse, $3; parking, $1 ● *Petrified Gardens,* Route 29, 584–2421. Hours: June to Labor Day, daily 9 A.M. to 5 P.M. Adults, $2; children 6–12, $1 ● *Saratoga National Historic Park,* US 4, 664–9821. Hours: daily 9 A.M. to 5 P.M. Free ● *Schuyler House,* US 4, Schuylerville, 695–3554. Hours: Memorial Day to Labor Day, daily 9 A.M. to 5 P.M. Free ● *Saratoga Circuit Tours,* 417 Broadway, Saratoga Springs, 587–3656. Two-hour sightseeing tour with guide. Drink Hall, opposite Congress Park. Hours: 10 A.M. to 1 P.M. Adults, $8; children under 12, $5.

FOR FURTHER INFORMATION Contact Chamber of Commerce, 494 Broadway, Saratoga, NY 12866, 584–3255.

Litchfield and Lake Waramaug: A Connecticut Double Feature

Lake what? Even in Connecticut, lots of people haven't heard of this placid blue oasis just north of New Milford in the Litchfield Hills. Just over eight miles around, ringed by wooded hills and as smooth as a looking glass, Lake Waramaug has a small public beach at one end, and at the other, a state park, with boating and swimming facilities as well as walking trails—and not a commercial facility in sight. All you'll find around the lake are summer homes and four fine small country inns.

Each of the inns is different and has something special to offer. The largest, the Inn at Lake Waramaug, is a mini-resort with its own beach and dock, sailboats and canoes, a little paddlewheel showboat to cruise you around the lake, tennis, and an indoor pool. There are a few rooms in the inn building, a 1795 Colonial house, but most are nicely furnished motel-type modern lodges on the grounds. Hopkins Inn across the way is a pretty yellow house with a porch looking out at the lake, with 10 modest colonial bedrooms upstairs, and the best dining room in the area. Make reservations for dinner even if you don't stay here.

The Boulders Inn, literally built with boulders in its fieldstone walls, is the most appealing of all. The antiques-filled living room has fine lake views from a big picture window, as does the dining room and a pleasant outdoor dining deck. Boulders accommodates 45 people, a dozen in the pretty inn rooms and the rest in cottages on the grounds, and all share the shimmering view.

Finally, there is The Birches, located away from the others on the west shore of the lake, with just six rooms in the outbuildings and a dining room in the old white main house, whose menu reflects the Austrian background of the owners.

A pleasant inn, good food, and plenty of outdoor activity could fill a weekend on its own, but an added attraction at Lake Waramaug is its proximity to some of Connecticut's loveliest Colonial towns. Prime among them is Litchfield, invariably on every list of the most beautiful Main Streets in America and considered by many experts to be the finest unrestored, unspoiled Colonial town in America.

One of the nicest things about visiting Litchfield is that its three dozen or so choicest homes, those forming the center Historic District around the village green, are easily strollable, concentrated on two long blocks, North and South streets, just off the green.

You may recognize the steepled Congregational Church on that green; it shows up in countless photographs of typical New England scenes. Next door is the 1787 parsonage where Harriet Beecher Stowe's family lived when she was born here in the 1800s.

Across the way on South Street are two homes that help to explain why Litchfield has remained unique and unchanged. The Moses Seymour House was completed in 1817 for Jane Seymour, who married Dr. Josiah G. Beckwith. The Beckwith family has remained in the house to this day. The Seymour House next door, one of the best examples of Federal architecture of this period, was built by Moses for his son Ozias; later occupied by Origen Seymour, chief justice of Connecticut; and remained in the Seymour family until 1950. Litchfield's families didn't move on to green pastures; they stayed to tend to their green.

Tapping Reeve opened the nation's first law school in his superb 1773 home with his brother-in-law, Aaron Burr, as his first pupil. Eventually, the pupils outgrew the house and a school building was erected in 1784. Among its alumni were 3 Supreme Court justices, 28 senators, more than 100 congressmen, 2 vice-presidents, 14 governors, and 16 chief justices of Connecticut.

John C. Calhoun was a student here, lodging in the rectory next door and planting some of the elms that remain along the street. Farther down the street is the 1736 home where Ethan Allen, Revolutionary War leader of the fabled Green Mountain Boys, is believed to have been born.

Beautiful white Colonials of the 1700s seem to go on and on, including the home of Oliver Wolcott, Jr., now the town library, and the obligatory structure boasting "George Washington slept here," in this case the Elisha Sheldon Tavern. With the exception of the law school and the town Historical Society, under renovation and expected to reopen in 1988, almost all of these homes are private residences. Like so many towns, Litchfield has one day set aside for its annual open house of historic homes. It is usually the second Saturday in July (check with the Historical Society to be sure), and it is well worth timing your visit to coincide. Make it a Saturday visit in any case, as both the Reeve House and the Society are closed on Sunday.

There are a few shops in Litchfield, on the green, in Cobble Court (a nineteenth-century courtyard with cobble streets) and in Litchfield Commons on Route 202, where you'll also find Wickets, one of the best restaurants in the area, and some very tempting desserts to go at the Uncommon Strudel Bakery Café.

If the day is fine, you may prefer to forget the shops and head for the White Memorial Foundation Conservation Center, just west on Route 202. It is the state's largest nature center, with 4,000 acres and many appealing hiking trails in the hills and valleys. Bantam Lake is also part of the center, offering swimming at Sandy Beach and boats for renting at the landing at Folly Point.

For anyone interested in flowers, particularly unusual perennials, White Flower Farm is a must. This is no ordinary nursery. Garden lovers make pilgrimages here to see the eight-acre formal display garden and to browse among the 1,200 varieties of unusual plants over 20 acres of growing fields. Delphiniums are a specialty, as are tuberous begonias.

It would be easy to spend a week, rather than a weekend, enjoying the out-of-doors and the other Colonial towns around Lake Waramaug—Washington, Kent, and Woodbury, to name just a few. At least mark this down for a return visit in the fall, when flaming foliage rings the lake in a blaze of color.

Connecticut Area Code: 203

DRIVING DIRECTIONS Henry Hudson Parkway to Saw Mill River Parkway. Route 684 north to Brewster, Route 84 east to Danbury, exit 7 to Route 7 north to New Milford, then Route 202 east to New Preston and Route 45 to Lake Waramaug.
Total distance: 85 miles.

ACCOMMODATIONS *The Inn on Lake Waramaug,* North Shore Road, New Preston, 868–0563 or (212) 724–8775, $$$$ MAP (three-day minimum in summer) ● *Boulders Inn,* Route 45, New Preston, 868–7918, $$$$ MAP ● *Hopkins Inn,* Hopkins Road, New Preston, 868–7295, $ EP (closed in winter) ● *Birches Inn,* West Shore Road, 868–0229, $$ MAP

DINING *Inn on Lake Waramaug* (see above), $$–$$$ ● *Hopkins Inn* (see above), $$ ● *Boulders Inn* (see above), $$ ● *Le Bon Coin,* Route 202, New Preston, classic French in a country house, $$$ ● *Wickets,* Route 202, The Commons, Litchfield, 567–8744, bright and airy, Cricket decor, new American cuisine, $$ ● *Tollgate Hill,* Route 202, Litchfield, 482–6116, 1700s Colonial, traditional menu, $$–$$$

SIGHTSEEING *Litchfield Historical Society,* Litchfield Green, 567–5862. Currently under renovation. Phone for date of this year's open house tour ● *Tapping Reeve House and Law School,* South Street, Litchfield, 567–4501. Hours: mid-May to October, Thursday to Monday noon to 4 P.M. Adults, $1; children, free ● *White Flower Farm,* Route 63 south, Litchfield, 567–0810. Hours: April to October, weekdays 10 A.M. to 5 P.M.; weekends 9 A.M. to 5:30 P.M. Free ● *White Memorial Foundation Center,* Route 202, Litchfield, 567–0857. Hours: grounds open daily, museum open Tuesday to Saturday, spring through fall, 8:30 A.M. to 4:30 P.M.; winter, 9 A.M. to 5 P.M.; Sunday 11 A.M. to 5 P.M. year-round. Adults, $1; children, $.50. Grounds: free. Museum phone: 567–0015.

A Midsummer Escape to Shelter Island

Some say the name came from the Quakers who found refuge from religious persecution on the island. Others believe it comes from the Indian term, *Manhansack-aha-quashawamock,* "an island sheltered by islands."

Whatever the origin of the name, here's a place for anyone saying "gimme shelter" from the usual commercial summer resorts.

Shelter Island's 12 square miles are tucked between the north and south forks of Long Island's east end, reachable only by ferryboat from Greenport to the north and Sag Harbor to the south. Though the population of 2,000 swells to about 8,000 in the summer, the effects of the influx are limited since most of the summer visitors own or rent homes—also limited in number, thanks to strict zoning. About a third of the island, 2,200 acres known as Mashomack Preserve, remains unpopulated.

The current visitors' guide lists about a dozen small hotels and/or restaurants, a couple of gift and/or antiques shops, a general store/ice cream parlor, and a few places where the locals buy clothing, food, and other necessities. Besides building and selling houses for summer people, the only local industry is fishing. The big summer events are the annual country fair and the Fireman's Barbecue in August. That's it.

So, what do you do on Shelter Island? You bike. Or hike. Sunbathe on crescent beaches. Rent a sailboat or go fishing. Play a little tennis or golf. Drive around to see the varied topography and homes. Mainly, you just plain relax and adjust to the calm pace of island life.

Despite its lack of commerciality today, and its onetime reputation as a refuge for pirates (Captain Kidd is reputed to have hidden treasure here), Shelter Island was founded by four merchants. They were in the business of supplying sugar from Barbados and found the many white oak trees on the island could be used for making barrels. One of them, Nathanial Sylvester, built the first home here in 1652. The present manor house, the residence of a descendant, was constructed in 1773. Sylvester Manor became a haven for Quakers who had been driven out of Boston, and Friends groups still conduct services here regularly. They also gather each fall at the Quaker Cemetery on the outer boundary of the manor to remember those who brought their faith to Long Island. The 1852 windmill nearby was restored in 1952 as a memorial to Sylvester.

The Shelter Island Historical Society maintains a small museum of local history in Manhanset Chapel and has furnished the 1743 Haven House, where the Haven Family lived for seven generations, as a House Museum. It is located on Route 114 about a mile from the South Ferry.

This is an interesting island to explore because the contours change so rapidly, from steep hills to flat valley to beach. If you arrive via the North Ferry from Greenport, you are within walking distance of the Victorian homes in an area called The Heights. This is pretty much the center of activity, the site of the Chequit Inn, with its veranda for gazing out at the sailboats that often race in Dering Harbor. A walk down the hill brings you to Bridge Street and the town, such as it is, where you'll find the day-trippers over from the Hamptons.

If you keep to the right instead of going down Bridge Street from the Chequit, you pass a nine-hole public golf course and descend a steep hill to Crescent Beach, a major gathering spot for the island's resident tourists, with a motel and a couple of hotels in the vicinity. Back across town is the modern Dering Harbor Condominium overlooking the harbor. It is on Winthrop Road, which leads to the village of Dering Harbor, the smallest but perhaps the richest per capita municipality in the state—200 acres and 30 homes. Adjoining is an area called Hay Beach, a subdivision of new homes, and the Gardiner's Bay Country Club.

Two causeways lead to the more rugged terrain of Big and Little Ram Islands with Gardiner's Bay on one side and calm Coecles Harbor on the other. Mashomack Forest is to the south across the harbor. Once private, it is now a public preserve maintained by the Nature Conservancy. It abounds with saltwater marshes, forests, beaches, and wildlife. Guided tours are offered on some weekends; check the current schedule. Among the intriguing sights are the huge nests of osprey, the eagles of the sea, which can be spotted atop the poles in the preserve and on the Ram Island Causeway.

On the other side of Route 114 are two other residential areas: Shorewood, populated mostly by summer renters, and Silver Beach, a retirement colony. Adjacent to Silver Beach is Westmoreland Farms.

Though the number of hotels is not large, there is a choice of atmosphere. Chequit Inn is a gingerbread Victorian circa 1870 and puts you in the middle of what action there is in town. Dering Harbor is built motel-style with private terraces, a pool and tennis courts, and a busy harbor where many guests arrive by boat. The Pridwin is an old-time resort with a big porch, white wicker chairs in the lobby, and cabins for guests who prefer them. Senior citizens groups like to come here in the off season. There is a private beach plus pool, water skiing and sailing, and three tennis courts for guests, as well as such diversions as croquet, shuffleboard, and Ping-Pong. Then there is the delightful Ram's Head Inn, the prototype country inn—16 rooms, way off by itself on one of the most scenic areas of the island with tennis, private beach, and sailing.

The Chequit has a piano bar, the Ram's Head Inn may have music on weekends, and there is entertainment in a converted barn called Inn Between on North Ferry Road. So much for Shelter Island nightlife.

Most vacationers on the island don't come expecting nighttime action and are perfectly happy being active in the day and turning in early. The one peril is bad weather. But if the clouds do roll in, while Hamptons visitors get off the ferryboat looking for new diversion, you can board and head the other way to Sag Harbor. The old whaling center is nicer when you can really walk around, but it is a pleasant port in all but a real storm.

Wear a slicker if need be, and take the short walking tour beginning on Main Street that leads you past the town's exceptional architecture that goes from early Colonial saltbox to Greek Revival mansions that once belonged to wealthy sea captains. Go into one of the mansions, the home of the Suffolk County Whaling Museum, to see the big scrimshaw collection and many other relics of the town's early industry. Then visit the Old Customs House and the Whaler's Church with its hand-carved whaling motifs.

There are plenty of shops to browse through in town. The Kramoris Gallery has whimsical folk art plus fine stained glass, Fisher's Main Street Antiques is filled with temptations, the American Hotel is the perfect old-fashioned spot for a drink and fancy dinner, and the Long Wharf Restaurant on Bay Street right off Main will serve you informal meals with a harbor view. A stop at the information center off Main will provide a map and all the guidance you need to plot your way through the little village.

If this is the tail end of the weekend, you can drive directly home from Sag Harbor. Otherwise, you can take the four-minute ferry ride back to Shelter Island and leave the rest of the world behind.

Shelter Island Area Code: 516

DRIVING DIRECTIONS Midtown Tunnel to I-495, Long Island Expressway to exit 73, Riverhead. Turn right and take Route 58, Old Country Road, east for about two miles to the traffic circle. Continue east past Central Suffolk Hospital for about two more miles on 58 until it turns into Route 25. Continue to Greenport and watch for a large sign, SHELTER IS FY, west of the shopping area to guide you off Front Street (Route 25) onto Fifth Street going south. Turn left at Wiggins Street (Route 114) to ferry landing. North Ferry Service runs from 6 A.M. to 11:45 P.M., 1:45 A.M. in July and August, continuously, every 15 minutes. Information, 749–0139. Continual shuttle service to North Haven and Sag Harbor via South Ferry is from the southern end of Route 114, 6 A.M. to 11:50 P.M. Information, 749–1200.

Total distance: 102 miles.

PUBLIC TRANSPORTATION Sunrise Express Bus Service 6 A.M. to 11:50 P.M. from New York City to Shelter Island (477–1200) or Long Island Railroad to Greenport (information, 212–739–4200). No need for a car on Shelter Island if you stay near the North Ferry Station or ride a bike.

ACCOMMODATIONS (Expect minimum stays in season) *Chequit Inn,* Shelter Island Heights, 749–0018, $–$$$; dinner entrées $$ ● *Pridwin Hotel and Cottages,* Crescent Beach, Shelter Island, 749–0476, $$$$ MAP; less weekdays and off season; more holiday weekends; dinner entrées, $$ ● *Ram's Head Inn,* 108 Ram Island Drive, Shelter Island Heights, 749–0811, $$$ with continental breakfast (more expensive rooms have private baths); dinner entrées $$$ ● *Dering Harbor Inn,* PO Box A.D., Shelter Island Heights, 749–0900, $$$–$$$$.

DINING All of the above, plus the following: *The Terrace, Chequit Inn* (see above), delightful outdoor setting, $$ ● *The Dory,* Bridge Road, 749–8871, $–$$$ ● *Dering Harbor Inn* (see above) $$–$$$ ● *Clam Diggers,* 15 Grand Avenue, 749–2005, $$$ ● *Cogan's Country Restaurant,* Route 114 749–0018, $$–$$$ ● *Bob's Fish Market,* Route 114, 749–0830, no frills, fresh fish, $–$$.

SIGHTSEEING *Shelter Island Historical Society, Manhanset Chapel Museum,* and *Haven House,* Route 114. Hours: Memorial Day through Labor Day, Thursday to Monday 11 A.M. to 4 P.M. Admission $1.75 ● *Sag Harbor Whaling Museum,* Main Street, Sag Harbor, 725–0770. Hours: Monday to Saturday 10 A.M. to 5 P.M.; Sunday 1 P.M. to 5 P.M. Adults, $1.50; children, $.50.

FOR FURTHER INFORMATION *Shelter Island Chamber of Commerce,* Box 598, Shelter Island, NY 11964, 749–0399.

Concerts and Colonial Greens: Bedford and Caramoor

Bedford Village is a bit of New England transplanted to the New York suburbs—village green, white-steepled church, Colonial homes and all.

Caramoor is a bit of the Mediterranean, a house-museum filled with treasures from European palaces set on 100 sylvan acres, with a Venetian theater that is the site of the most elegant kind of outdoor summer music festival.

Put them together and you have a gracious summer getaway not much more than an hour from home.

Those who liken Bedford to a New England village are not far wrong, for it was actually part of Connecticut when settled in 1680. A royal decree settled a border dispute by placing Bedford in Westchester County, where it prospered and became the county seat.

In the mid-1800s, when the railroad made the town more accessible to New York, Bedford's scenic beauty attracted wealthy families who built their country estates on the hilltops nearby and acquired the nickname of "hilltoppers." A local historian of the period noted kindly that the newcomers—many of them world-famous—were generally "unobjectionable." The estates still make for pleasant sightseeing along the country roads near town.

The buildings surrounding the village green were built after the Revolution, since most of the town was burned by the British in 1779. Bedford's early residents set out to replace each building on its original site. Most of the structures still stand, thanks to the unusually active Historical Society.

In 1916 when the Methodists stopped holding services in their aging church on the green, the church was bought at auction by someone who planned to convert it into apartments. An indignant band of citizens raised the money to buy the building back, repair it, and turn it into a community house. That was the beginning.

The 1787 Court House, the oldest public building in Westchester County, was restored to appear just as it did early in the last century when William Jay, son of the first chief justice, presided on the bench. On the second floor the Bedford Museum was built to trace 300 years of the town from its earliest Indian origins.

One ticket covers a visit to this building and the restored one-room schoolhouse across the green. The ticket also provides a printed walking tour of the village, a stroll that takes you past the Old Burying Ground (1681), the general store (1838), the post office (1838), the library (1807), and beautiful homes from the early 1800s.

One of the white-pillared structures once housed an A & P, which was an unusual link in the chain because the storefront was not painted red. The tradition-conscious owner made it a condition of the contract that the facade not be altered.

That building is now Bedford Green, a shop offering three floors of fine antiques. Turn off the main avenue to Court Road, and you'll find more shops in charming Colonial homes. Among them are the Richard Oliver House, for men's country clothes; Savoir Faire, a potpourri of porcelain, pewter, silver, and gifts; and Ida B.'s Stitchery, a haven for needlepoint enthusiasts.

Even trees are considered worth saving in preservation-minded Bed-ford. Take a drive just north of town on Route 22 to see a towering white oak estimated to be 500 years old. Somehow that tree became a symbol of the town's attachment to the past. The owner, Harold Whit-man, deeded its ground to the town of Bedford in memory of his wife back in 1947, making it the Bedford Oak in truth as well as sentiment.

Of all our founding fathers, few filled so many high offices as John Jay. He served as president of the First Continental Congress, first chief justice, governor and chief justice of New York State, minister to Spain, and author of the Jay Treaty. The Jay Homestead, located a few miles farther north on Route 22, has been designated a state historic site. An enlarged 1787 farmhouse, it is part clapboard, part shingle, and part stone, a blend of both Hudson Valley and New England build-ing traditions. It was still occupied by the family as late as 1958. Their presence is tangible. Each of the generations added the conveniences and tastes of its own era, providing a dimension unusual in historic homes. Costumed hostesses will take you around, pointing out the fine furnishings and the periods represented by each of the rooms. The two kitchens are especially intriguing, each fully outfitted with fascinating paraphernalia.

Follow Route 22 south again and turn left onto Route 137 to reach Caramoor, a totally different kind of homestead. Best known for its Venetian Theater, Caramoor was the country home of Walter Tower Rosen, a lawyer and investment banker. Mr. and Mrs. Rosen built their pink stucco Mediterranean villa amid acres of woodland and for-mal gardens, then filled it with treasures from European palaces and villas. In fact, they installed whole rooms, complete down to wall panelings, molded ceilings, and priceless wall coverings. Down the narrow vaulted hallway, behind heavy carved wooden doorways, are rooms representing styles from fifteenth-century Gothic to sixteenth-century Renaissance to eighteenth-century neoclassical. Some are hung with silk and wallpaper painted in China in the eighteenth century.

You visit an intimate library from a château in southern France, a small room from a palace in Turin, an English pine-paneled chamber from a home in Dorsetshire, a French Regency sitting room, or a Jaco-bean bedroom. You'll come upon Pope Urban VIII's bed and a chair owned by Spain's Ferdinand and Isabella, along with the most exten-sive collection of needlepoint upholstery in the Western Hemisphere. The needlework, both French and Italian, is displayed in almost over-whelming profusion in an 80-foot music room; the ceiling was carved for a palace in Italy 400 years ago.

To enter the theater area, you pass through great black and gold wrought-iron gates acquired by Mr. Rosen in Switzerland. The stage of the Venetian Theater is built around a set of pink marble columns that once stood in a fifteenth-century garden near Venice. On a moonlit night this is a magical setting for muisic.

Caramoor is much too elegant a place for sprawling on blankets, but there are picnic tables in an apple grove near a grape arbor. Seating is on folding chairs, both in the main theater and in the Spanish courtyard where Sunday afternoon concerts are held. The music varies from opera to symphony to chamber music in the afternoons; the season runs from late June to late August.

If you don't want to hear music on Sunday, you can take a drive to North Salem to one of Westchester County's most unexpected attractions, the Oriental Stroll Gardens at the Hammond Museum. There's no more serene setting for a summer stroll than these 15 formal Oriental landscapes where weathered tree trunks, weeping willows, dwarf fruit trees, flowering shrubs, artfully placed stones, moss and pebbles, reflecting pools, and a mirror-still lake blend to form a setting of rare tranquillity.

The Hammond's other special claim to fame is an elegant three-course luncheon service in a shaded flagstone courtyard centered by a fountain and dotted with cheerful red geraniums. It has been aptly compared to lunching in the French countryside.

The museum building itself is attractive, with a soaring beamed great hall. It calls itself a museum of the humanities, and exhibits range widely, from religious artifacts to modern art to places of entertainment to Mexican tapestries.

Another excellent place for art is the Katonah Gallery, a new wing at the side of that town's library. It holds six major exhibitions a year borrowed from other museums, galleries, and private sources.

One final nearby attraction to note is Ward's Pound Ridge Reservation, a 4,600-acre park with some excellent hiking trails through the woods.

Though lodgings in this area are strictly motel variety, the dinner possibilities are atmospheric and varied. Some local favorites are Emily Shaw's Inn, in Pound Ridge near the Bedford line, a restored farmhouse; Box Tree, an elegant Colonial in Purdy's; and The Arch in Brewster (tiny, so make reservations well in advance). If you want super-elegant four-star French cooking (and prices to match), La Cremaillère in Banksville isn't very far away.

Westchester Area Code: 914

DRIVING DIRECTIONS Take the Hutchinson River Parkway north to the intersection of I-684, then north on 684 to Route 35, Katonah. Turn right and follow route 22 south into Bedford Village; Caramoor is at the intersection of Route 137, about half a mile east of 22. *Total distance:* roughly 50 miles.

PUBLIC TRANSPORTATION Metro North offers Metro North "Caramoor Specials" from New York on concert Saturdays; includes train fare, shuttle bus, house tour, pre-concert lecture, and concert. For reservations and fees, phone (212) 340–3141.

ACCOMMODATIONS *Ramada Inn,* Route 22, Armonk (south of Bedford), 273–9090, $$$$ ● *Holiday Inn,* Holiday Drive, Mount Kisco, 241–2600, $$$ ● Also see Ridgefield, CT (page 130), about 20 minutes away.

DINING *Emily Shaw's Inn,* Route 137, Pound Ridge, 764–5779, dinner $$–$$$; lunch $–$$ ● *The Arch,* Route 22, North Brewster, 279–5011, $$$$ (complete dinner, $42) ● *Village Inn,* Route 22, Bedford, 234–9843, $$–$$$ ● *La Cremaillère,* four miles on righthand side from exit 31, Merritt Parkway, Banksville, 234–9647, $$$–$$$$ ● *Box Tree,* Routes 22 and 116, Purdy's, 277–3677, charming French restaurant in 1775 home, $$$ ● *Le Chateau,* Route 35, South Salem, 533–6631, elegant J.P. Morgan mansion, $$$–$$$$ ● *La Camelia,* 234 N. Bedford Road, Mount Kisco, 666–2466, Spanish, $$$.

SIGHTSEEING *Bedford Museum,* Bedford Village, 234–9328. Hours: Wednesday to Sunday 2 P.M. to 5 P.M. Adults, $.75; children, $.25 ● *John Jay Homestead State Historic Site,* Route 22, Bedford Village, 232–5651. Guided tours. Hours: Memorial Day to Labor Day, Wednesday to Saturday 10 A.M. to 5 P.M.; Sunday 1 P.M. Call for off-season hours. Free ● *Caramoor,* Route 137, PO Box R, Katonah, 232–5035. One-hour guided tours mid-April to November. Hours: Thursday and Saturday 9 A.M. to 4 P.M.; Sunday 1 P.M. to 4 P.M. Adults, $4; children, $2; children under 10 not admitted. Write or call for summer music festival schedule and prices. ● *Katonah Gallery,* Bedford Road, Katonah, 232–9555. Hours: Tuesday to Friday 2 P.M. to 5 P.M.; Saturday 10 A.M. to 5 P.M.; Sunday 1 P.M. to 5 P.M. Free ● *Ward Pound Ridge Reservation,* Route 121 at Route 35, Cross River, 763–3493. Hours: 9 A.M. to sunset. Parking: nonresidents, $2; residents, $1 ● *Hammond Museum,* Deveau Road off Route 24, North Salem, 669–5135. Hours: Wednesday to Sunday 11 A.M. to 5 P.M. Adults, $2; children under 12, $1. Stroll Gardens open mid-May to late October, $2 and $1.

Crafts (Small and Otherwise) on the Connecticut Shore

Farm animals used to graze on the wide village green in Guilford, Connecticut. Colonial neighbors discussed the day's news under the shade of the trees, the local militia drilled here, and for a time the green even doubled as the local cemetery until someone decided such a central location really ought to be reserved for the livelier residents of the town.

The green remains the hub of Guilford centuries later, surrounded these days by shops instead of sheep. And come the middle of July each year, it is livelier than ever as it plays host to top craftsmen from all over New England: potters, weavers, glassblowers, smiths, carvers, and others who show their wares at the Guilford Handicrafts Exposition. Many are members of Guilford's excellent Handcraft Center.

Except for the annual big show held in Springfield, Massachusetts, this three-day affair is probably the area's biggest crafts exhibit. It is a perfect time to get acquainted with the quaint and historic towns that line the Connecticut shore from Guilford to Old Lyme.

Towns like Guilford, Madison, and Old Lyme owe their flavor more to their Colonial heritage than to their proximity to the Long Island Sound. They have long histories, many fine homes, some excellent small museums, and almost as an afterthought, proximity to the beach.

Most of the summer visitors here are people who own or rent the shingled cottages near the shore, so there is wonderfully little commercialism, yet there are some very appealing lodgings in the area. The Madison Beach Hotel has simple rooms and the grandest of views, right smack on the water. Water's Edge in Westbrook is a handsome hotel that also has water views and its own stretch of beach. For inn lovers, there is a homey place in Westbrook, and two real winners in Old Lyme. Whether you select the Bee and Thistle, an informal yellow Colonial house, or the Old Lyme Inn, an 1850s mansion with an elegant French menu in the dining room, you have a perfect base for exploring a very special little town. In fact, wherever you decide to stay, you may well want to begin your sightseeing in Old Lyme and work your way back to Guilford, saving the crafts for Sunday.

Old Lyme's entire wide shaded main street lined with Colonial homes has been declared a historic district. One residence housed one of the nation's first art colonies. The columned Georgian mansion is known as Florence Griswold House for "Miss Florence," who put up and fed a group of painters, including Henry W. Ranger, Willard Metcalf, and Clark Voorhees. They eventually developed the "Ideal Lyme landscapes" that brought national attention to the area. The house is now headquarters for the Lyme Historical Society and contains paintings and panels left by the artists, an extensive china collection, and completely furnished period rooms such as the front parlor, circa 1830s, and the lady's bedroom from the early 1900s.

Next door the Old Lyme Art Association was founded in 1914 as a showcase for local artists and remains a prestigious gallery with changing exhibits of prominent current work.

Old Lyme's third attraction is a weird one, a Victorian house transformed into a Nut Museum. Curator Elizabeth Tashjian is tour guide in her own home for offbeat exhibits including the world's tallest nutcracker, as well as nut art, music, and lore. She also has a small sculpture garden outside.

Heading back down the coast, take time out for the picturesque harbor and excellent seafood restaurants in Old Saybrook. If you opt for an informal take-out lunch, you can sit outside on the docks and watch the boats go by.

Should you choose to spend Saturday afternoon at the beach, you can try two small beaches near Old Lyme off Route 156 (beach stickers required, available from the Town Hall on Lyme Street), or you can drive to Hammonasset, between Clinton and Madison (one mile south of I-95 exit 62), the largest Connecticut shoreline park. You'll still have to put up with the pebbles that are unavoidable nuisances on Sound beaches, but the sand here stretches for two wide miles and the vistas of endless small boats offshore are a bonus.

Of course, if you choose a beachside lodging, all you have to do is come home for the afternoon.

If you want to see Madison's historic house, the Allis-Bushnell House and Museum, you'll have to squeeze it in on Saturday between 1 P.M. and 4 P.M. It's a bit unusual for its corner fireplaces and its reproduction of a doctor's office of the early 1900s. There are also children's toys and costumes from the late 1700s to 1900s.

If you do miss this house, take a drive instead down Madison's main and side streets and admire the handsome homes that are still private residences. This is also an ideal town for a shoreline drive to see those big rambling summer cottages.

Evenings are on the quiet side here—a long dinner, maybe a movie, or a local concert here and there. Ask at your inn what's happening currently.

Sunday, take a slow drive back to Guilford on US 1, detouring for some of the antiques stores along the way.

When you get to the Crafts Exposition, pick and choose carefully among the dozens and dozens of exhibitors. Buying hastily can be a mistake because you never know what's waiting in the next tent. When you've bought your ceramic pitcher, goblets, carvings, or whatever, take time to see the three historic sites of Guilford.

This town boasts the oldest stone house in the country, constructed around 1639 by Reverend Henry Whitefield, founder of Guilford. It was built like a manor house in the English midlands that its owner used to call home, with a steeply pitched roof, small windows, and a great hall 33 feet long with a huge fireplace at either end. A partition in the middle hinged to a second floor joist either turns the room into two or swings up to the ceiling out of the way. It's an unusually interesting house-museum and offers some exhibits of early crafts such as weaving and metalworking.

The Hyland House is also an early home, a 1600 saltbox with a "new" lean-to added about 1660. It is completely furnished as though a family could be living in it still, and has beautiful paneling and original hardware. Thomas Griswold House, circa 1735, is pretty enough to have once adorned a commemorative stamp, and it is a repository for many of the historic artifacts of the town's long history.

If you are into outlet bargains, you may want to continue beyond Guilford to Branford, where a new outlet center on Route 1 has shops for Chaus, Manhattan, Van Heusen, and American Tourister, among others. On the way you'll pass the Branford Craft Village at Bittersweet Farm on Route 1, where crafts are always on the agenda. Bishops Farm south of Guilford is a good spot to pick up fresh produce of the season.

One last possibility in Branford finally does take you out to sea. Legend has it that Captain Kidd visited the Thimble Islands, offshore, west of Guilford, and deposited his booty somewhere in the area when he fled the British in 1699. No one has found gold here yet, but a short cruise around the little known islands does make for a rewarding and scenic tour. Take exit 56 off I-95 and follow signs to Stony Creek; boats at Branford's Stony Creek dock make the trip regularly during the summer.

Connecticut Area Code: 203

DRIVING DIRECTIONS Take I-95 to exit 70, Old Lyme; Guilford is at exits 57 to 59.

Total distance: about 104 miles.

ACCOMMODATIONS *Bee and Thistle Inn,* 100 Lyme Street, Old Lyme, 434-1667, $$–$$$ • *Old Lyme Inn,* 85 Lyme Street, Old Lyme, 434-2600, $$ CP • *Madison Beach Hotel,* 94 West Wharf Road, Madison, 245-1404, $$$–$$$$ CP • *Water's Edge Inn and Resort,* 1525 Boston Post Road, Westbrook, 399-5901, out of state, (800) 222-5901, $$$–$$$$ • *Captain Stannard House,* 138 South Main Street, Westbrook, 399-7565, $$ CP.

DINING *Bee and Thistle Inn* (see above), $$–$$$ • *Old Lyme Inn* (see above), $$$–$$$$ • *The Dock,* Saybrook Point, Old Saybrook, 388-4665, good seafood with a harbor view, clam bar, $$–$$$ • *Saybrook Fish House,* 99 Essex Road, 388-4837, fish nets, wrapping paper for tablecloths, and the freshest seafood on the menu, $$–$$$ • *The Wharf,* Madison Beach Hotel (see above), fresh flowers, sea view, and mixed menu, $$–$$$ • *Friends & Company,* 11 Boston Post Road, Madison (on the Guilford line), 245-0462, informal, snacks or full meals, $–$$ • *Dock House,* Lower Whitfield Street, Guilford, 433-6884, seafood with a water view, $$–$$$ • *Little Brick House,* Lower Whitfield Street, Guilford, 453-2410, restaurant and seafood market near the water, $$–$$$ • *Sachem Country House,* Goose Lane, Guilford, 453-5261, an eighteenth-century house, $$ • *Century House,* 2455 Boston Post Road, Guilford, 453-2216, fine French food, $$–$$$.

SIGHTSEEING *Guilford Handicrafts Exposition.* For dates and this year's admission prices, contact the Chamber of Commerce, 669 Boston Post Road, Guilford, CT 06437, 453-9677, or the Guilford Handcraft Center, PO Box 221, Guilford, CT 06437, 453-5947. Handcraft Center shop and gallery hours: Monday to Saturday 10 A.M. to 4 P.M.; Sunday noon to 4 P.M., free • *Whitfield House Museum,* Whitfield Street, Guilford, 453-2457. Hours: April to November, open Wednesday to Sunday 10 A.M. to 5 P.M.; November to April, 10 A.M. to 4 P.M. Adults, $1.25; children 6–17, $.50, children under 6 free • *Hyland House,* 84 Boston Street, Guilford, 453-9477. Hours: June to early September, open Tuesday to Sunday, 10 A.M. to 4:30 P.M.; September to mid-October, Saturday and Sunday only. Adults, $1.50, children under 14 free • *Griswold House,* 171 Boston Street, Guilford, 453-3176. Hours: mid-June to mid-September, open Tuesday to Sunday 11 A.M. to 4 P.M. Adults, $1, children, $.50; under 12 free • *Florence Griswold House,* 96 Lyme Street, Old Lyme, 434-5542. Hours: June to October, Tuesday to Saturday 10 A.M. to 5 P.M., Sunday 1 P.M. to 5 P.M., rest of year, Wednesday to Sunday 1 P.M. to 5 P.M. Adults, $1; children free • *Lyme Art Association,* Lyme Street,

Old Lyme, 434-7802. Hours: May to mid-October, Tuesday to Friday noon to 5 P.M., Sunday from 1 P.M. Donation ● *Nut Museum,* 303 Ferry Road, Old Lyme, 434-7636. Hours: May to November, Wednesday, Saturday, and Sunday 2 P.M. to 5 P.M. Adults, one nut and $2; children 6–16, one nut and $1 ● *Thimble Island Cruises: Sea Mist II,* Mike Infantino, Jr., 64 Thimble Island Road, Stony Creek Dock, Branford, 481-4841, or *Volsunga III,* Captain Dwight Carter, PO Box 3332, Jepson Island, Stony Creek Dock, Branford, 448-9978.

Harmonious History
in New Jersey

The Colonial dame, wearing a mobcap and a long homespun dress, was sweeping her front step. She smiled and nodded as we passed, as though this group in jeans and sneakers could have been just the Colonial family next door.

The village around her, too, seemed perfectly natural in its surroundings, a clearing next to the Morris Canal. Despite the visitors strolling its paths, it might have still been the settlement known as Andover Forge during the Revolutionary War.

Today it is called Waterloo Village and is a restoration consisting of 26 buildings along the canal in Stanhope, New Jersey. It isn't the biggest or most elaborate restoration you'll ever see, but there's something extraordinary about the place—a sense of entering a time warp and walking into the past.

There is a church, a stagecoach inn, several houses and barns, a working gristmill, a smithy's shop, an apothecary shop, and a general store, all seemingly occupied by people going about their daily affairs. A potter works at his wheel, the smithy's hammer clangs, herbs are hung on the racks in the drying room at the apothecary.

You watch them at work, maybe chat as they dip the candles, weave the cloth, or grind the grain, and there you are, back in the past. There are no guides to break the illusion. It's a self-guided tour at your own pace, with plenty of time to pause under a tree or have a snack of wine and cheese at a table beneath the low beams in the general store.

This is a pleasant experience anytime, but come warm weather there is double incentive to make the trip because Waterloo's annual Festival of the Arts fills the area with activity. In May, September, and October crafts and antiques shows are on the docket. In the summer, the field in front of the village turns into a music arena presenting everyone from the Festival Symphony Orchestra to the Metropolitan Opera to John Denver. (The "Met in the Park" concerts are on weeknights and are free.) If you want to have dinner before the Saturday concerts, bring a picnic or reserve ahead for the buffet served in the Meeting House.

Two very pleasant inns have opened recently in the Waterloo area. Right in Stanhope is the Whistling Swan, a gracious Victorian with warm ambience that reflects its friendly owners. The Inn at Millrace Pond in Hope is especially convenient if you want to spend some time enjoying the scenery and the great outdoors at the Delaware Water Gap National Recreation Area. The delightful, authentically furnished Colonial inn is part of a complex of historic buildings that includes a gristmill now transformed into a restaurant. Hope, a tiny town packed with history, merits a little walking tour on its own. Otherwise, Chester or Morristown may be your best bets for lodging.

Whatever your schedule, reserve some time for driving around one of the wealthiest areas in New Jersey—or anywhere else, for that matter—the hunt country of Somerset and Morris counties. They rank themselves among the top 20 counties in wealth in the country, and you won't doubt it if you travel down to Chester through towns like Far Hills, Peapack, Gladstone, Mendham, Liberty Corners, and Basking Ridge. The very heart of the area is south of Route 24 and north of I-78 and the very best addresses are south of Mendham, Jacqueline Onassis's Far Hills country place among them.

Don't stick to the main roads. Try 525 or those wiggly lines on the map with no numbers to see the best estates of the horsey set. In the towns along the way you can explore the eclectic stores that occupy appropriately atmospheric Victorian houses. Antiques shops are legion, especially in Mendham and in Oldwick, to the west.

A few backroads, some sightseeing and shopping stops, and Waterloo Village make for a Saturday well spent, leaving you with a pleasant decision between history in Morristown and the great outdoors at the Delaware Water Gap on Sunday.

Morristown was actually the nation's military capital for a while, the site of Washington's headquarters and the main encampment of the Continental Army during the winter of 1779–80, when the general was fighting to rally and rejuvenate his starving, freezing, and sometimes mutinous forces. Morristown National Historical Park has three parts, each representing a different element of that crucial year.

The first, off Morris Avenue, is the museum, where you can see a color film about the area and exhibits of weapons and other pertinent artifacts. In front of the museum building is the Ford Mansion, the finest home in town in the 1770s, which was offered as headquarters to Washington and his wife by Mrs. Jacob Ford, a widow who obligingly moved with her four children into two rooms to create space for them. The house still has many original Ford furnishings.

Fort Nonsense, not far from the Morristown Green, got its name because no one could remember why soldiers had been obliged to work so hard to dig its trenches and embankments.

The actual Jockey Hollow encampment area is a few miles south of Morristown off 202. It contain typical log huts where the troops might have been quartered, as many as twelve to a shelter, plus the officers' huts, the parade ground where troops were drilled, and Wick Farm, a prosperous farm of the day used as headquarters for General Arthur St. Clair. It, too, retains some of its original furnishings. The area also includes a wildlife sanctuary with wooded hills, streams and flowers, and hiking trails.

There's more history to be tracked down in Morristown. Speedwell Village was the home and factory of Stephen Vail, who manufactured the engine for the first steamship that crossed the Atlantic. It was also the home of Vail's son, Alfred, who perfected the telegraph with Samuel Morse, demonstrating it publicly for the first time right here. The house has period furniture and there are various exhibits of engines and the history of the telegraph.

But how much can a person absorb on one summer afternoon? Maybe it's time for a different destination, such as the Frelinghuysen Arboretum, a 127-acre estate with rolling lawns, gardens, and stately trees in a traditional English park design. There are also nature trails here and the unusual fern configurations of a swamp area.

Or if the day is fine, maybe you'll decide to forego sightseeing altogether and head instead for the nature trails, waterfalls, and canoeing at the Delaware Water Gap, 70,000 acres of pristine woodland preserved by the National Park Service to provide a much-welcome wilderness respite for city dwellers. The area also has several interesting sites of its own, including a restored country village and a crafts village.

At the end of the day, you may want to check for just one more historic setting—a place to enjoy a fine dinner before you head home. A word to the wise: If you're in the mood for a splurge, dinner at Le Délice is worth a detour off Route 80 to Whippany.

New Jersey Area Code: 201

DRIVING DIRECTIONS To Waterloo Village, take I-80 to Route 206 (exit 25), drive north 2½ miles to Waterloo Road, then left another 2 miles to Waterloo Village. Watch for signs. Follow Route 206 south

to Chester and Bernardsville, Route 202 or 287 to Morristown, Route 80 west to Delaware Water Gap.
Total distance: 50 miles.

ACCOMMODATIONS *Whistling Swan Inn,* Box 791, 110 Main Street, Stanhope, 347-6369, $–$$ CP ● *The Inn at Millrace Pond,* PO Box 359, Hope, 459-4884, $$–$$$ CP ● *Chester Inn,* 11 Main Street, Chester, 879-6878, rooms upstairs over an 1810 tavern, $$ CP ● *Old Mill Inn,* Route 202, Bernardsville, 766-1150, motel adjoining a historic inn restaurant, $$–$$$ CP ● *Best Western Morristown Inn,* 270 South Street, Morristown, 540-1700, $$$–$$$$ ● *Headquarters Plaza,* 3 Headquarters Plaza, Morristown, 898-9100, stylish (and expensive) new hotel, $$$$.

DINING *Black Forest Inn,* Route 206, Stanhope, 347-3344, German and French dishes in a turn-of-the-century stone house, $$–$$$ ● *Silver Springs Farm,* Drakestown Road, Flanders (south of Stanhope), 584-6660, French haute cuisine—reserve ahead, $$$ ● *Black Horse Inn,* Route 24, Mendham, 543-7300, Victorian Inn, $$–$$$$ ● *Governor Morris Inn,* 2 Whippany Road, Morristown, 539-7300, comfortable, reliable, typical Colonial, $$–$$$ ● *The Tarragon Tree,* 225 Main Street, Chatham, 635-7333, French and fine, $$–$$$; prix fixe on weekends ● *The Old Morris Canal,* 2 Walton Place, Stanhope, 347-9434, $$, well recommended ● *Rod's 1890s Ranch House,* Madison Hotel, Route 24, Convent Station, 539-6666, $$ ● *Llewellyn Farms,* Route 202 and SR 10, Morris Plains, 538-4323, comfortable, country fare, $$$–$$$$ ● *Giraffe,* 96 Morristown Road, Basking Ridge, 221-0017, $$–$$$ ● *Le Délice,* 302 Whippany Road, Whippany, 884-2727, fine French, $$$$ ● *The Mountain House,* Mountain Road, Delaware Water Gap, PA, (717) 424-2254, simple old-fashioned charmer, $–$$.

SIGHTSEEING *Waterloo Village,* Waterloo Road off Route 206, Stanhope, 347-0900. Hours: mid-April to December, Tuesday to Sunday 10 A.M. to 6 P.M. Adults, $7.50; senior citizens, $5; children 6–12, $3. Concerts vary in price, roughly $15 to $22 for seating in tent, $10 for lawn. Phone for current schedule and prices ● *Morristown National Historical Park,* Morris Avenue, Morristown, 539-2016. Hours: Wednesday to Sunday 9 A.M. to 5 P.M. Adults, $.50 (paid at Historical Museum for all sights); under 16 and over 62 free. ● *Speedwell Village,* 333 Speedwell Avenue, Morristown, 540-0211. Hours: May to October, Thursday and Friday noon to 4 P.M.; Sunday 1 P.M. to 5 P.M. Adults, $1; senior citizens and children 12–18, $.50, children under 12 free ● *Frelinghuysen Arboretum,* Whippany Road (entrance from East Hanover Avenue), Morristown, 285-6166. Hours: mid-March to early December, Monday to Friday 9 A.M. to 5 P.M., weekends till 6 P.M. Free ● *Delaware Water Gap National Recreation Area,* I-80 at New Jersey–Pennsylvania border, (717) 588-6637, free. Information station at Kittatinny Point exit, New Jersey, open April to October daily, rest of year, Friday to Sunday only. For complete schedule of park activities, write to Superintendent, Delaware Water Gap, Bushkill, PA 18324.

Stone-House Hunting in Ulster County

It may seem an unlikely place to look for the past. First there are the fast-food signs, then the funky shops filled with students from the local college. But drive on to the end of Main Street (just before the bridge)—and the clock turns back 300 years.

A national historic landmark that celebrated its tercentennial in 1978, Huguenot Street is the oldest street in America with its original homes intact. The sturdy, steep-roofed stone houses on the block, their Old World architecture unique to New Paltz and its Ulster County environs, still evoke the feel of a rural European village as they did for the homesick French Huguenot families who built them so long ago.

The houses are an unusual start to a weekend of beautiful back-roads Ulster County scenery and a visit to one of America's unique hotels, Mohonk Mountain House.

The settlers of New Paltz were a small band of Huguenot families from Flanders villages. Fleeing from the religious persecution of Louis XIV, they first moved to the Rheinland Pfalz, or Palatinate, in Germany. Eventually they emigrated to America and the Dutch settlements of Kingston (then known as Wiltwyck) and Hurley in the Hudson River Valley. In 1677 a dozen of these families banded together to buy from the Indians their own tract of land beside the Wallkill River. They named it New Paltz for the Rheinland Pfalz.

Happy to have found a safe haven at last, the Huguenots moved onto their land in the spring of 1678 and there they put down firm roots. Although their homes were enlarged as new generations grew and prospered, five of the first six houses on the street remained virtually unchanged for 250 years and were occupied by descendants of the original builders.

Even today many names of those original settlers—Deyo, Bevier, Elting, DuBois, and Hasbrouck—remain prominent in New Paltz life. These families were largely responsible for forming the Huguenot Historical Society in the 1950s to begin buying and restoring the earliest homes. Each house museum is supported by a family association of descendants.

A tour of the homes begins at Deyo Hall on Broadhead Avenue, half a block off Huguenot Street. Here, displays give visitors some insight into the history of the area. An excellent introduction is the Jean Hasbrouck Memorial House, whose steep, shingled roof, great chimney, and jambless fireplace have earned it a citation as the most outstanding example of medieval Flemish stone architecture in America. The gigantic internal chimney is one of the only originals of its kind in existence. Many of the furnishings, including the tavern table, Hudson Valley rush-bottom chairs, Dutch *kaas* (chests), and a cradle, belonged to the Hasbrouck family prior to 1700.

In the Abraham Hasbrouck House, unusual family heirlooms include an English four-panel chest that commemorated a 1609 marriage. There's also a rare seventeenth-century Dutch writing table with mother-of-pearl inlay and a cozy Dutch bed hidden behind paneled doors. The pride of this house is the mammoth medieval fireplace in the central "room of seven doors." As in most of the homes, you can still see much of the original woodwork, huge beams, and wide floorboards.

The two Hasbrouck houses, along with the equally interesting Hugo Freer and Bevier-Elting houses, represent living styles from the town's earliest days. The LeFevre House, built in 1799 with three stone walls and a front of brick, marks a transition to the Federal period on the street. Deyo House, dating from 1692, was remodeled in the 1890s into an elegant Edwardian residence.

Huguenot Street's annual Heritage Day, usually the first Saturday in August, adds demonstrations of weaving, blacksmithing, and other arts and crafts of the past to the regular house tours.

Also on the street are two churches. A careful reconstruction of the 1717 French Church has been placed next to the original Huguenot Burying Ground. The 1839 red brick Dutch Reformed Church is a sign of the growing influence of Dutch neighbors on the Huguenots.

After you've seen Huguenot Street, then head four miles south on Route 32 to Locust Lawn, the other Huguenot Society property in the area. Built by Josiah Hasbrouck in 1814, this Federal-style house reflects the owner's travels to Washington and Virginia, and its furnishings are a textbook of period decoration, from Queen Anne to early Victorian. Also nearby is the Terwilliger Home, where the Hasbroucks lived until Locust Lawn was completed. Many consider this appealing home their favorite of all the stone houses.

Just west of Locust Lawn, 20 acres of woodland, thicket, and pond have been set aside as a wildlife sanctuary. Nature trails through the area may be reached from the entrance on Jenkinstown Road.

There's more spectacular nature awaiting, however, six miles west of New Paltz at Mohonk Mountain House. This absolutely huge old-fashioned Victorian fantasy of towers and turrets is wrapped around one end of a natural marvel, a mountain lake atop the Shawangunk Mountains. The dark blue, 60-foot-deep, spring-fed lake lies in a small fault running across the main line of the mountain, surrounded by cliffs—a truly spectacular sight.

It was the natural beauty of this place 1,200 feet high that captivated the twin Smiley brothers, Alfred and Albert, in 1869. Albert bought up 300 acres and a rundown tavern for $28,000, mortgaging his future in the process, while Alfred stayed at his teaching job to bring in some much needed cash. To add more to their income, a ten-room hotel was opened in 1870—with drinking, smoking, dancing, and cards outlawed by its Quaker owners.

More than 100 years later, Mohonk still belongs to the Smiley family. It has grown to 305 rooms; the grounds now total 7,500 acres (5,000 of them in protected undeveloped land known as the Mohonk Trust); and there are award-winning gardens, a cliff-top lookout tower to make the most of the view, artificial lakes, 30 miles of bridle trails, an 18-hole golf course and putting green, miles of gorgeous hiking trails, and tennis. There is still no bar and no smoking in the dining room, though drinks are allowed now at dinner or in your room. People come regardless of restrictions, for this remains a magnificent natural retreat.

You can happily spend a weekend or more at Mohonk, or you can stay in a nearby bed and breakfast and come as a day guest, paying admission to enjoy hiking in the woods, strolling the gardens, or taking out one of the horses for hire at the stable. If you have a meal in the dining room, there is no admission charge.

Some Sunday, continue driving to the end of the Mohonk Road and you'll reach High Falls, a tiny town with one of the Hudson Valley's finest restaurants, the Dupuy Canal House, a historic stone structure that was once a lively tavern back in 1797. The old Delaware and Hudson Canal passed through here. In a tiny and charming museum in an old church you can see replicas of the canal boats, panoramas of the canal and the adjoining towpath, and fascinating miniature dioramas of early life in High Falls.

This is choice antiquing territory. The Tow Path House by the D &

H Canal should be able to supply a free current guide to all nearby shops published by the Antiques Dealers Association of Ulster County.

It's also choice back-roads country, the kind of area to just get lost on the side roads admiring the quaint stone houses and farms and the unspoiled Ulster County scenery.

One pleasant drive west on Route 213 brings you to Stone Ridge and more antiques shops, including The Thumb Print, housed in a picturesque old barn. Continue north on Route 209 to Hurley, site of the first Huguenot settlements in the county, and you'll see stone houses still occupied here, transformed into attractive homes for today.

If you have more time, continue to Kingston, New York's first capital, with historical sites and museums, Hudson River cruises from the Rondout area, and its own store of stone houses. Or head up Route 28 and 375 to Woodstock, the artists' colony that is chockablock with intriguing shops.

If time is up, you can still fit in one last stop on the way home, at the Hudson Valley Wine Village in Highland. A winery tour followed by a tasting is a thoroughly pleasant way to wind up the weekend.

Ulster County Area Code: 914

DRIVING DIRECTIONS George Washington Bridge to Palisades Parkway to exit 9N, New York Thruway to exit 18, New Paltz. Turn left onto Route 299, which becomes Main Street, then right onto Huguenot Street just before the river.

Total distance: 85 miles.

ACCOMMODATIONS *Mohonk Mountain House,* Mohonk Road, New Paltz, 233-2244, $$$$ AP (inquire about many special weekends for nature lovers, photographers, tennis players, music fans—even fans of mystery novels) ● *Williams Lake Hotel,* Rosendale, 658-3101, pleasant resort, $$$$ AP (advance reservations in summer by the week only, but a possibility for last-minute accommodations) ● Many delightful bed-and-breakfast inns in this area. (For a complete list write to Ulster County Information Office.) Here are some of the best: *The Barn,* 156 Huguenot Street, New Paltz, 255-4591, stunning contemporary home with pool, $$$ CP ● *Baker's B&B,* RD 2, Box 80, Stone Ridge, 687-9795, 1780 stone farmhouse on 16 acres, $$ CP ● *Hasbrouck House Inn,* PO Box 76, Stone Ridge, 687-0736, 1757 estate manor house, pool, $$–$$$ CP ● *Captain Schoonmaker's,* Route 213, Box 37, High Falls, 687-7946, 1760 stone house, canopy beds, waterfall on the grounds, $$ CP.

DINING *DuPuy Canal House,* Route 213, High Falls, 687-7700, $$$$, prix fixe full dinner $37 and $48 ● *Mohonk Mountain House* (see above), $$ ● *The Locust Tree Inn,* 215 Huguenot Street, New Paltz, 255-7888, an old stone house in convenient location, continental menu, lunch $, dinner $$–$$$ ● *Dominick's,* 30 N. Chestnut, New Paltz, 255-0120, basic Italian, $–$$ ● *Egg's Nest,* Route 213, High Falls, 687-7255, for gourmet pizza with interesting toppings, $.

SIGHTSEEING *Huguenot Street,* New Paltz, 255-1660. Hours: 9:30 A.M. to 4 P.M. Wednesday to Sunday, late May to September. Individual houses: adults, $1.50; children, $.75. Guided tours at 9:30 A.M. and 1:30 P.M. Complete tour: adults, $5 (short tour, $2.50); children 7–12, $2; children under 7 free ● *Delaware and Hudson Canal Museum,* Mohonk Road, High Falls, 687-9311. Hours: May through October, Wednesday to Sunday 11 A.M. to 5 P.M. Donation ● *Ulster County Fair,* held annually in August at New Paltz fairgrounds. Dates available from Ulster County Information Office ● *Woodstock–New Paltz Arts & Crafts Fair,* held annually both Memorial Day and Labor Day weekends at fairgounds, information from Quail Hollow Events, PO Box 825, Woodstock, 679-8087. For Woodstock and Kingston sightseeing, see pages 138–39.

FOR FURTHER INFORMATION Ulster County Public Information Office, PO Box 1800, Kingston, NY 12401, 331-9300.

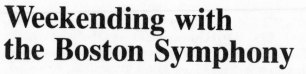

Weekending with the Boston Symphony

Is there anybody out there who doesn't know about Tanglewood?

The summer home of the Boston Symphony has been one of the most popular destinations in the Northeast ever since the concerts began in 1936. The 6,000 seats in the open-air shed are often sold out, and as many as 10,000 more people may be found on the lawn, spreading wicker baskets and wine bottles on blankets and settling back to enjoy a symphony concert under the stars.

Some people like the lawn even better on Sunday afternoon, when you can really appreciate strolling the 210 acres of William Aspinwall Tappan's former estate, viewing the formal gardens and the re-creation of the red house where Nathaniel Hawthorne worked, no doubt inspired by the beauty around him. The view of lake and mountains from the main house (now the administration building) is magnificent.

Does Tanglewood even need mentioning here, especially since the Berkshires come up again for other reasons in fall and winter? The answer is yes, since the fare of music as well as dance and theater is so rich in the summer that plans for a weekend seem in order, if only to inspire those who haven't gotten around to making the trip.

For first-timers, then, a word about tickets and accommodations. As for tickets, lawn seats are always available, but write ahead to Tanglewood or watch for the very first ad that appears in the Sunday *New York Times* to order tickets if you want to be sure of reserved seating for the concert of your choice. As for accommodations, the list is long and there are many terrific choices, everything from an Italian villa to simple country inns, with dozens of motels in between. You must make reservations several months ahead for the choicest of the inns, and even the motels may require you to stay a minimum of three nights. There are few bargains here with so much demand.

On warm summer days, it helps to have a pool nearby, so my first pick of inns provides this nice extra. At the delightful Apple Tree Inn, a 22-acre antiques-filled hilltop retreat, the pool as well as the many-windowed gazebo dining room come with soaring mountain views. This inn is also conveniently set near a gate to Tanglewood.

A sleeper way out in the country is the Colonel Ashley Inn, a bed-and-breakfast home off Route 41 in Sheffield. This is a Colonial charmer whose very private poolside looks up to fabulous views of Mount Everett.

Weathervane Inn in South Egremont and Williamsville Inn in West Stockbridge are both country hostelries with antiques, warmth, and that all-important pool. And if money is no object, you can live like a king at Blantyre, a veritable hilltop castle, or the imposing mansion next door at the Cranwell Resort, and Wheatleigh shows you the good life as enjoyed by the contessa who once owned this villa.

In addition to these, a number of old mansions turned inn in Lenox offer spacious and gracious quarters, and there are other possibilities in Lee and Stockbridge, including the Red Lion, the granddaddy of all the inns, where everyone who is anyone shows up sooner or later.

Now that you have the basics, here's a quick rundown on some of the attractions you have to choose among, in addition to planning a night and/or afternoon at the symphony. Jacob's Pillow Dance Festival, the oldest such event in America, takes place in a rustic 100-acre setting in a barn named for its founder, Ted Shawn. You'll see the whole gamut of dance performed over the summer here. A recent season included the Joffrey II dancers; companies from India, Spain, and

Brazil; modern dance; the Boston Ballet; a week of premieres by the resident ballet; and an American sampler from classic to folk. The Berkshire Ballet, a home-grown group, offers classical and contemporary dance at the Koussevitsky Arts Center in Pittsfield.

The Berkshire Theater Festival in Stockbridge, housed in a building designed in 1886 by Stanford White, was only the second summer theater in the nation when it began performances in 1928. Now there's top-grade summer stock here in the Mainstage, and avant garde new American plays at The Unicorn, where there are special events and children's matinees in the courtyard.

If drama is a special interest, don't overlook the excellent Williamstown Theater Festival, which has done some experimental productions that attracted much critical acclaim.

The bard is the thing at Shakespeare & Company, played in a natural amphitheater on the grounds of The Mount, Edith Wharton's former estate high above Laurel Lake. There are normally two plays alternating, and you can picnic on the lovely grounds. The house itself is open for daytime tours.

Aston Magna presents baroque concerts during July at St. James Church in Great Barrington, the new Berkshire Opera offers weekend performances at the Cranwell Estate in Lenox, and South Mountain gives chamber music concerts in a hall atop South Mountain in Pittsfield. The latter series begins late and lasts through September, when many of the other attractions are gone.

You won't have a lot of time to worry about sightseeing, especially if you have sunshine during the day and a pool or a pond at your disposal. A couple of possibilities for lake swimming are Pontcosuc Lake in Pittsfield, York Lake in New Marlboro, and Beartown State Forest near Great Barrington.

Save a little time for a drive around and a walk through both Lenox and Stockbridge, the former a town that was the summer mountain retreat for millionaires in its heyday, the latter a picture-book New England town with a Norman Rockwell museum honoring the man who immortalized the town in his paintings. One nice way to see the sights in Lenox is on a guided bicycle tour offered by a local group know as Continuous Cycle.

If the clouds roll in, consider Saturday and Sunday matinees at the various theaters in the area, or go shopping in West Stockbridge, or antiquing in South Egremont or Sheffield, or visit the marvelous Clark Art Institute in Williamstown. If you need further suggestions, check the attractions mentioned in the fall and winter Berkshire itineraries on pages 134 and 206.

You'll probably make plans to come back, because if a Berkshires weekend proves anything, it's that you really can't get too much of a good thing.

Berkshire Area Code: 413

DRIVING DIRECTIONS Saw Mill River Parkway north to the Taconic Parkway to the New York State Thruway Berkshire Spur (Route 90), then east to exit 2. Follow Route 102 to US 20 into Lenox. Tanglewood is on West Street, Route 183 in Lenox.
Total distance: 153 miles.

PUBLIC TRANSPORTATION Amtrak serves Pittsfield; Bonanza Bus services much of the Berkshire area. You might be able to stay close enough to walk to Tanglewood, but it is difficult to get around to other places without a car.

ACCOMMODATIONS Rates given are for weekends in July and August concert season and foliage season. All are less on weekdays and in September, much less after October. All inns have minimum stays in season. *Apple Tree Inn,* 224 West Street, Lenox, 637-1477, $$$–$$$$ CP (less expensive rooms are in a modern lodge on the grounds) ● *Colonel Ashley Inn,* Bow Wow Road (off Route 41), Sheffield, 229-2929, $$$ CP ● *Williamsville Inn,* Route 41, West Stockbridge, 247-6580, $$$–$$$$ CP ● *Weathervane Inn,* Route 23, South Egremont, 528-9580, $$$$ MAP ● *The Red Lion Inn,* Main Street, Stockbridge, 298-5545, $$–$$$ ● *Birchwood Inn,* 7 Hubbard Street, Lenox, 637-2600, spacious historic house with canopy beds, handsome garden, $$–$$$$ CP ● *Cliffwood Inn,* 25 Cliffwood Street, Lenox, 637-3330, Belle Epoque showplace, breakfast on the veranda overlooking the grounds, $$$$ CP ● *Underledge,* 76 Cliffwood, Lenox, 637-0236, manor house on four acres, $$$$$ CP ● *Seven Hills,* Lenox, 637-0060. Manor house and lodge being spruced up, lovely grounds, pool, tennis, music-student waiters and waitresses perform, $$$–$$$$ CP ● *Berkshire Thistle Inn,* Pine Street, Stockbridge, 298-3188, nicely decorated and conveniently located village home, $$$$ CP ● The top of the line: *Blantyre,* Route 20, Lenox, 298-3806, impressive 1902 manor, pool, tennis, rooms *begin* at $175 CP ● *Cranwell Resort and Conference Center,* Route 20, Lenox, 637-1364, elaborate Tudor mansion with views, pool, tennis, health club, and golf, will be center of a condo community, carriage house rooms begin at $150 EP ● *Wheatleigh,* West Hawthorne Road, Lenox, 637-0610, elegant villa with pool, fine chef, rooms begin at $145 EP.

DINING *Wheatleigh* (see above), continental, prix fixe, $$$$$ • *Apple Tree Inn* (see above), continental with an Italian accent, $$–$$$ • *Williamsville Inn* (see above), continental, $$$ • *Weathervane Inn* (see above), American-Continental, $$ • *The Old Mill,* Route 23, South Egremont, restored gristmill, American menu, long a local favorite, $$–$$$ • *Federal House,* Route 102, South Lee, 243-1794, highly rated continental, $$$ • *Gateways Inn,* 71 Walker Street, Lenox, 637-2532, continental, $$$ • *Red Lion Inn* (see above), New England fare, $$–$$$ • *The Painted Lady,* 285 South Main Street, Great Barrington, northern Italian, $$–$$$ • *20 Railroad Street,* same address, Great Barrington, 528-9345, burgers to dinners, fair prices, $$ • For lunch, in Stockbridge, try *The Café* in the Mews around the corner from the Red Lion; in Lenox, *Café Lucia,* 90 Church Street, or *The Quiet Corner,* 104 Main Street; and in West Stockbridge, *Shaker Mill Tavern,* which also has light supper fare and entertainment. For Tanglewood takeout, call *The Elegant Picnic,* 637-1621, or *A Moveable Feast,* 637-1785, for just what the names imply.

SIGHTSEEING Check all for current dates, ticket prices, and starting times. *Tanglewood,* West Street (Route 183), Lenox, 637-1940, 637-1666 from June to August. Concerts: July to August • *Jacob's Pillow Dance Festival,* off Route 20 on George Carter Road, Becket, 243-0745. Performances: Tuesday to Saturday • *Shakespeare & Company,* the Mount, Route 7, Lenox, 637-1197. Tuesday to Friday 11 A.M. to 4 P.M., Saturday and Sunday 9:30 A.M. to 4 P.M. • *South Mountain Concerts,* Route 7, one mile south of Pittsfield, 443-6517 • *Berkshire Theater Festival,* Main Street, Stockbridge, 298-5576. • *Williamstown Summer Theater,* Park and Main (intersection of Routes 7 and 2), Williamstown, 458-8146 • *Aston Magna Foundation,* PO Box 28, Great Barrington, 528-3595 • *Berkshire Ballet,* 210 Wendell Avenue, Pittsfield, 442-1307 • *Berkshire Opera,* Cranwell Resort, Lenox, 637-3073 • *Continuous Cycle,* Walker House, 74 Walker Street, Lenox, 637-0904, bicycle rentals and guided tours. Tickets to all area events can be purchased at the Berkshire Ticket Booth at the Lenox Chamber of Commerce, Lenox Academy Building, 75 Main Street, open daily 1 P.M. to 5:30 P.M.

FOR FURTHER INFORMATION *Lenox Chamber of Commerce,* Lenox Academy Building, 75 Main Street, Lenox, MA 01240, 637-3646, for general local information and lodging referral service; *Berkshire Visitors' Bureau,* The Common, Pittsfield, MA 01201, 1-800-BERKSHR (except in MA, 443-9186), for information and lodging listings in the entire area.

Rhode Island's Unsung Shoreline

It was Sunday noon on a mid-July weekend, and all was right with the world at Weekapaug Beach—hot sun, ocean breeze, cloudless sky, and beach blankets spaced in a discreet checkerboard to allow everyone a patch of privacy to enjoy it all.

It is a scene repeated many times along 25 miles of sandy shoreline edging the area officially labeled Washington County but affectionately known to everyone in Rhode Island only as "South County." The county's five state parks, spaced between Westerly and Point Judith, draw their full share of sun worshipers, but the town beaches in between (by New York standards, at least) have plenty of room for all. And so does this relatively unheralded vacation area.

South County doesn't ape the chicness of the Hamptons or the quaintness of Cape Cod. It's a down-to-earth, wide-open area with a couple of nice inns, a scattering of adequate motels, a smattering of small towns, lots of nature preserves and fishing grounds, and just enough shops to fill the bill on a rainy day. There's little traffic, less serious hassle—and few better places for a truly relaxing weekend.

Westerly, population 14,497, is the hub of the western end of the county, and within the bounds of Westerly township is a variety of accommodations that should suit almost anyone. One of the best choices is Shelter Harbor Inn, about four miles out of town, an informal restored country farmhouse and barn that offers seclusion, a pleasant sundeck, a tennis court, big full breakfast included in the rates, and guest passes to that delightful residents-only beach at Weekapaug.

Weekapaug Inn is quite another matter—a handsome, weathered, shingled summer place that has been run by the same family for three generations and had some of its guests for almost as long. Here you'll find rockers on the porch, beautiful grounds with a water view, bowling on the lawn, tennis, sailing, golf privileges, and a private beach. It's expensive and has the atmosphere of a private club.

West of Weekapaug are two beaches that are poles apart. Misquamicut is a state beach, crowded with roller rink, water slide, seafood stands, tavern, discos, and all the other amusements of a slightly tacky beach area. Nevertheless, on one end is the nicest direct beachfront accommodation on the shore, the Pleasant View House.

Farther on, on a spit with Little Narragansett Bay on one side and the ocean on the other, is Watch Hill, an enclave of big Victorian homes and old wealth. But you can't exactly categorize Watch Hill. The shops here include expensive antiques and exclusive stores, but there are also souvenir places, a wonderful old used bookstore called the Book and Tackle Shop, and a very plain restaurant that is a local institution called the Olympia Tea Room.

The street runs directly across from the harbor so one of the major events of the day here is watching the sun go down over the masts of the sailboats. Park benches are thoughtfully provided.

The oldest carousel in the country is at the end of the block, with horses hung on chains, and it fills the street at night with music to serenade strollers out for a homemade ice cream cone or fresh buttered popcorn.

Mansions notwithstanding, there's nothing forbidding about Watch Hill—it's a delightful place despite the fact that the lodgings are not the greatest. The huge old wooden Ocean House, the last remaining grand hotel, has seen better days. Hartley's Guest House also seems a bit down at the heels, but it has a great location between Main Street and the ocean beach. (The latter is free, reached by a craggy hidden path; the bay beach charges admission.) The best bet is Watch Hill Inn, also an easy walk to the ocean beach, with simply furnished rooms and a front deck on the harbor that is the best spot in town for cocktails and sunset watching.

Narragansett, whose famous old casino was lost in a hurricane some years ago, was quiet until recently when a mini-building boom began. Now it boasts the biggest lodging along the shore, the Village Inn, a weathered modern hotel complex overlooking Narragansett Bay and the busy town beach. At this end of the shoreline, you'll find more space for sunbathing at Scarborough Beach, and you'll be near the picturesque fishing village of Galilee and the Block Island Ferry, as well as closer to Newport if you choose to drive over for a day.

If the weather is with you, you'll be more than content with just a place to stay and a few restaurant recommendations on the Rhode Island shore. But if the clouds roll in or you're beginning to burn, all is far from lost. Visit some of the lovely conservation areas along the shore, and take advantage of nature walks and field trips scheduled at the Kimball Wildlife Refuge and the Ninigret Conservation Area. If you are here the first Sunday in August, don't miss the annual all-day seafood festival at Ninigret, a feast of good eating. And remember that this is fisherman's paradise—write ahead to the state tourist office for a free guide telling you where to cast for what.

Or go to Westerly and its library—not to read a book but to admire the wood paneling, fireplaces, stained glass, marble mosaic floors, and leaded-glass hanging lamps in this surprisingly lovely building. Look out back for another surprise. Wilcox Park is one of the prettiest to be found anywhere in a city this size. The park is used for free summer concerts, so check in the library for a schedule.

Also in Westerly, though open only on Sunday afternoons, is the 1732 Babcock Smith House, one of Rhode Island's architectural landmarks, restored and elegantly furnished by the local historical society.

A growing sightseeing complex is the South County Museum on 175 acres of Canonchet Farm in Narragansett, where old-time crafts and farming techniques are demonstrated. Exhibit areas include a carpenter's shop, cobbler's shop, tack shop, and general store. Kids enjoy the collections of old toys, desks, and slates, and the kitchen equipped with pre-electricity tools like rug beaters, cheese presses, irons, and washing machines, all powered by human energy.

For antiquing head for the Mentor in North Kingstown on Route 1, the North Kingstown and Wickford Antique Centers, both on Route 102, and the Dove and Distaff on Main Street in Wakefield, which has really fine collectors' pieces. While you are in Wakefield, have a meal at the Larchwood Inn, a gracious antiques-filled home in town. You can stay here, too, if you want to be a bit inland. (For more shops, ask for the free printed guide to antiques stores on the South Shore; most stores have them.)

Other pleasant shopping stops are Windswept Farm (also a restaurant) on Route 1 outside Westerly, for antiques and gifts, and Charlestown's Fantastic Umbrella Factory, a crazy mishmash of pottery, china, posters, clothes, gifts, and what-have-you in ramshackle, old farm buildings with a few goats and chickens still wandering in the barnyard. For lunch or dinner, there's a good little restaurant in the complex.

Some other dining possibilities: Shelter Harbor is a good choice (the place to sample Rhode Island jonnycakes), as is the Watch Hill Inn for Italian food and the Olympia Tea Room, which serves fresh seafood and homemade bread as well as tea. George's in Galilee is the special spot for seafood, and Narragansett has turned into the shore's dining center, with several good new restaurants. Evening diversion is the Theater-by-the-Sea in Matunick, which specializes in summer stock musicals.

By all means, stop at some of the roadside stands near the beach (especially those near Weekapaug) where lobster goes for about $6, a dozen clam cakes cost $3, and you take your meal and your chowder outside to the picnic tables in the back. The food, like the area, doesn't come in fancy wrappings, but it can't be beat.

Rhode Island Area Code: 401

DRIVING DIRECTIONS Take I-95 to Route 2 (exit 92), Westerly exit. Follow Route 2 into Route 78 (Westerly bypass) to US 1 and bear north for Shelter Harbor Inn, Charlestown, or Narragansett (watch for town signs to guide you). Route 1A south leads to Watch Hill, Misquamicut, and Weekapaug.
Total distance: 145 miles.

ACCOMMODATIONS _Shelter Harbor Inn,_ Route 1, Westerly, 322-8883, $$$ including full breakfast ● _Weekapaug Inn,_ Weekapaug, 322-0301, $$$$$ AP ● _Pleasant View House,_ 65 Atlantic Avenue, Misquamicut, 348-8107, $$$$–$$$$$ MAP ● _Hartley's Guest House,_ Larkin Road, Watch Hill, 348-8253, $–$$ ● _Larchwood Inn,_ 176 Main Street, Wakefield, 783-5454, $$ ● _General Stanton Inn,_ Route 1, Charlestown, 364-8888, $$–$$$ ● _Watch Hill Inn,_ Bay Street, Watch Hill, 348-8912, $$$$ CP ● _The Village Inn,_ 1 Beach Street, Narragansett, 783-6767, $$$–$$$$ ● Some modest and appealing small bed-and-breakfast choices: _The Inn at Foster Farm,_ 85 Beach Street, Route 1A, Westerly, 596-6384, $ CP; _J. Livingston's Guest House by the Sea,_ 39 Weekapaug Road, Weekapaug, 322-0249, $$$ CP; _Fairfield by the Sea,_ 527 Green Hill Beach Road, Green Hill, 789-4717, $ CP; _The Summer House Inn,_ 87 Narragansett Avenue, Narragansett, 783-0123, $$–$$$ CP. For a long list of bed and breakfast in homes in Narragansett, contact Bed and Breakfast by the Sea, c/o Narragansett Chamber of Commerce.

DINING _Shelter Harbor Inn_ (see above), $$ ● _Larchwood Inn_ (see above), $$ ● _Fantastic Umbrella Factory Café,_ Route 1, Charlestown, 364-3935, $–$$ ● _George's,_ near the fishing dock, Galilee, 783-2306, $–$$ ● _Olympia Tea Room,_ Watch Hill, 348-8211, $$ ● _Watch Hill Inn_ (see above), The Deck, informal, snacks, $, and Positano, Italian, $$ ● _Spain,_ The Village Inn (see above), Narragansett, really excellent Spanish fare, $$ ● _Coast Guard House,_ 16 Ocean Road, Narragansett, 789-0700, seafood with a sea view, waterfront deck, $$ ● _Sweet Meadows Inn,_ 10 Point Judith Road, Narragansett, 792-3700, Colonial home, patio dining, American-Continental menu, $$–$$$ ● _Basil's,_ 22 Kingston Road, Narragansett, 789-3743, unpretentious French, $$–$$$ ● _Terminesi's,_ 85 Boon Street, Narragansett, 783-7939, no-frills, good Italian, $ ● Two other good choices in the Mariner Square shopping center on Route 108, Point Judith Road, Narragansett, are: _Antipasto's Restaurant,_ 789-3000, Italian with a bountiful salad-antipasto bar, $$, and _Mercedes Ocean House,_ 789-3380, seafood and

Cajun specialties, $$ ● Just f.y.i.: Almost everyone in Narragansett has breakfast at *Dad's Place,* 142 Boon Street, 783-6420.

SIGHTSEEING *Westerly Public Library,* Westerly, 596-2877. Hours: Monday, Tuesday, Wednesday 8 A.M. to 9 P.M.; Thursday 8 A.M. to 5 P.M.; Friday and Saturday 9 A.M. to 2 P.M. Closed Saturdays in July and August. Free. Ask at library for schedule of free concerts in Wilcox Park ● *Ninigret Conservation Area,* Route 1A (off Route 1), Charlestown, 364-3106, open daily sunrise to sunset. Free ● *Kimball Wildlife Refuge,* Route 1, take Windswept Farms exit. Hours: daily, sunrise to sunset. Free. Ask at either refuge for current free nature programs ● *Babcock-Smith House,* 924 Granite Street, Westerly, 596-4424. Hours: Sunday 2 P.M. to 5 P.M., also Wednesday in July and August. Adults, $2; children under 12, $.50 ● *South County Museum,* Route 1A across from the Narragansett Pier Bathing Pavilion, Narragansett, 783-5400. Hours: Memorial Day to Labor Day, Wednesday to Sunday 11 A.M. to 4 P.M., weekends only September and October. Adults, $2; children, $1; families, $6.

FOR FURTHER INFORMATION Greater Westerly Area Chamber of Commerce, 159 Main Street, Westerly, RI 02891, 596-7761. Charlestown Tourist Information Center, Route 1, north of Route 216, Charlestown, RI 02813, 322-1131. Narragansett Chamber of Commerce, "The Towers," Ocean Road, Narragansett, RI 02882, 783-7121. South County Tourism Council, Inc., PO Box 651, Narrangansett, RI 789-4422.

A Taste of Victoriana at Nyack-on-Hudson

There was a lively argument the other day on a street corner in Nyack, New York. A young man, gesturing upward toward the round towers of an ornate Victorian home, kept insisting that this was the house to buy. His wife continued to shake her head and point across the street to an old house with a wraparound porch perched above the Hudson.

Neither house was for sale that day, but Nyack is a town that inspires first-time visitors to wishful househunting. An antiques and handicrafts shopping center, Nyack is also an old-fashioned village filled with delightful gingerbread Victorian homes. It is a town that proudly declares itself one of the last remnants of "Small Town, USA."

The town's scenic location on the west bank of the Hudson once made it a busy river landing and later allowed it to decline gracefully into a peaceful resort community. Grover Cleveland spent summers here, Ben Hecht and Carson McCullers found the atmosphere conducive to writing, and Helen Hayes bought a gracious white house on North Broadway, where she still lives today. Nyack's best-known native son, Edward Hopper, memorialized his town's homes in his paintings.

Nyack had come on hard times, however, and its charm seemed threatened by the specter of housing developments and shopping centers. Instead, the combination of low rents and artistic atmosphere inspired the town's renaissance as a shopping and strolling mecca. On a pleasant weekend, the sidewalks are filled with visitors, especially when street fairs are in swing in May, July, and October.

A good plan would be to arrive Saturday morning, take in a few of the scores of shops on Broadway and Main Street, then buy a picnic lunch (there's a deli on Broadway) and go two miles north to Hook Mountain State Park. Picnic tables are right at the river's edge; the view is hard to beat. Thus refreshed, you'll be ready to explore the town at length.

Nyack's homes remain its pride. Most are not mansions but well-kept examples of comfortable Victoriana in its turn-of-the-century heyday, displaying the gables and porches, balconies and bay windows, cupolas and whimsical carving that give this style its special appeal.

To appreciate the houses, you must get out and walk, preferably accompanied by the *Village Guide and Walking Tour,* a booklet available in most shops for about $2. It will give you a fast lesson in spotting Victorian architecture, and then point out the most interesting houses on the five different loops along the tree-lined village streets and the waterfront. If you're on your own, an easy route to follow is south on Broadway to Washington Avenue, then one block left to Piermont at the water's edge.

All roads eventually lead to Broadway and the shops. On one block alone (South Broadway between Hudson and Cedar Hill avenues), there are at least two dozen stores offering everything from baskets to beads, furniture to works of art. Stroll the side closest to the river and you can prowl among places like Thieves Market (chocolate molds, signs, and tins), Christophers (lots of handsome oak furniture and a greenhouse), and Hand of the Craftsman with original crafts. The Vintage Car Store will gladly sell you a souped-up Ferrari for about

$22,000. If you've left your checkbook at home, you're still welcome to browse.

There are more stores on Main Street, and if you continue on Route 9W into Upper Nyack you'll find another cache of shops, including a group gallery that calls itself the Upper Nyack Antiques Center.

When hunger pangs strike, there are lots of pleasant possibilities. For lunch, Strawberry Place (an ice cream parlor) has an interesting sandwich menu; and Old Fashion is a chop house with seafood and hot sandwiches in a tavern atmosphere. At dinner time, the River Club on the waterfront and the Bully Boy, an English pub not far away in Congers, are popular locally.

Make it an early dinner, and you can then drive across the Tappan Zee Bridge for music under the stars at Lyndhurst. Concerts are held every Saturday night from July through mid-August on the 67-acre grounds of this Gothic revival mansion overlooking the Hudson River. It is located on Route 9, half a mile south of the bridge, and you can picnic there, too.

Spend the night at the Tarrytown Hilton or the Marriott with an indoor pool, and you can spend Sunday sunning or swimming or hitting a few tennis balls.

You'll also be perfectly situated to explore Sleepy Hollow Country, beginning with three restorations that provide a look at life in early Hudson River days. Starting with the farthest point, Van Cortlandt manor at Croton-on-Hudson, you can visit a Revolutionary War estate where Benjamin Franklin was once a guest. Beautifully situated overlooking the river, the gracious 1680 stone house with railed porch, double stairway, and pitched roof is surrounded by eighteenth-century gardens, peach, pear, and apple trees, and a brick-paved Long Walk lined with lush flowerbeds. Costumed hostesses take you through the house, pointing out the prized furnishings and telling of life during the home's heyday.

Philipsburg Manor in North Tarrytown was also the preserve of a prominent family, one that once owned about a third of what is now Westchester County. The trilevel home bears witness to New York's Dutch-English origins. One of its most appealing rooms is the big beamed kitchen, where the hostesses show you how food was prepared in Colonial times. At the gristmill and barn on the grounds, you'll learn about some of the daily activities on an early Colonial farm.

The last of the restorations, Sunnyside in Tarrytown, was the home of Washington Irving, who immortalized the area with his stories of Rip Van Winkle and Ichabod Crane, the legends of Sleepy Hollow. Irving once described his Victorian home as "a little old-fashioned stone mansion, all made up of gable ends, and as full of angles and corners as an old cocked hat.'' The house stands on the east bank of the Hudson surrounded by orchards, gardens, and wooded paths planned by Irving himself. Much of his original furniture and personal possessions also remain, including his massive desk in the library.

In addition to these properties, Sleepy Hollow Restoration oversees the Union Church of Pocantico Hills, a modest stone sanctuary with exquisite stained glass windows by Matisse and Chagall, a sight that should not be missed. Another architectural landmark, Montgomery Place at Annandale-on-Hudson, is in the process of restoration and may be open by the time you read this.

You may want to return to Lyndhurst for a house tour, stepping back into a gilded age when Jay Gould lived here very much like a king. The house is maintained by the National Trust for Historic Preservation.

If all that house-hopping has built up an appetite, have a last dinner at the Tappan Hill restaurant, a scenic spot high on a hill at Benedict and Highland avenues, only about four blocks off Route 9 near the center of Tarrytown.

Nyack and Tarrytown Area Code: 914

DRIVING DIRECTIONS Take the George Washington Bridge to New Jersey, then the Palisades Interstate Parkway to exit 4. Continue north on 9W until you come to Broadway, then bear right into the center of Nyack. The parkway also leads back to the Garden State Parkway and the connection to the Tappan Zee Bridge, which leads directly across the river into Tarrytown.

Total distance: about 25 miles.

PUBLIC TRANSPORTATION For Nyack only: Take the IND A Train to the George Washington Bridge Bus Terminal at 175th and Broadway in Manhattan, then board one of the Red & Tan buses that leave for Nyack every hour weekdays and weekends. Metro North serves Tarrytown.

ACCOMMODATIONS *Tappan Zee Town House,* Route 9W, Nyack, 358–8400, $$ • *West Gate,* Polhemus Street, Nyack, 358–8100, $$ • *Tarrytown Hilton Inn,* Route 9, Tarrytown, 631–5700, $$$$ • *Marriott,* 670 White Plains Road (Route 119), Tarrytown, 631–2200, $$$$.

DINING *Old Fashion,* 83 South Broadway, Nyack, 358–8114, $–$$

• *River Club*, foot of Burd Street on River, Nyack, 358–0220, seafood, $$–$$$ • *Bully Boy Chop House*, 117 Route 303, Congers, 268–6555, $$–$$$ • *Tappan Hill*, Highland Avenue, Tarrytown, 631–3030, $$–$$$ • *Caravela*, 532 North Broadway (Route 9), Tarrytown, 631–1863, seafood, Portuguese specialties, $$–$$$ • *Lago Di Como*, 27 Main Street, Tarrytown, northern Italian, $$–$$$ • *Maison Lafitte*, Route 9, Briarcliff Manor, 941–5556, classic French in a country inn, $$–$$$ • For lunch or light fare in Tarrytown, try *Horsefeathers*, 94 North Broadway (Route 9) or *Washington Irving Boat Club*, foot of Main Street, a nautical bar and grill with a view downriver.

SIGHTSEEING *Sleepy Hollow Restorations*, three properties all along Route 9, Tarrytown, NY 10591, 631–8200. Hours: daily 10 A.M. to 5 P.M. Each house: adults, $5; children, $3. Combination tickets: adults, $12; children, $7 • *Union Church of Pocantico Hills*, Route 448, North Tarrytown, tours April to December, Wednesday, Thursday, Friday, and Sunday, 1 P.M. to 4 P.M., $3 donation. (Ask whether Montgomery Place is also available for tours.) • *Lyndhurst*, Route 9, Tarrytown, 631–0046. Hours: April to October, Tuesday to Sunday 10 A.M. to 4:15 P.M. Adults, $5; children and senior citizens, $2.50.

FOR FURTHER INFORMATION Free map, street fair calendar, and shopping guide booklet are available by mail from the Art, Craft, and Antique Dealers Association of the Nyacks, PO Box 223G, Nyack, NY 10960, 358–8443.

Long Island Beaches for Beginners
Part 1: The Fabled Hamptons

Yes, that was definitely Billy Joel and Christie Brinkley at the next table in the restaurant. And yes, that was unmistakably George Plimpton coming down the aisle of the John Drew Theater. And it could well have been Robert DeNiro stopped next to you at the last red light.

Celebrities are commonplace in the Hamptons. Socialites spend their summers in Southampton, artists and writers and publishing executives in East Hampton—and prominent faces from the worlds of arts and entertainment are easy to spot in either town or in any of the villages in between. But their presence is possibly the least of the reasons for planning a weekend on Long Island's eastern end.

The main attraction remains the thing that brought the beautiful people here in the first place—the beach. There are miles and miles of it, broad stretches of soft sand lined with sheltering dunes, some of it still amazingly unpopulated. You'll search hard to find better beaches anywhere, and if you are an ocean lover and a sun worshiper, you may never notice or care who else is around sharing nature's bounty with you.

There are other reasons for making the trip, of course. Lots of people enjoy the browsing possibilities in an area filled with chic shops and art galleries. Others are attracted by resort towns where picturesque windmills still stand and where a Colonial heritage remains dominant in spite of the influx of summer visitors. There are many fine restaurants to choose from. And let's face it—it's fun to peek at the mansions behind the hedges.

All in all, the popularity of the area is well deserved, and though you'll encounter annoying traffic not only driving out from the city but also clogging the streets of the shopping centers after you arrive, this remains a prime summer destination.

The Hamptons officially begin with Westhampton, which is considerably closer to the city than the rest, but that proximity seems its only advantage. It is by far the most built up of the towns, with houses and condominiums lining the beach road.

Adjoining Westhampton Beach, however, is Quogue, a quiet village that is almost all gracious private homes, one of them an inn worth noting. The Inn at Quogue is an elegant place done with country pine, chintz, and quilts. The breakfast room overlooks a garden of wildflowers. If you can afford the tab, it's easy to feel at home here—and it's less than a mile to the very private town beach. Mark this one down as a sleeper.

Southampton was discovered long ago—even earlier than you might have guessed. The marker at Conscience Point off North Sea Road bears a plaque reading, NEAR THIS SPOT IN JUNE 1640 LANDED THE COLONISTS FROM LYNN, MASS., WHO FOUNDED SOUTHAMPTON, THE FIRST ENGLISH SETTLEMENT IN THE STATE OF NEW YORK.

Visit the Old Halsey House here and you'll be entering the oldest frame house in the state. The Southampton Historical Museum offers relics even older, all the way back to Indian days—not to mention a whaling captain's living room, a Colonial bedroom, a one-room schoolhouse, a country store, a carpenter's shop, and exhibits of early farm equipment. The restored Silversmith Shop on Main first opened about 1750.

Many tourists overlook all the history, preferring instead to head for Job's Lane to look at the galleries and antiques shops and the fashions both staid and strictly kicky in boutiques along the way. The antiques shops on Job's Lane don't deal in junk-tique; if you don't believe it, just check the price tags.

While you're on Job's Lane, don't get so carried away with window shopping that you miss the Parrish Art Museum. The changing exhibits are well worth a look.

Southampton has long been a favorite watering hole for society, and its mansions are legendary. Best roads for seeing them are parallel to the ocean on Meadow Lane (also the site of the handsome town beach) and Gin Lane, and on intersecting streets such as Halsey Neck, Cooper's Neck, and First Neck lanes. Wait until you see the size of these shingled "cottages"—and the cars in the driveway.

If you want to stay in Southampton and share that inviting public beach, the Village Latch Inn on Hill Street is a delightful inn-resort that puts you within walking distance. The nearby Southampton Inn is motel-like but also convenient, and the Old Post House feels like what it is—an inn with a lot of history behind it.

Driving farther east on Route 27 you'll pass through appealing small villages such as Water Mill (named for its windmill) and Bridgehampton, each with many shops for later exploring, and into East Hampton, where you could well be driving into another era. The approach as you turn left onto Main Street is pure Colonial, handsome white houses facing a green and a narow pond that was a cattle watering hole for early settlers and is a gathering spot for ducks today. The first stretch of Main Street is labeled Woods Lane, probably because it once ran through a forest.

East Hampton is another settlement founded more than three centuries ago, and in this case many descendants of the original families remain. Most of the older homes have been declared historic landmarks, and this town would make interesting strolling even if it were landlocked.

Almost every old home has a story to tell. On the west side of the pond, the second house from the V where Woods Lane turns into Main Street is The Studio, the home of noted watercolorist Thomas Moran. Two doors down at 217 is the home that was summer White House for President John Tyler. Across the green is the South End Burying Ground, and on James Lane, a short street bordering the eastern edge of the cemetery, are some of the oldest homes in town. Among them are Winthrop Gardiners's saltbox, Mill Cottage, and Home Sweet Home, a 1750 home named in honor of its owner, John Howard Payne, who wrote the song of the same title. It is open to visitors. Mulford

Farmhouse next door, built in the 1650s, is the oldest of all the homes and was a working farm until the late 1940s.

Back on Main Street is Guild Hall, art museum and home of the John Drew summer theater and cultural center of East Hampton. Across the way is the town library and next door, Clinton Academy, the first chartered secondary school in New York state. It is currently home to the East Hampton Historical Society, which regularly holds exhibits and lectures. Next is Towne House, a tiny 1930 structure that has been both schoolhouse and town hall and is currently being restored.

Hook Mill at the end of town is very much a landmark, and tours of the wind-powered grinding mill, which is still in working order, are a favorite with children. Hook Mill Burying Ground is even older than the South End cemetery, and it is not unusual to see people taking rubbings of the stones, which date to 1650.

The East Hampton Chamber of Commerce at the corner of Main Street and Newtown Lane has free walking guides to the village and lots of other printed information. Shops in town begin on Main and continue down Newtown. They grow more numerous and more interesting every year.

The beach in East Hampton is at the end of Ocean Avenue, a right turn south at a blinker as you approach town. Lily Pond Lane, which runs west off Ocean Avenue, is this town's mansion row.

For your own weekend home there are some very appealing inns back on Main Street. The Maidstone Arms, across from the green, is sunny and simple with a Victorian feel and lots of wicker. The 1770 House lives up to its name with Colonial decor, wide-planked floors, antiques, and canopy beds. Across the street, the Huntting Inn, which dates to 1751, is also Colonial, though the accommodations are secondary to the restaurant downstairs, an outpost of New York's classy The Palm. The Palm has a second location at The Hedges, an even more appealing inn.

Farther east is the town of Amagansett, which is really a Hampton in all but name. Boutiques and shopping complexes have altered what used to be a small charming town with Colonial flavor, diluted only by the modernistic beachhouses near the shore. But they haven't overrun the place yet; there are still enough saltbox homes, Colonial shutters, and geranium boxes to make the town wonderfully appealing, even if the famous once-authentic farmer's market has succumbed to commercialism.

All the new shops do make for interesting browsing, and Balasses House, an old standby on Main Street, has beautiful English country antiques. If you need other diversions there is a little marine museum on Bluff Road, as well as a historical museum known as Miss Amelia's Cottage, with excellent period furniture, particularly clocks and other pieces made by the Dominy family, well-known Colonial craftsmen of East Hampton.

Amagansett has several town beaches. One of them, Coast Guard Beach, is a popular singles territory, sometimes called "Asparagus Beach" for all the bodies standing around.

One of the most appealing places to stay in the whole area is in Amagansett. Just off Main, the Mill Garth is a 100-year-old main house with another half dozen or so studios and apartments winding around a complex of lawns and gardens, all antiques-filled and offering charm as well as privacy. It is only half a mile to the beach, but if you are feeling lazy, they will lend you a bike or provide parking passes. Gansett Green is a more modest but similar complex.

Hamptons weekends can't be run by schedules. Both East Hampton and Southampton can easily take half a day just for sightseeing, but if the weather is right, the beach and the ocean may be the only sights you care to see.

Not only is Amagansett pleasant to visit, but Water Mill and Bridgehampton also have many interesting specialty shops worth a stop, particularly for the folk art, Appalachian art, and quilts in Bridgehampton. All of Route 27, in fact, offers galleries and shops that will tempt you to pull off the road for a bit.

If you want tennis, golf, or fishing, all are available; just ask at your lodging for the most convenient spot. And you can take a trip to Montauk, Sag Harbor, or Shelter Island.

There's enough to keep you busy here for many a day—and many a weekend. Why do you think all those people spend the summer here?

Hamptons Area Code: 516

DRIVING DIRECTIONS Long Island Expressway to exit 70, right for three miles to Sunrise Highway (Route 27) eastbound. Follow 27 to Southampton; it continues to be the only main route to Montauk and the end of the island.

Total distance to Southampton: 96 miles.

PUBLIC TRANSPORTATION Long Island Railroad has regular service to the Hamptons, (718) 739–4200 or (516) 369–1666. Hampton Express, (212) 233–4403 or (516) 369–1666, and Hampton Jitney, (212) 936–0440 or (516) 283–4600 provide bus service. There are also small commuter airlines; check chambers of commerce for current schedules.

ACCOMMODATIONS Many places have three-day minimums in summer. *The Inn at Quogue,* 288–1300, $$$$ • *The Village Latch Inn,* 101 Hill Street, Southampton, 283–2160, $$$–$$$$ • *The Old Post House,* 136 Main Street, Southampton, 283–1717, $$$$ CP • *The Southampton Inn,* Hill Street at First Neck Lane, 283–6500, $$$$ • *The Maidstone Arms,* 207 Main Street, East Hampton, 324–5006, $$$–$$$$ CP • *1770 House,* 143 Main Street, East Hampton, 324–1770, $$$$ CP • *Huntting Inn,* 94 Main Street, East Hampton, 324–0410, $$$–$$$$ • *East Hampton House,* Montauk Highway, East Hampton, 324–4300, particularly nice motel with many kitchenettes, seven-days minimum but worth a try for last minute weekend accommodations, $$$–$$$$ • *The Mill Garth,* Windmill Lane, Amagansett, 267–3757, $$$$ • *Hedges Inn,* 74 James Lane, East Hampton, 324–7100, $$$$ • *Gansett Green Manor,* Main Street, Box 799, Amagansett, 267–3133, $$, efficiencies, $$$–$$$$.

DINING *The Inn At Quogue* (see above), fresh-caught seafood, fresh-grown vegetables, $$$ • *John Duck Jr.,* North Main Street, Southampton, 283–0311, no atmosphere, just delicious home-style roast duckling and lots of it, $$–$$$ • *The Old Post House* (see above), pleasant outside dining, $$–$$$ • *Athena,* 75 Main Street, Southampton, 283–9867, Greek, $$–$$$ • *1770 House* (see above), prix-fixe dinner, $$$$ • *Maidstone Arms* (see above), $$$ • *Fresno Place* (on Fresno Place—follow Race Lane to end, turn right, then right again), East Hampton, 324–0727, tiny spot specializing in sushi and other Japanese dishes, $$$ • *Wings Point,* 295 Three Mile Harbor Road, East Hampton, 324–6100, $$$ • *The Palm* at Huntting Inn and at the Hedges (see above), $$$ • *Michaels,* 28 Maidstone Park Road, East Hampton, 324–6725, seafood, $$–$$$ • *Leif Hope's Laundry,* 31 Race Lane, East Hampton, 324–3199, brick walls, skylights, mixed menu, popular, $$–$$$ • *Gordon's,* Main Street, Amagansett, 324–9793, longtime local favorite, $$–$$$ • *Oceans,* Route 27, Amagansett, 267–6622, grill, outdoor dining, $$ • In the evening, *East Colony Comedy Club* at the Southampton Inn and the piano bar at *Bobby Van's,* Main Street, Bridgehampton, 537–0590, are possibilities, and for the younger set, there's *Danceteria* and *Oceans* on Route 27 in Amagansett.

SIGHTSEEING *Southampton Historical Museum,* 17 Meeting House Lane off Main Street, 283–2494. Hours: mid-June to September, daily except Monday 11 A.M. to 5 P.M. Adults, $1; children,

$.25 ● *Parrish Art Museum,* 25 Job's Lane, Southampton, 283–2118. Hours: Thursday to Monday 10 A.M. to 5 P.M., except Sunday, 1 P.M. to 5 P.M. Free ● *Halsey Homestead,* South Main Street, Southampton, 283–3527. Hours: mid-June to mid-September, daily except Monday 11 A.M. to 4:30 P.M. Adults, $1; children, $.25 ● *Olde Mill,* Route 27, Water Mill, 726–4594. Hours: mid-June to September, Monday, Wednesday, and Saturday 10 A.M. to 4 P.M.; Sunday 1 P.M. to 4 P.M. Donation ● *Home Sweet Home House and Windmill,* 14 James Lane, East Hampton, 324–0713. Hours: May to November, Monday to Saturday 10 A.M. to 4 P.M.; Sunday 2 P.M. to 4 P.M. Adults, $1.50; children, $1 ● *East Hampton Historical Society,* 101 Main Street, 324–6850, and all its properties: *Osborne-Jackson House,* 101 Main Street; *Historic Mulford House,* James Lane; *Clinton Academy,* 151 Main Street. All open July and August, Tuesday to Sunday 1 P.M. to 5 P.M.; June and September, weekends only. One ticket for all properties: adults, $2; children, $1 ● *Hook Mill,* 36 North Main Street, East Hampton, 324–0173. Hours: late June to Labor Day, daily 10 A.M. to 4 P.M. Adults, $1.50; children, $1 ● *Guild Hall Museum and John Drew Theater,* 158 Main Street, East Hampton, 324–0806. Hours: June to October, Wednesday to Friday 10 A.M. to 5 P.M., Saturday and Sunday 1 P.M. to 5 P.M. Donation at exhibits. Check for current summer theater schedule at John Drew Theater, 324–4050 ● *Miss Amelia's Cottage,* Main Street, Amagansett, 267–3020. Hours: Tuesday to Sunday 1 P.M. to 4 P.M. ● *East Hampton Town Marine Museum,* Bluff Road, Amagansett, 267–6544. Hours: July to Labor Day, Tuesday to Sunday 10:30 A.M. to 5 P.M.; June and September, weekends only. Adults, $2; children $1.

FOR FURTHER INFORMATION Contact the Southampton Chamber of Commerce, 79 Main Street, Southampton, NY 11968, 283–0402. East Hampton Chamber of Commerce, 74 Park Place, East Hampton, NY 11937, 324–0362.

Long Island Beaches for Beginners
Part 2: Unaffected Montauk

Boutiques and babies don't always mix. Small children and country inns aren't always comfortable with each other. And people who love wide open seascapes and shell searching often hate tourist-clogged sidewalks and busy town beaches.

That's why many people prefer to keep right on going when they get to the Hamptons. Instead of heading for the action, they want to get away from it on the easternmost end of Long Island.

The scene changes dramatically on Route 27 as soon as you pass the outer limits of Amagansett. No more shops. After a while, no more clumps of beach houses. At Napeague there is a lineup of condominium resort complexes along the shore. Many owners rent out their units, and these are choice lodgings with tennis, pools, and long stretches of very private beach. Sea Crest and Driftwood are among the oldest and best of these.

Finally, when the condos end, there is nothing ahead except beach grass and dunes and the unmistakable scent of the sea growing stronger all the time.

Bear right onto Old Montauk Highway and you'll see the sea, Hither Hills State Park, and a few exceptional places for beach lovers. Gurney's Inn is the oldest and best known. Panoramic View, terraced up a steep hillside, offers dramatic sea views, private beach and pool, simpler accommodations, and a smaller tab. Wave Crest, now a condo, is another nearby spot for wave watching. All of these provide comfort and extraordinary private powdery beaches. Leave the small groups clustered in front of each hotel, and in either direction there's open space for walking, jogging, or shelling as far as the eye can see and the feet can carry you.

Children are in the definite minority here—very young ones, at least. They're more likely to be found farther on in Montauk, where about a dozen motels are grouped near the ocean, few of them offering much in the way of charm but all providing something equally hard to come by—direct access to the beach. There couldn't be a better place for young families. It's easy for one parent to take a little walk back to put the baby in for a nap while the other stays on the beach with the rest of the family. Many of these motels offer refrigerators and/or cooking facilities, helping to save on restaurant bills. And if there are children too old to want to sit around with parents in the evening but too young to drive, Montauk offers a special bonus. The beach (and the beach motels) are only a block off the Main Street of town, meaning that it's an easy walk to the local movie or mini-golf course or pinball parlor.

Almost all of the oceanfront motels recently have become condominiums, which is both bad and good, depending on your budget. Many have been fixed up quite a bit, but their prices have risen as well. You have to look hard these days if you want to pay less than $100 a night for a motel room. Check the chamber of commerce and the bed-and-breakfast listing in the front of this book for less pricey accommodations.

If you want to enjoy Montauk's easy atmosphere and still live in style, the place is Montauk Manor, an old landmark high on a hill that is now a virtual castle of a condominium, decorated by Bloomingdale's. You're away from it all here, but the free mini-bus will whisk you to the beach or to dinner or anywhere you have a yen to go. Another posh local spot is the Montauk Yacht Club, ideal whether you need a place to park yourself or your yacht.

But don't be misled by these luxury accommodations. At heart this is still a fisherman's town. Until recently, the best place in town to find anything, including clothes, was White's Drug Store. The town center is filled with modest eating places serving breakfast, lunch, and dinner, a pizza place, and a handful of modest shops—nothing remotely like the shopping a few miles to the west.

So what do you do in Montauk when you're not on the beach? Get back to nature. Go hiking or biking on dirt roads beside the ocean, sound, lake, and fresh ponds. Watch for birds—you're in the crossroads of a major migratory pattern. Go berry picking for shadberries, blackberries, or blueberries—or, in September, for beach plums and wild grapes. Go horseback riding on the beach or sign up for lessons in wind surfing or sailing.

There are many ways to go out to sea in Montauk. You can sign on for the deep-sea fishing trips that go out of the harbor daily; or rent a sailboat or take a day-long whale-watching expedition aboard the *Finback II*, a working scientific research boat. Or you can take the ferry to Connecticut or Block Island, just a 1½-hour cruise away.

Whether you get on a boat or not, you'll surely want to watch them returning to the docks with the day's fresh catch of fish. One prize spot for viewing is Gosman's Dock, where fresh fish is available in the fish store as well as in the restaurant, one of the most popular places on all Long Island.

Gosman's lobsters are legendary; there is often at least an hour's wait for a table on weekend evenings. There are no reservations; you'll just have to wait your turn, keeping occupied with a drink from the bar and the activity of the boats around you. If you don't want to wait, there is a clam bar and a takeout where you get "lobster in the rough" to eat at picnic tables nearby. If not as pleasant as the restaurant, it is, at least, cheaper. (The crowds at Gosman's, incidentally, have inspired the opening of the only shops in town that might qualify as touristy—all right at the dock.)

The other "don't miss" attraction in Montauk is its lighthouse, which has stood on the very eastern tip of Long Island since 1795. Kids absolutely love clambering up the rocks here, and grown-ups with cameras go crazy looking for the best angle on the cliff-top view.

If you find yourself stuck indoors with kids in the rain, there are just enough diversions within driving distance to save the day. Two stand-bys are the whaling museum in Sag Harbor and East Hampton's windmill. If the children are old enough to appreciate a bit of history, you can also visit the museums in the various Hamptons towns.

Are the motels in Montauk tacky? Does the town lack class? Some Hamptons lovers might say so, but you couldn't prove it by the many people who swear by the place and can't wait to get back.

Long Island Area Code: 516

DRIVING DIRECTIONS Follow directions to Southampton (page 105); continue east on Route 27 to Montauk.
Total distance: 120 miles.

PUBLIC TRANSPORTATION Same as Hamptons, page 105.

ACCOMMODATIONS Expect minimum-stay requirements in season. All rates down after Labor Day. • *Gurney's Inn*, Old Montauk Highway, 668–2345, $$$$$ MAP • *Panoramic View*, Old Montauk Highway, 668–3000, with kitchenettes and terraces, $$$–$$$$ • *Wave Crest*, Old Montauk Highway, Box 952, 668–2141, $$$$ • *Royal Atlantic Motel*, South Edgemere Street, 668–5103, pool, some kitchenettes, $$$$ • *Ocean Beach Motel*, PO Box 728, 668–5790, refrigerators in rooms, $$$$ • *Ocean Surf*, South Emerson Avenue, 668–3332, some efficiencies, $$$$ • *Sea Crest*, Montauk Highway, Napeague, 267–3159, efficiencies, pool, tennis, $$$$ • *Driftwood*, Montauk Highway, Napeague, 668–5744, pool, tennis, efficiencies, $$$$ • *Sun Haven Motel*, Montauk Highway, Route 27, Napeague, 267–3448, efficiencies, pool, tennis, $$$–$$$$ • Three lower-priced Montauk choices within easy walking distance to the beach: *Oceanside Beach Resort*, S. Eton Street and Montauk Highway, 868–9825, $$$; *Beach House*, S. Embassy and S. Elmwood, 668–2700, $$$; *Malibu Motel*, Elmwood Avenue, PO Box 353, 668–5233, $$$ • Top of the line in Montauk: *Montauk Manor*, Edgemere Street, Box 226C, Montauk, 668–2521, kitchens, pool, tennis, $$$$; *Montauk Yacht Club & Inn*, Star Island, Montauk, 668–3100, $$$$; *Surf Club*, S. Essex and Surfside Avenue, 668–3800, beachside condos, pool, tennis, $$$$.

DINING *The Inn at Napeague,* Route 27, 267–8103, $$ • *Gurney's Inn* (see above), $$–$$$$ • *Gosman's Dock,* at the end of the docks, 668–5330, $$–$$$ • *Port Royal,* Navy Road, 668–3599, outside deck, bay views, good duckling, $$ • *Royal Atlantic Restaurant,* Edgemere Road, 668–5510, good food and bountiful salad bar, $$ • *The Fish Factory,* South Embassy Street, 668–3445, $–$$ • *The Crow's Nest Inn,* Route 127 1½ miles east of village, 668–3700, wonderful water views, early-bird lobster specials, good chowder, $$–$$$ • For lunch: *The Lobster Roll,* Route 27, Napeague, $ • *Mimosa Beach Café,* right on the beach in Montauk, $.

SIGHTSEEING AND ACTIVITIES *Bicycle rentals, Pfunds Hardware Store,* Main Street, 668–2456 • *Wind-surfing and sailing lessons and rentals: Wind and Surf Shoppe,* Montauk Yacht Club, Star Island, off West Lake Drive, 668–2300 • *Waterskiing instruction and boat rentals: Uihleins,* Montauk Harbor, West Lake Drive Ext., 668–2545 • *Horseback riding: Indian Field Ranch,* Montauk Highway, 668–2744; *Deep Hollow Riding Academy,* Montauk Highway, 668–5453 • *Fishing trips, ferry to Block Island and Connecticut, sunset sightseeing cruises: The Viking Fleet,* Montauk Harbor, 668–5709. Phone for current rates; *Okeanos Whale Watching Cruises,* PO Box 776, Hampton Bays, 728–4522. Daily cruises from Montauk Marine Basin at 10 A.M., returning approximately at 4 P.M. Adults, $25; children under 13, $15. Reservations required • *Montauk Point State Park,* end of Route 27, 668–2461. Parking, $3.50.

FOR FURTHER INFORMATION Contact the Montauk Chamber of Commerce, Box CC, Montauk, NY 11954, 668–2428.

Shipping Out in New London

The call of the sea is still strong in New London, Connecticut.

Once brave whalers shipped out from New London's piers, making the town wealthy and world renowned. Today it is the home of the Coast Guard Academy, the proud seagoing service whose mission since 1790 has been to rescue lives and property at sea.

It is a salty history that the town celebrates in style each summer with a succession of gala weekends at the city pier. Sail Festival Weekend, held in mid-July, is a three-day affair that includes name bands, street fairs, moonlight cruises, and a Saturday night fireworks extravaganza over the Thames River. The recently instituted Harbor Festival, held over Labor Day, focuses on seafood and good eating.

But the day that everyone most looks forward to is the Coast Guard Weekend in early August when the majestic *Eagle,* America's only tall ship, glides into port to hold open house. The Coast Guard's actual birthday is August 4, but the date of the open house varies from year to year, depending on when the *Eagle* completes her annual cadet-training cruise.

Even in the nuclear age, the romance of the great sailing ships still captures the imagination, and the *Eagle,* the 295-foot barque that led America's Bicentennial Tall Ships Parade, remains the object of fascination for all ages. There is usually a band on hand to add to the festive spirit of the day. Often it is either the spiffy Coast Guard Band or the Cadet Band ready to trumpet a salute to their service.

Though New London's summer celebrations offer many special events, any time you visit this historic nautical area you will find pleasures awaiting. Together, New London and its neighbors, Groton and Mystic, cover the historic waterfront, comprising not only an old whaling center but the nation's submarine capital and the living museum at Mystic Seaport, the largest maritime complex in the east. As an added bonus, New London offers a scenic sandy shoreline along the Long Island Sound and an amusement park at Ocean Beach.

Not too long ago New London was a city gone downhill, but it is now fighting hard to reclaim some of its illustrious past. The New London Historic Walking Tour is posted prominently along the main street, a restored pedestrians-only mall known as Captain's Walk. The tour begins with the city's pride, its beautifully restored nineteenth-century train station, and includes the restored Nathan Hale Schoolhouse. It moves on to the 1930s Customs House, whose front door was once part of the frigate *Constitution,* and then to the four imposing, columned whaling merchant's mansions now known as Whale Oil Row. The compact tour covers other historic homes, including the Shaw Mansion, now the headquarters and museum of the New London Historical Society.

As you proceed south from Whale Oil Row, you'll find several fine old homes on Hempstead Street. One of Connecticut's oldest, Hempstead House, is a 1637 homestead that was maintained by the family of the original owners until 1937. The only house remaining that escaped burning by British troops in New London in 1781, it is open to the public for a look into the past.

Head back to town via Starr Street, where the old homes have been restored to form a charming contemporary neighborhood. Back near the waterfront, Bank Street is another area being refurbished store by store, adding atmosphere, dining places, and nightlife to the city.

Drive out toward Ocean Beach Park to 325 Pequot Avenue and you'll find Monte Cristo Cottage, the boyhood home of playwright Eugene O'Neill. The Victorian home has been restored, and tours are available weekdays or by appointment. Eugene O'Neill Theater Center in nearby Waterford holds an annual summer series of readings by promising new playwrights. Check to see what is scheduled while you are in town.

New Yorkers may find a familiar look to New London's Ocean Beach, done by the designer of Jones Beach. There's a mile-long boardwalk, rides, a pool, miniature golf, and a wide beach on the sound.

New London's best lodging is also in this area. The Lighthouse Inn, the Victorian mansion of steel baron Charles S. Guthrie, has been renovated into a totally elegant enclave just a block from a private beach. You'll find rich paneling and a carved spiral staircase leading to lavish guest rooms, including four huge front bedrooms with canopy beds and water views. There are also rooms in an adjacent carriage house, and an excellent dining room. In town, the Radisson Hotel offers attractive modern quarters within a walk of the pier, and the Queen Anne Inn is a pleasant modest bed-and-breakfast inn in a Victorian home a short drive from the center.

Continuing with sightseeing, a few miles west of New London in Waterford on a breezy promontory is the luxurious summer estate of Edward and Mary Harkness—27 buildings on 235 acres, including spacious lawns, formal Italian gardens, and 200-year-old trees. Now known as Harkness Park, about half the area is open to summer visitors, including the gardens, the mansion, a bird-painting exhibit, and a beach for strolling (no swimming allowed).

Back on the other side of I-95 in New London on Mohegan Avenue is the Coast Guard Academy, a cluster of handsome, traditional red brick buildings on 100 acres high above the Thames. It has inviting grounds, a well-endowed museum, and a multimedia center at river's edge, where you can learn about the service's glory days from the era of George Washington to the present. There's a bonus when the *Eagle* is in port. Each summer the barque is a magnificent floating classroom for cadets who learn the ways of wind and water on the cruise of a lifetime.

Across from the academy on Mohegan Avenue is the campus of Connecticut College and the Lyman Allyn Museum, named in memory of a famous sea captain. It contains art, antiques, and a wonderful

collection of dollhouses, dolls, and toys. Also on the campus is the
Connecticut Arboretum, a particularly fine nature preserve, which offers 415 acres with hiking trails.

Across the Thames at Groton, the U.S. Navy Submarine Base, the
largest in the world, provides still another perspective on America's
maritime traditions. The submarine has a longer history in the New
London area than most visitors realize. The first submarine, *The Turtle,* invented by David Bushnell of nearby Saybrook, was launched in
1776. Although an attempt to sink a British flagship failed, the seven-
and-a-half-foot vessel paved the way for today's underwater fleet.

At the USS Nautilus Memorial at the base, you can trace the progress of submarines from those days to the nuclear age, and board the
world's finest nuclear-powered sub. Working periscopes, an authentic
submarine control room, and mini-theaters are part of the exhibit.

Groton has its own share of nautical history. Up the hill from town is
Fort Griswold State Park, where Colonial troops were massacred by
Benedict Arnold's British forces in 1781. An obelisk standing 127 feet
high marks the spot, and the fort still offers the same commanding
view of the river that made it ideal as a lookout for British ships.

Monument House nearby holds the D.A.R. collection of both Revolutionary and Civil War memorabilia. The Ebenezer Avery House is
furnished with household accoutrements from Colonial times. It was
moved from its original site on Thames Street, but it is the very same
building in which the wounded from the battle were brought to be
treated.

Groton is not a city that wears its history well, but the Groton Bank
Historical Association publishes an interesting pamphlet that tells the
long story of the town. Available in local stores, the pamphlet indi-
cates excellent examples of the two-and-a-half centuries of architecture
from the Colonial era through the whaling days, places easy to miss on
your own. It begins with the oldest home in town, the Joseph Latham
House on Meridian Street, and guides you to Thames and Broad
streets.

All of this sightseeing is hardly going to leave enough time to do
justice to Mystic Seaport, one of America's prime maritime attractions. There are the majestic sailing vessels to board; a whole nineteenth-century village with working shops to explore; buildings filled
with rare boats, ship's models, figureheads, scrimshaw, and art; the
chance to watch boats being built; and continuing demonstrations of
arts such as sail setting, ropework, oystering, or fireplace cooking. It
might be well to save Mystic for a weekend of its own or tack an extra
day onto your present tour.

Note that each of these sea-centered communities offer ample opportunity to actually get out on the water. In New London, ferries ply back and forth to Fishers Island, Block Island, and Orient Point. The *River Queen II*, a pint-size replica of a Mississippi paddle-wheeler, tours the Thames Harbor from Groton. Visitors to Mystic Seaport can have a half-hour day cruise on the jaunty little coal-powered steamboat *Sabino*, or a 90-minute river cruise at night, often with music.

And should all that nautical atmosphere move you to want to go farther out to sea, you can ship out on one of the windjammers, replicas of the old two-masted nineteenth-century schooners that sail out of Mystic regularly for one-, two-, or five-day cruises.

Connecticut Area Code: 203

DRIVING INSTRUCTIONS I-95 to exit 83 for New London, exit 85 for Groton.
Total distance: about 125 miles.

PUBLIC TRANSPORTATION Amtrak has trains to New London from Grand Central, but it's hard to get beyond the center of town without a car.

ACCOMMODATIONS *Lighthouse Inn,* 6 Guthrie Place (off Pequot at Lower Boulevard, one-half mile east of Ocean Beach Park), 443–8411, $$$–$$$$ CP ● *Radisson Hotel,* 35 Gov. Winthrop Boulevard and Union Street, 443–7000, $$$ CP ● *Queen Anne Inn,* 265 Williams Street, 447–2600, $$–$$$ CP (with afternoon tea) ● *Thames Harbour Inn,* 193 Thames Street, Groton, 445–9111, motel on the river, some efficiencies, $$–$$$. See also Mystic, page 29.

DINING *West Bank Bistro,* 52 Bank Street, 444–0803, stylish new café with great water view from the deck, $$–$$$ ● *Bulkeley House,* 111 Bank Street, 443–9599, Colonial tavern, $$ ● *Thames Landing Oyster House,* 2 Captain's Walk, 442–2650, popular for seafood near the station and pier, $–$$ ● *Lighthouse Inn* (see above), elegant, with water view, $$ ● *Two Sisters Deli,* favorite local spot for lunch, $. See also Mystic, page 29.

SIGHTSEEING *Shaw Mansion,* 11 Blinman Street, New London, 443–1209. Hours: Tuesday to Saturday 1 P.M. to 4 P.M. Adults, $1; children, $.50 ● *Nathan Hale Schoolhouse,* Captain's Walk next to City Hall, New London, 443–2861. Hours: Memorial Day to Labor Day, Monday to Friday 10 A.M. to 3 P.M. Free ● *Hempstead House,*

11 Hempstead Street, New London, 247–8996. Hours: May 15 to October 15, Tuesday to Sunday 1 P.M. to 5 P.M. Adults, $2; children, $.50 ● *Ocean Beach Park,* Ocean Avenue, New London, 447–3031. Hours: daily 9 A.M. to 10 P.M. Adults, $1; children $.50. Parking, $3, weekends, $5 ● *U.S. Coast Guard Academy,* Mohegan Avenue, New London, 444–8270. Hours: May to October, daily 10 A.M. to 5 P.M.; rest of year, 9 A.M. to 4 P.M. Free ● *Harkness Memorial State Park,* Route 213, Waterford, 443–5725. Hours: mansion open daily, Memorial Day to Labor Day, 10 A.M. to 5 P.M.; grounds open all year. Parking weekdays, $1, weekends, $2 ● *Connecticut Arboretum,* Connecticut College Campus, New London, 447–7700. Hours: daily during daylight hours. Free ● *Lyman Allyn Museum,* 625 Williams Street (near college), New London, 443–2545. Hours: Tuesday to Saturday 1 P.M. to 5 P.M.; Sunday 2 P.M. to 5 P.M. Donation ● *Monte Cristo Cottage,* 325 Pequot Avenue, New London, 443–0051. Hours: Monday to Friday 1 P.M. to 4 P.M. and by appointment. Adults, $2; children, $.50 ● *USS Nautilus Memorial,* U.S. Naval Submarine Base, Route 12, Groton, 449–3174. Hours: April 15 to October 14, Wednesday to Monday 9 A.M. to 5 P.M.; rest of year to 3:30 P.M. (closed the third week of March, June, and September and second week of December). Free ● *Ft. Griswold State Park,* Monument and Park avenues, Groton, 445–1729. Hours: Memorial Day to Columbus Day, daily 9 A.M. to 5 P.M. Free ● *Ebenezer Avery House,* at Ft. Griswold, Groton, 446–9257. Hours: June to August, Saturday and Sunday 2 P.M. to 4 P.M. Free ● *Mystic Seaport,* Route 27, Mystic, 536–2631. Hours: daily 9 A.M. to 5 P.M. Adults $10; children, 6–12, $5.

FOR MORE INFORMATION Southeastern Connecticut Tourism District, Ye Old Towne Mill, 8 Mill Street, New London, CT 06320, 444–2206.

Gingerbread by the Sea in Cape May

With more than 600 prize gingerbread Victorian houses within 2.2 square miles, how do you ever decide which ones deserve special status? In historic Cape May, New Jersey, they didn't even try. They simply declared the whole town a national landmark.

Hop aboard the sightseeing trolley or join one of the guided walking tours of the nation's oldest seashore resort and you'll soon know why.

While erosion has diminished Cape May's once lavish beaches, fire has leveled the legendary nineteenth-century hotels that hosted presidents and royalty, and the usual quota of innocuous resort motels and eateries have sprung up around the beach, nothing has touched the tree-lined residential streets of old Cape May. They remain a serene world apart, a gracious enclave of pastel paint and lacy curlicues, mansard roofs and fish-scale shingles, ornate railings and columned porches, with widows' walks, cupolas, towers, and turrets looking out to sea.

Because of its unique heritage, the largest collection of Victorian homes in America, Cape May is a seaside retreat like no other—and possibly at its most appealing during the tail end of summer, after Labor Day. The water remains warm, there is more room for strolling on the beach promenade, and you have a better chance of getting reservations in the guest houses in the historic district where you will sample the best of Victorian living.

If you wait until early October, you can take in the Victorian Week festivities, a ten-day gala encompassing two weekends. There are special house tours, period fashion shows, and lectures on Victorian arts as well as an antiques show, entertainment, and other special activities.

On a Cape May tour, you'll learn that a destructive fire in 1878 accounts for the unusual concentration of 1880s homes. Before that date Cape May was the prime vacation spot on the East Coast. It had attracted Colonial luminaries from Philadelphia as early as the 1770s, and in the years following local guest house and hotel registers included the names of seven U.S. presidents, including Andrew Jackson and Abraham Lincoln, as well as Henry Clay, Horace Greeley, actress Lily Langtry, and composer John Philip Sousa. Huge old wooden hotels like the Mansion House, the Mount Vernon, and the United States had been vulnerable to fires all along, but the blaze of 1878 was so devastating that 30 acres of the town were laid bare by the flames.

Ironically, it was that disaster that prompted so many wealthy people, most from the Philadelphia area, to come in and build on the suddenly available tracts of land. They were further encouraged by the railroad, which offered a year's free transportation for anyone who would help recoup their tourist trade.

The homes that went up were smaller than Cape May's original structures, but were even showier, products of an era when having money meant flaunting it in the form of elaborate exterior home decoration. "The fancier the better" seems to have been the Victorians' motto.

Trolley tours of the town run regularly, but you'll get a much better look at the architecture on a walking tour sponsored by the Mid-Atlantic Center for the Arts. It takes you down streets like Ocean and Beach, Gurney and Stockton, Columbia and Howard, with an enthusiastic local resident to fill you in on who was who in the homes and hotels along the way. You'll learn how the Chalfonte Hotel on Howard Street, the only remaining survivor of the 1878 fire, once qualified for a local liquor license by counting linen closets and bathrooms as "accommodations"; about the wife of a sea captain living near Howard and Ocean who confessed in her diary that she was afraid when her husband went to sea, leaving her to deal with the Indians and pirates who roamed the Cape; and about the socialite from Baltimore who came to the Columbia Hotel in the summer of 1917 to plan her coming-out party. Her name was Wallis Warfield, later known as the Duchess of Windsor.

Most of the homes are private residences, but you can get a feel for their interiors by visiting some of the guest houses in the historic district. The acknowledged showplace in town is the Mainstay Inn, also know as the Victorian Mansion, once an elegant gambling club, still with its original 14-foot ceilings, tall mirrors, ornate plaster moldings, elaborate chandeliers, and cupola with an ocean view. The current young owners, Tom and Sue Carroll, have kept many of the original furnishings, and they offer tours and tea in the parlor (on the veranda, weather permitting) on Saturdays and Sundays at four.

Catty-corner from the Mainstay at the corner of Gurney is The Abbey, an 1869 Gothic villa that once belonged to coal baron John B. McCreary. It is furnished with tall carved walnut headboards, marble-topped dressers, and ornate lighting fixtures from its original era, and the first floor also can be toured at teatime on weekends. The second-floor bedrooms have private baths; if you stay on the third floor you share the Tower Bath, big as a bedroom, with claw-foot tub, pedestal sink, brass fixtures, Oriental rug, and stained glass.

These two homes are the pick of the guest-house accommodations, and two or three months ahead is none too soon for reservations. Some other pleasant inns are Victorian Rose, the Queen Victoria, The Brass Bed, and Captain Mey's. No rooms at the inns? You'll have to settle for a motel and teatime tours.

Cape May's beaches are a lot slimmer than they used to be, but there is still enough room for sunning and the promenade is perfect for walking or jogging with an ocean view. A 30-minute bike ride from town takes you to Cape May Point, where the Atlantic meets Delaware Bay and where you can sift through the sand for pieces of polished quartz known as Cape May diamonds. These have more sentimental than monetary value, but they are pretty and, when polished, can be set into jewelry souvenirs. Cape May Point State Park has a pleasant bird sanctuary and also one of the country's oldest lighthouses, dating to 1744. The Point's Sunset Beach is the favored local spot for sunset watching.

Back in Cape May you can play tennis at the Cape May Tennis Club, next to the Physick Estate at 1048 Washington Street, and while you are in the neighborhood have a look at the elegant restoration of an 1881 home, finely furnished with Victorian pieces. The Cape May County Art League holds changing exhibits in the carriage house on the estate.

On Washington Mall you'll find three blocks of shops as well as sidewalk cafés, ice cream parlors, and a bookstore where you can pick up the Sunday papers. Just off the mall is the Pink House, an antiques shop that is the ultimate in Victorian frills. It's the house you see most of the time when you see a photo of Cape May.

You'll hardly need any further diversion if the weather is right, but for cloudy days or a very worthwhile detour on the way home, don't overlook Wheaton Village, about an hour away in Millville, New Jersey. This relatively unknown attraction is a re-created Victorian village on the site of a former glass factory. The 1888 Factory has been restored and gives demonstrations of early glass-blowing techniques daily at 11 A.M., 1:30 P.M., and 3:30 P.M. The crafts arcade demonstrates nineteenth-century arts such as weaving, woodcarving, printing, and pottery making; and an old barn provides an agricultural history of South Jersey, with lots of waterfowl and farm animals to delight the kids. Young visitors also love the ¾-mile train trip around the lake in an old-fashioned train.

But the main attraction here is the Museum of Glass, one of the best collections of its kind anywhere, in an attractive building around a court that makes excellent use of its tall windows to highlight the glass displays. You'll view the first hand-blown bottles, used for drinks, strong and otherwise; goblets, pitchers, ornamental glass, medicine bottles, perfume and ink bottles, early lamps, pressed glass, cut glass lead crystal, works of art by Tiffany, art nouveau glass, art deco glass—just about every kind of glassware ever made by hand or machine. You can buy glassware in the Village store and paperweights in a shop that has a most comprehensive collection of this art ranging in price from $3 to $3,000.

Wheaton Village is a surprise in this quiet, nontouristy farm area, and it is a fascinating look at another kind of 1880s—a perfect counterpoint to a weekend in Victorian Cape May.

Cape May Area Code: 609

DRIVING DIRECTIONS Garden State Parkway south to last exit.
Total distance: 160 miles.

PUBLIC TRANSPORTATION Bus service via NJ Transit from the New York Port Authority; for schedules and rates, phone (201) 762–5100 (in northern NJ, 800–772–2222, in southern NJ, 800–582–5946).

ACCOMMODATIONS *Mainstay Inn,* 635 Columbia Avenue, 884–8690, $$–$$$ CP ● *The Abbey,* Columbia and Gurney streets, 884–4506, $$–$$$ CP ● *The Brass Bed,* 719 Columbia Avenue, 884–8075, $$–$$$ ● *Victorian Rose,* 715 Columbia Avenue, 884–2497, $–$$ ● *Queen Victoria,* 102 Ocean Street, 884–8702, $$–$$$ CP ● *Chalfonte Hotel,* 301 Howard Street, 884–8409, last of the pre-1878 biggies, $$$–$$$$ ● *Captain Mey's Inn,* 202 Ocean Street, 884–7793, $$–$$$ CP. If these are full, there are many more inns, plus motels. Write to the Chamber of Commerce for complete list.

DINING *The Mad Batter,* 19 Jackson Street, 884–5970, nouvelle cuisine in a gingerbread house, $$–$$$; brunch $ ● *Chalfonte Hotel* (see above), southern specialties, complete dinner, $$$ ● *The Lobster House,* Fisherman's Wharf, 884–8296, nautical decor and menu, $$–$$$ ● *Watson's Merion Inn,* 106 Decatur Street, 884–8363, an old standby, $$–$$$ ● 410 Bank Street (at that address), 884–2127, popular, $$$ ● *Washington Inn,* 801 Washington Street, 884–5697, grandiose 1856 home, $$–$$$ ● *Alexander's,* 653 Washington Street, 884–2555, elegant, $$$ ● *Trattoria,* Carpenter's Lane, 884–1144, informal Italian, $$.

SIGHTSEEING For current schedules and rates of walking tours, trolley tours, and house tours, see the free pamphlet "This Week in Cape May," available at all lodgings, or contact Mid-Atlantic Center for the Arts (MAC), 1048 Washington Street, PO Box 164, 884–5404 ● *Physick Estate,* 1048 Washington Street, 884–5404. Tours Tuesday to Sunday in summer season, 11 A.M. to 3:30 P.M. Adults, $4, children, $2 ● *Wheaton Village,* Route 552, Millville (from Cape May take Route 47 north and west and watch for signs), 825–6800. Hours: April to December, daily 10 A.M. to 5 P.M.; January to March, closed Monday and Tuesday, reduced rates. Adults, $4; children 6–17, $2; children under 5 free; family of 2 adults and 2 children, $7.50.

FOR FURTHER INFORMATION Greater Cape May Chamber of Commerce, PO Box 109, Cape May, NJ 08204, 884–5508. Current activity schedule is available from the Mid-Atlantic Center for the Arts, PO Box 164, Cape May, NJ 08204.

The Pick of the Past in Massachusetts

Brimfield. The Founding Fathers must have had a premonition when they named the place, because brim it does—on every field as well as sidewalk and front porch and any other place where there is room to set up a booth.

Brimfield, Massachusetts, a tiny town near the southern border of the state, is the flea-market capital of the world, the place where some 2,000 vendors congregate three times a year for a sale that must be seen to be believed. Trinkets, trunks, beer bottles, brass beds, Victorian sofas, vintage postcards—you'll be hard pressed to name any item that won't be for sale somewhere in Brimfield during these weekend gatherings held in May, July, and September each year.

The early September date usually brings the best weather for browsing and makes for a perfect end-of-summer weekend, for when you've made the rounds and gathered all the tea caddies and copper pots and other treasures that you can afford, you'll find yourself right next door to the sights of Sturbridge and perfectly positioned for a back-roads meander home through some quaint and undiscovered Connecticut towns.

The gathering of the flea market clans began more than 20 years ago, brainchild of an entrepreneurial dealer named Gordon Reid, who hosted the first affairs at his farm, Antique Acres. Reid's daughters, Jill and Judith, run things now on the same spot, with the flair that must be hereditary, since the show seems to grow both in crowd and dealers yearly. Between them, the Reids corner the cream of the dealers who come to town, but they aren't quite the whole show. There is almost no end in sight to the variety of vendors who show up to take advantage of the crowds. Try to come early, when you can pick and choose with the least amount of elbowing. Whole busloads of shoppers tend to show up as the day goes on.

Sturbridge is only a five-minute drive east of Brimfield on Route 20. The best-known attraction here is Old Sturbridge Village, a 200-acre re-creation of a rural New England village of the early nineteenth century, and one of the outstanding developments of its kind. It's a wonderful place no matter what your age, beautifully landscaped and with more than 45 old buildings moved from their original sites to form a realistic town where costumed ''residents'' go about the everyday activities of an earlier time.

You'll see the farmer hoe his crops or plow his fields, watch spinners weave wool carded at the waterpowered carding mill, find the cobbler's daughter sewing shoe uppers at home, or a woman binding books at the printing office. You just might also be on hand when the farmer appears at the blacksmith shop with a broken hoe to be mended, or find a farm wife picking vegetables to cook over an open hearth for the noon meal, or encounter the members of the Ladies' Benevolent Society gathering for their regular meeting.

Every day there are fireplace cooking demonstrations and a dozen different early nineteenth-century crafts in the making. You can hop aboard the horse-drawn wagon or look in on Meetinghouse services, and almost every weekend brings a special event. September weekends in recent years have included an Antiquarian Book Fair, demonstrations of cider making, and a Militia Day when historically dressed militiamen practice gunfiring drills and hold a mock battle.

Sturbridge Village can take an hour or a whole day, depending on how much time you have to give it. Snacks and refreshments and whole meals are available on the premises, and there are picnic tables if you want to bring your own fare.

There's a real village of Sturbridge to be explored as well, an authentic New England town with its original green and many historic buildings intact. If you can handle more shopping, here's a town full of shops. The Shaker Shop has fine reproductions of Shaker furniture designs, there's Basketville and Quilters Quarters on Route 20, antiques stores on the green, and Sturbridge Antiques to the east on Route 20 with 25 dealers under one roof. To the west on Route 20, watch for Route 148 north and signs for Cheney Orchards for sweet cider and the best of the new apple crop.

If you do Brimfield on Saturday morning, the real Sturbridge in the afternoon, and Sturbridge Villiage on Sunday, your visit will be more than complete. But if you can tear yourself away with time left for exploring on the drive home, there are some detours along the Connecticut back roads that are delightful alternatives to turnpike driving. One of these is Woodstock, not the famous one but a country cousin slightly east on Route 169, a little town of stone walls and historic houses that date to 1686.

There is no Main Street as such here, just clusters of homes and occasional shops. About midway through the town on the crest of a long ridge is Woodstock Hill, where huge old trees shade handsome country houses spanning a couple of centuries in architecture. One that stands out is Roseland Cottage, a bright pink Gothic-style house built in 1864 for a wealthy gentleman named Bowen, a New York newspaper publisher, who installed the best of everything, right down to a private bowling alley. The house and gardens and barns are open to visitors, owned and operated by the Society for the Preservation of New England Antiquities. Woodstock Academy is almost directly across the common and about a mile south of 169 in Quasset School, a little red-brick schoolhouse (open to the public in the summer months only). The Woodstock Fair each Labor Day weekend is a real old-fashioned country fair, worth keeping in mind for another time.

Woodstock offers its own small group of shops. In addition to a sampling of local crafts and antiques, there is the Irish Crystal Company with beautiful imported lead crystal. Windy Acres has dried and silk flowers as well as fresh blooms, and the Christmas Barn and Shop has 12 rooms of gifts, candles, tree decorations, and fabric. A mile off 169 on Woodstock Road in East Woodstock there's another furniture showroom where handcrafted pieces in pine and oak are available.

Keep heading south on 169 for Brooklyn, another of those out-of-the-way discoveries off the tourist paths. Brooklyn's New England Center of Contemporary Arts is a charming rustic gallery with monthly new exhibits of work by recognized living artists. There is usually an artist in residence to talk about his or her work. The Golden Lamb Buttery is a delightful dinner stop.

It's a gentle way back to reality and if you connect with Route 205 below Brooklyn and then Route 14, you'll soon be back on I-395, the Connecticut Turnpike, and speeding back to the present with all your newfound treasures from the past.

Brimfield Area Code: 413
Sturbridge Area Code: 617 (508 after July 16, 1988)

DRIVING DIRECTIONS   New England Thruway or Hutchinson River Parkway and Merritt Parkway to I-91 north; at Hartford cut off to I-86 and continue to Sturbridge, exit 3. Brimfield is about 7 miles west of Sturbridge on Route 20.
Total distance: about 160 miles.

PUBLIC TRANSPORTATION   Amtrak train service to Worcester, half an hour's drive.

ACCOMMODATIONS   *The Publick House,* Main Street (Route 131), 347–3313, a charming 1771 inn, $$$. If you like smaller inns, ask for the *Colonel Ebenezer Crafts Inn,* a restored 1786 home under Publick House management, $$$ ● *Country Motor Lodge,* also run by Publick House, $$ ● *Old Sturbridge Village Motor Lodge,* Route 20 west, Sturbridge, 346–3327 (adjacent to the Village itself), $$ ●

Oliver Wight House, 1789 home turned inn, part of Lodge complex, $$–$$$ ● *Sheraton Sturbridge Resort,* Route 20, 347–7393, indoor pool, tennis, $$$–$$$$ ● *Wildwood Inn,* 121 Church Street, Ware, (413) 967–7798, antiques-filled Victorian home, five rooms, serving homemade breads and muffins for breakfast—20 minutes from Sturbridge and a bargain, $–$$ with continental breakfast ● *General Samuel McClellan House,* Routes 169 and 171, South Woodstock, CT (203) 928–5360, another pleasant country inn, $–$$.

DINING *The Publick House* (see above), $$ ● *Salem Cross Inn,* West Brookfield (north of Sturbridge), 867–2345, restored 1705 inn, Yankee fare, $–$$ ● *Bald Hill,* Route 169, South Woodstock, 974–2240, setting of plants and flowers, $–$$; Sunday brunch, $ ● *Golden Lamb Buttery,* Hillandale Farm, Route 169, Brooklyn, (203) 774–4423, exceptional, $$$$ ● *Samuel McClellan House* (see above), is a good stop for lunch, $.

SIGHTSEEING *Brimfield Flea Market,* Route 20, Brimfield. Outdoor fair dates: early May, mid-July, and mid-September. For current season dates, phone J&J Promotions, 245–3436 ● *Old Sturbridge Village,* Route 20, 347–3362. Hours: daily April to October 9 A.M. to 5 P.M.; shorter hours off season. Adults, $9.50; children 6–15, $4; children under 6 free ● *Roseland Cottage,* Route 169, Woodstock, CT, (203) 928–4074. Hours: Memorial Day to mid-September, Wednesday to Sunday noon to 5 P.M.; to mid-October, weekends only. Adults, $2.50; children under 12, $1.25.

FOR FURTHER INFORMATION Contact Sturbridge Information Center, Route 20, Sturbridge, MA 01566, 347–7594.

Fall

Antiquing in Old Connecticut

Any experienced actress knows that a well-staged revival can be big box office. So June Havoc says that although they called her the "Madwoman of the Crossing" when she began in 1978, she had high hopes when she set about to bring Cannon Crossing back to life.

This tiny crossroads village, bounded by the red and white Cannondale railroad station on one side and the Norwalk River on the other, was a serious victim of neglect at the time—paint peeling, roofs sagging, walls on the verge of tumbling down. Today it is as spiffy as a stage set and sometimes close to SRO on a busy weekends, when visitors come to browse for antiques, watercolors, candles, fabrics, and other finds housed in the nostalgic nineteenth-century buildings.

A shopping expedition alone doesn't quite justify a whole weekend, of course, not even in such an unusual setting. But by good luck Cannon Crossing is within easy reach of Ridgefield, a beautiful Connecticut town with a long history, a wide Main Street canopied by stately elms, four highly regarded restaurants, and some fine country inns. And to cap things on Sunday, you can journey farther up Route 7 to Kent, another country charmer with a tiny jewel of a museum where tools become works of art.

Route 7, the road north of Norwalk that leads to the Crossing, used to be known as Antiques Row for its abundance of shops. Shopping centers have taken their toll on the small dealers, but if you drive past some of the more mundane establishments, you'll still find a few choice stores in the Wilton area. Watch for names like Den of Antiquity and Attic Treasures and you'll know you're on the right track.

Just about everything is for sale at the Wayside Exchange, a high-quality consignment shop packed full of wooden and upholstered furniture, stacks of dishes and silver, trunks, books, copper pots, and endless miscellany. A stop here might net you a hand-painted child's chest and matching mirror, a tall grandfather's clock, or a silvery dinner bell.

Vallin Gallery is well known for its exquisite Oriental antiques. Chests, tables, lamps, vases, porcelains, and scrolls may be found, all of high quality and priced accordingly. Neighboring Toby House specializes in early porcelains, particularly English Wedgwood and lusterware. Figurines and paintings of dogs are another specialty.

The Dovetail, featuring handmade reproductions of eighteenth-century furniture, is on Route 7 at the turnoff to Cannon Crossing.

When you spot the sign for the Crossing, turn east and you'll soon have a whole cache of shops to explore, a mix of antiques and crafts. The formerly run-down general store is now called the Mercantile and has a variety of country pine furniture and other finds beyond the wide front porch. Some other high spots are Penny Ha' Penny, with fine imported foods as well as crafts, and The Enchanted Cottage with a potpourri of wares. Behind all this is a barnlike structure with outbuildings containing a fireplace shop, a tinsmith, more antiques, and who knows what else—anything from unusual foods to crafts in shops that are delightfully unpredictable.

Miss Havoc, incidentally, lives in the restored mill house at the river's edge.

Take a break at the Old Schoolhouse Café and Riverside Garden, where the blackboards now bear menus instead of multiplication problems, and then it's on to Ridgefield.

There are more shops to explore on the way to the turnoff on Route 35, as well as on Route 33, an alternative country road connection to Ridgefield that takes you past many lovely Colonial homes. Ask for a complete listing of area antiques shops if you want to do further shopping; it is available in most of the stores. You might take scenic Route 33 anyway, just to see the sights the next time you return to Route 7.

Either way will bring you onto Ridgefield's broad Main Street, lined with mansions that were once the summer retreats of wealthy residents of New York. The principal bit of history on the street is Keeler Tavern, which was in operation from 1772 to 1907 and has been meticulously restored with authentic furnishings and accessories. Costumed hostesses will show you the sights, including the cannonball that remains embedded in the shingles outside as a memento of a British attack during the Revolutionary War.

Down the street in a 1783 white house, the Aldrich Museum is a surprise in this tradition-oriented town. Its three floors are filled with the latest in modern art, and there is an abstract sculpture garden in back.

Ridgefield's highly regarded eating places, all favoring continental fare, are The Inn, The Elms, and Le Coq Hardi in town, and Stonehenge, a 1799 house off Route 7, where fresh trout from the collecting pool behind the waterfall is a house specialty.

The Inn and The Elms offer lodging, as does the West Lane, an elegant Victorian beauty, with mahogany paneling, designer fabrics, and working fireplaces in four of the fourteen rooms. There are also half a dozen simple rooms in a separate building at Stonehenge.

If you are at West Lane, they'll let you sleep late and serve you breakfast until 11. Then it's Route 7 time again and the drive north to Kent, another pretty Colonial town loaded with shops, plus a special treasure, the Sloane-Stanley Museum. The late artist Eric Sloane's outstanding collection of early American tools is housed here in a rustic barnlike building donated to the state by the Stanley Tool Works as a gift marking that company's 125th anniversary.

Sloane saw handcrafted tools as the nation's first works of art, and you'll likely agree when you see his artistic displays of wooden bowls, buckets, and barrels; tiny hinges and huge plows; tools carefully crafted to follow the shape of the grain of the wood they are made from; and others, such as hoes, rakes, and handles, with shapes by nature that could not be improved upon. Some of the most interesting displays show how the tools were used. Many of the wooden pieces, elegantly carved and highly polished, are unmistakably pieces of art.

Outside there is a small cabin reflecting the austere conditions of frontier life, and just below the museum are the ruins of an iron furnace. Partial restoration of the Kent Furnace is planned for the future.

You can see a totally different kind of craftsman at work, giving new twists to an old art, at Bull's Bridge Glass Works. Stephen Fellerman is usually present to demonstrate his award-winning glassblowing techniques, creating art glass in flowing shapes and glowing colors. Iridescent lusterware is one of his specialties. Bull's Bridge, incidentally, is the name of the covered bridge just west of Route 7 across the Housatonic River.

Another pleasant distraction is a visit to Kent Falls State Park, also right on Route 7. An easy footpath leads to the top of the 200-foot falls, with the sight and sounds of the cascading water beside you all the way.

Should you like Kent so much you want to make a return trip, there are some lovely bed-and-breakfast lodgings in town, as well.

For Sunday dinner, Kent's best offering is the Fife and Drum, where you'll enjoy not only excellent food but also entertainment by owner-pianist Dolph Trayman, a top musician. Then it's back home to find the right places for all your newly acquired treasures, permanent souvenirs of the weekend.

Connecticut Area Code: 203

DRIVING DIRECTIONS Hutchinson River Parkway to the Merritt Parkway, exit 40, Route 7 north. Cannondale and Cannon Crossing are a right turn clearly marked; Routes 33 or 35 lead to Ridgefield.

Total distance: 60 miles.

ACCOMMODATIONS *West Lane Inn,* 22 West Lane, Ridgefield, 438–7323, $$$$ CP ● *Stonehenge,* Route 7, Ridgefield, 438–6511, $$$ CP ● *The Elms,* 500 Main Street, Ridgefield, 438–2541, $$$ CP. ● Kent lodgings are in prize small Colonial homes, but note that few rooms have private baths: *The Saltbox Inn,* Route 7, Kent, wonderfully restored and authentically furnished Colonial saltbox, 927–4376, $$$$ CP; *Flanders Arms,* Route 7, Kent, 927–3040, eighteenth-century Colonial, Laura Ashley decor, $$–$$$ CP; *The Country Goose,* Route 1, Kent, 927–4746, another eighteenth-century Colonial, $$ CP; *Constitution Oak Farm,* Beardsley Road, Kent, 354–6495, a working farm in the country, like a visit to Grandma's house, $$ CP; *Fife and Drum,* Route 7, Kent, 927–3509, rooms in a modern lodge are spacious and well decorated, $$$.

DINING *Stonehenge* (see above), $$$, prix-fixe dinner, $$$$$ ● *Inn at Ridgefield,* 20 West Lane, Ridgefield, 438–8282, $$$, prix-fixe dinner, $$$$$ ● *The Elms* (see above), $$$ ● *Le Coq Hardi,* Big Shop Lane, Ridgefield, 431–3060, $$$ ● *Fife and Drum* (see above), $$–$$$. (Note: All Ridgefield inns require jackets for dinner.)

SIGHTSEEING *Cannon Crossing,* Cannondale, off Route 7 north of Norwalk. Hours: shops open Tuesday through Sunday 11 A.M. to 5 P.M. ● *Keeler Tavern,* 132 Main Street, Ridgefield, 438–5485. Hours: Wednesday, Saturday, and Sunday 1 P.M. to 4 P.M. Adults, $1.50; children, $.50 ● *Aldrich Museum of Contemporary Art,* 258 Main Street, Ridgefield, 438–4519. Hours: Saturday and Sunday 1 P.M. to 5 P.M., Tuesday to Friday 2:30 P.M. to 4:30 P.M. Adults, $1; children, $.50 ● *Sloane-Stanley Museum,* Route 7, Kent, 566–3005, May through October, Wednesday to Sunday 10 A.M. to 4:30 P.M. Adults, $1.25; children 6 –17, $.50.

Shakers and Scenery in the Berkshires

The tri-level round stone dairy barn is not only the most striking building at Hancock Shaker Village, but also an apt symbol for the extraordinary people who once lived on this site.

The barn's shape is as ingenious as it is beautiful. Hay wagons could enter at the top, traverse the interior on a sturdy balcony, and dump the hay into the center to a middle level where as many as 54 head of cattle, radiating around the central manger stanchions, could easily be fed by a single farmhand.

The Shakers had a way of finding the most functional way of doing things. The simple classic lines of their chairs and chests made more than a century ago were a precursor of modern design. They were the first to think of packaging garden seeds and herbal remedies, and such handy devices as the circular saw, the flat broom, and the common clothespin were their inventions. They made work easier for themselves as well as for an eager public who bought these products, and thus helped support the community that thrived here for more than 100 years.

The order had all but vanished, done in perhaps by its own rule of celibacy, when the last surviving buildings were acquired in 1960 by a group resolved to create a memorial to the sect by restoring its unique village. It is a fascinating place to visit, conjuring a vivid picture of the life-style of a unique people.

Since the village is also near the heart of the Massachusetts Berkshires, it is an ideal autumn destination, allowing you to enjoy the year-round attractions of the area while the mountains are aflame with autumn color.

Of the original 100 structures on 1,250 acres, 20 have been restored. The visitors' center outside the historical village sells tickets and will provide you with a pamphlet to lead you through the various buildings, where guides are posted to answer questions. Exhibits at the center and through the buildings will tell you about the community from its founding in 1790 to the opening of the restoration in 1960. You'll learn that the Shakers were actually an outgrowth of the Quakers, but took a different path, believing that Christ had already returned in the person of their founder, Mother Ann Lee. Mother Ann decreed that religion was to be the dominant force in every area of their lives, requiring separation from the world, communal property, regular confession of sin, and celibacy. Though the sexes were separated, they were considered equal, a very advanced notion in the 1700s. In England they acquired the name Shaking Quakers for the ritual dances that were part of their worship, literally shaking off sin, and were eventually simply dubbed Shakers.

Mother Ann fled from England, where her ways were frowned upon, and came to America to preach her special gospel. Hancock was the third of the 18 communities the sect eventually established throughout the Northeast and Midwest. At the town's height in the

1830s there were six "families" in residence with a total membership of about 300.

At the restoration you'll visit the Garden House and Herb Garden, which is planted with materials that constituted some of the major crops of the Hancock herb and extract industry. One of the most important buildings is the Brick Dwelling, which housed 100 and contained the communal dining room and meeting room used for weekday worship. The basement level contains the Great Cook Room and the appropriately named Good Room, where homemade baked goodies are still made and sold to visitors. Also in the building are typical sleeping quarters, a pharmacy, a nurse shop, the children's room, and the schoolroom.

In the Brethren's and Sister's shops you'll see the chair, broom carpentry, cobbling, and clockmaking industries run by the men; and the dairy, medical department, and weaving rooms that were the women's province. The famous Shaker chairs are displayed in the Brethren's Shop, and reproductions are sold in the Ministry Shop.

A few other sights are the most recently completed structures, the Hired Men's Shop and the Printing Office plus the Wash House, Tan House, Laundry, Machine Shop, and Meeting House, all contributing to a realistic picture of what life was like for this devout band who left the world to build a successful self-sufficient community for themselves.

It takes at least half a day to really appreciate Hancock Shaker Village, and with lunch you'll have just a couple of daylight hours left. Considering the season, you might choose to spend them enjoying the scenery from one of the two prime viewing points, Mount Greylock, the area's highest peak, to the northeast in North Adams, or the next highest point, Mount Everett, to the south in Mount Washington. Mount Washington, a sky-high village with just 100 residents, also gives you a view of Bash Bish Falls, which makes a spectacular 50-foot plunge.

All the inns and restaurants that serve music lovers in the summer are available in fall as well, so you'll have many pleasant choices for dinner and lodgings.

On Sunday you can see some of the sights that are often missed in the busy summer season in Lenox and Stockbridge, which were magnets for both the wealthy and the literary greats of the mid-1800s. Drive around Lenox to see the fine homes in the town that was referred to as the "inland Newport." Longfellow, Melville, Hawthorne, Henry Adams, and Edith Wharton were among the literati who were attracted by the area's beauty, along with several prominent artists.

Tanglewood's grounds with their magnificent gardens are open for strolling year-round, and here you'll see a re-creation of the little house where Hawthorne wrote many of his novels.

A fine way to see the best of Lenox is by bicycle. You can rent a bike at Continuous Cycle or join one of its one- and two-hour tours.

The traditional New England main street of Stockbridge was immortalized by one of the area artists, Norman Rockwell, whose paintings can be seen in the Old Corner House on Main Street, a restored eighteenth-century home that is now a museum dedicated to Rockwell.

There are other interesting sights on the historic street.The oldest house, the 1739 Mission House, was the home of John Sergeant, who was a missionary sent to convert the Indians. It is filled with fine Early American furnishings and has an authentic Colonial herb garden out back. The Merwin House, also known as Tranquility, was built around 1825 and is Victorian in its decor. There are two old churches on the street and the Village Cemetery is the resting place of Indian chiefs as well as early Colonial settlers.

The Children's Chimes, erected in 1878 on the site of the original Mission Church, were built by David Dudley Field as a memorial to his grandchildren; they serenade the town every evening at sunset from apple-blossom time until frost.

If you aren't staying there, do stop for a drink or a meal at the Red Lion. It's the most delightful Colonial inn, full of eighteenth-century furniture and Colonial pewter, with charm in every corner. If it is still warm enough, the courtyard is a particularly nice place for refreshments. On Main Street and in other courtyards just off it, you'll also find a few interesting shops and galleries for exploring.

Another spectacular home just west of Stockbridge is Chesterwood, where sculptor Daniel Chester French created the casts for his famous "Seated Lincoln" for the Lincoln Memorial in Washington. You can still see the casts in the studio along with other bronzes and working models. The home itself, set beside the Housatonic River overlooking Monument Mountain, is certainly a setting that might lead to inspiration. French referred to his home simply as "heaven." Chesterwood has been beautifully maintained by the National Trust for Historic Preservation.

If you still have time to spare, West Stockbridge will hope to provide another kind of inspiration—the spending of cash for the jewelry, folk art, pottery, health foods, dried herbs, and what have you in the shops comprising a town that calls itself "New England's Yankee Market."

If you prefer to concentrate on antiques, drive south on Route 7 to Sheffield, a gracious town with a covered bridge and a main street lined with stately homes—at least a dozen of them transformed into antiques shops. There's no problem finding most of the stores, since they are right on Main Street, but one complex worth seeking out is Twin Fires Antiques on Route 41—12 shops in 2 large barns with lots of special pieces of antique English stripped pine furniture.

By the time you've done the shops, the autumn color should be fading into the twilight, telling you it's time to get back on the highway and home.

Berkshires Area Code: 413

DRIVING DIRECTIONS Saw Mill River Parkway north to the Taconic State Parkway to the New York Thruway (Berkshire Spur, Route 90), then east to Route 22; north on 22 to Route 295, east on 295 to Route 41, and north on 41. Hancock Shaker Village is at the junction of Routes 20 and 41, five miles west of downtown Pittsfield. To get to Lee and Lenox, take exit 2 off Route 90 and proceed north on Route 7. To Pittsfield from Lee or Lenox, continue north on 7, turn west at Route 20.

Total distance: about 163 miles.

ACCOMMODATIONS AND DINING See "Weekending with the Boston Symphony," page 91.

SIGHTSEEING *Hancock Shaker Village,* Route 20 at 41, Pittsfield, 443-0188. Hours: Memorial Day to October, daily 9:30 A.M. to 5 P.M. Adults, $6.50; children 6–12, $2.50 ● *Mission House,* Main and Sergeant streets, Stockbridge, 298-3239. Hours: May to mid-October, Tuesday to Saturday 10 A.M. to 4:30 P.M.; Sunday 11 A.M. to 3:30 P.M. Adults, $3; children 6–16, $1 ● *Merwin House,* 39 Main Street, Stockbridge, 227-3956. Hours: June to mid-October, Tuesday, Thursday, Saturday, and Sunday, noon to 5 P.M. Admission, $1.50 ● *The Norman Rockwell Museum,* Main Street, Stockbridge, 298-3822. Hours: daily except Tuesday 10 A.M. to 5 P.M. Adults, $3; children 5–12, $1 ● *Chesterwood,* Route 183, two miles west of Stockbridge, 298-3579. Hours: May to October, daily 10 A.M. to 5 P.M. Adults, $4; senior citizens and children 6–18, $1 ● Bicycle rentals and tours: *Continuous Cycle,* Walker House, 74 Walker Street, Lenox, 637-0904.

FOR FURTHER INFORMATION Contact Berkshires Visitors Bureau, The Common, Pittsfield, MA 01201, 443-9186.

An Autumn Palette in Woodstock

Take one of America's most famous art colonies, put it in a mountain setting with foliage-lit back roads just waiting to be explored, add a bevy of shops and galleries filld with fine art, crafts, and wares of every kind, and you have an autumn weekend, Woodstock style.

Artists discovered Woodstock, New York, a long time ago. The famed Byrdcliffe Crafts Colony was founded here way back in 1902, and the Art Students League summer school followed just a few years after. In 1910 the Woodstock Artists Association and its gallery came into being, and in 1916 the town hosted the nation's first summer chamber music series, the Maverick Concerts. The scenery attracted serious artists, some of whom began to give Woodstock a colorful reputation for their bohemian life-style. Then along came rock, the 1969 Woodstock Music Festival, and it seemed that things would never be the same.

Happily, Woodstock recovered. The artists remain, and the notoriety that brought new tourists spawned even more galleries and boutiques, making the town a delight for browsers.

Woodstock is deservedly popular and parking on the street is a problem, so when you arrive it's best to make use of the parking lots thoughtfully provided. One is to the right off Mill Hill Road as you approach the village green, another is past the green, a left turn from Tinker Street onto Tannery Brook Road. A third lot can be found on Mountain View Avenue off Rock City Road, a right turn from the circle at the green, and if all else fails, there is additional parking behind the First Church of Christ on Tinker Street.

In season, Woodstock hums with activity—theater at the Woodstock Playhouse and Byrdcliffe, music at the Maverick Chamber Concerts, Opus 40, and with any number of smaller groups that keep cropping up each year.

A few events carry over into the fall, and art and photo exhibits continue in full swing. Two main centers in town are the Woodstock Guild's Kleinert Arts Center gallery and the Crafts Shop next door. Either spot is a good place to ask about special events that may be going on, since the town information booth has uncertain hours after Labor Day.

You'll have little trouble finding the shops, since they are clustered on Mill Hill Road, which leads into town, and on Tinker, a continuation of Mill Hill beyond the green. Woodstock shopping is fun because the offerings are as diverse as the crowds that come to browse. There are artsy boutiques and high-quality galleries, along with stores stuffed with touristy gifts and gewgaws. Expect to find stained glass and coffee mugs, handmade teddy bears, handcrafted jewelry, and hand-dyed batiks. The Catskill House specializes in kaleidoscopes—and dragons! Collectors can have a field day picking up antique books at the Readers' Quarry, Scottish or Welsh records and books on Celtic mythology at Three Geese in Flight, and rare records at The Collector.

When you need to replenish your energy, there are plenty of restaurants on Tinker as well, housed in the same kind of picturesque old buildings as the shops.

After you've had your fill of shops and filled up at the cafés, take a scenic drive north from the green on Rock City Road up to Mead's Mountain for a fantastic view from the fire tower's Overlook Trail. There are more galleries on the way up, if you haven't already overdosed on art.

Woodstock lodgings are surprisingly modest for such a special town. The most convenient are Twin Gables, an old-fashioned guest house, and the no-frills Millstream Motel. Pinecrest Lodge, on the edge of town, is a rustic complex with rooms in cottages in the woods, and a swimming pool. The nicest inn of all, the Victorian Mt. Tremper Inn, is eight miles to the west. Even farther west in Shandaken is another good bet, Auberge des Quatre Saisons, modest motel accommodations once again, but with a great view and superb French food.

Woodstock and its environs can while away a pleasant Saturday, leaving you plenty of time for leaf watching and sightseeing on Sunday. There are many picturesque routes to choose from. Go west on Route 28 to 28A to make the circle around Ashokan Reservoir, where the foliage is twice as colorful reflected back in the blue water. The reservoir, set like a jewel in a crown of mountains, is a prize drive.

A worthwhile detour on the way occurs about three miles into Route 28A, where a left turn to Spillway Road brings you to Crafts People, a charming home displaying the work of 150 artisans, many of them local residents. The shaded lawns and gardens around the house make a great picnic spot, and you're welcome to linger for a while.

Keep going west on Route 28 to Arkville for another perspective on the scenery aboard the Delaware & Ulster Rail Ride. You'll be following the same wooded route that tourists used on steam trains to the mountains early in this century.

A special lure on another foliage loop, north on Route 212 to Saugerties, is the annual Chrysanthemum Festival, which takes place each year at Seamon Park the first three weeks of October. Arts and crafts exhibits and concerts are part of the festivities, as well as fine floral displays.

There's another good reason to head for Saugerties, if you can time your visit to coincide with the public viewing days at Opus 40, one of the most unusual outdoor sculpture displays to be found. It took the late Harvey Fite 37 years to create this monumental environmental display rising out of an abandoned quarry. The sculpture covers more than six acres and is made of hundreds of thousands of tons of fine bluestone, carefully fitted stone by stone into shapes. Fite also created the Quarryman's Museum on the grounds. Viewing dates seem to change from year to year, so it's best to phone for the current schedule.

If you'd like fresh-picked and edible souvenirs of your trip, stop at Sunfrost Farms, 217 Tinker Street, Woodstock, or outside Saugerties at Bill Boice, 5187 Old Kings Highway, Mount Marion, for home-grown fruit and vegetables and organic eggs. Westwood Farmers' Market on Route 28 in West Hurley is another spot to pick up the bounty of the harvest, including fresh-from-the-farm apples. Or, if you go home via Route 213, you can stop at either Stone Ridge Orchards or Mr. Apples in High Falls and pick your own.

Another very rewarding stop is Kingston, New York's first capital, where you can tour the 1676 Senate House, the old Dutch church, and the many fine stone houses. The Rondout section of Kingston on the riverfront is rapidly being developed into a maritime center. At the Hudson River Maritime Museum, you can see exhibits of the many kinds of ships that have plied the Hudson over the years and board the 65-foot Rondout Belle for a river cruise highlighted by a tour of the Rondout II Lighthouse, as well as by the humor in the captain's narration. The Kingston Urban Cultural Park next door to the museum has a boat shop where you can see boats under construction. There are increasing numbers of other river cruises available from this area as well, including some by sailboat, all wonderful ways to see the Hudson Valley at its autumn best. On land, you can indulge yourself at the Rondout Ice Cream & Cookie Company or try a taco at Rosita's, both on West Strand, or have a drink on the open deck of Mary P's on Broadway and watch the boats go by. You'll find tempting shops in the restored Rondout neighborhood as well, including Skillypot Antique Company, an association of 25 dealers.

Finally, driving back down the Hudson, you can wind up your weekend with another kind of harvest if you visit one of the many wineries of the Hudson Valley on your way home. Hudson Valley Wine Village in Highland welcomes visitors with a riverview and wine-making tours and samples, a perfect final toast to a fine autumn weekend.

Woodstock Area Code: 914

DRIVING DIRECTIONS New York State Thruway to exit 19 at Kingston, west on Route 28, right on Route 375 north, then left off Route 375 onto Route 212 for Woodstock.
Total distance: 108 miles.

ACCOMMODATIONS *Millstream Motel,* 38 Tannery Brook Road, Woodstock, 679–8211, $$ CP ● *Pinecrest Lodge,* 77 Country Club Road, Woodstock, 679–2814, $$ CP ● *Twin Gables Guest Home,* 73 Tinker Street, Woodstock, 679–9479, $ ● *Mt. Tremper Inn,* Route 212 and Wittenberg Road, Mt. Tremper, 688–9938, $$–$$$ CP ● *Auberge des Quatre Saisons,* Route 42, Shandaken, 688–2223, doubles in chalet-type motel with private bath, shared bath in lodge, $$– $$$ MAP ● Two other bed-and-breakfast possibilities in the vicinity: *Buena Vista Manor,* Route 9W, West Camp (north of Saugerties), 246–6462, special view, $$ CP; *Rondout Bed & Breakfast,* 88 W. Chester Street, Kingston, 331–2369, 1905 mansion on two acres, $– $$ CP.

DINING *Deming Street,* 4 Deming Street (off Mill Hill Road east of town), Woodstock, 679–7858, serves all three meals, both light and full dinners, $–$$ ● *Whistlers,* Route 212 west, Woodstock, 679– 9522, trendy menu, blackened fish, etc., $$ ● *Joshua's Café,* 51 Tinker Street, Woodstock, 679–9575, excellent Middle Eastern fare, $– $$ ● *The Little Bear,* Route 212, Bearsville, gourmet Chinese food beside a rippling brook, $ ● *La Duchese Anne,* Wittenberg Road, Mt. Tremper, 688–5260, country French in a rustic setting, $$ ● *Auberge des Quatre Saisons* (see above), worth a drive, $$ ● *Schneller's Restaurant,* 61–63 John Street, Kingston, 331–9800, good for lunch, entrées, and sandwich board, $ ● Don't overlook the pizza parlor in Woodstock—it makes a great whole-wheat crust.

SIGHTSEEING *Opus 40 and Quarryman's Museum,* High Woods, Saugerties, 246–3400, call for dates ● *Delaware and Ulster Rail Ride,* Route 28, Arkville, 586-DURR, phone for this year's schedules and rates ● *Chrysanthemum Festival,* Seamon Park, Malden Avenue, Saugerties, 9 A.M. to dusk, usually first three weeks in October. Free ● *Senate House Museum,* 312 Fair Street, Kingston, 338–2786. Hours:

Wednesday to Saturday 10 A.M. to 5 P.M.; Sunday 1 P.M. to 5 P.M. Free ● *Hudson River Maritime Museum,* 1 Rondout Landing, Kingston, 338–0071. Hours: Tuesday to Sunday noon to 5 P.M. Adults, $1; children, $.50. Rondout Belle hour-and-a-half boat ride and lighthouse tour, twice daily, $8 and $6 ● Best to phone for schedules and rates for other Hudson River cruises from Kingston, including, *Hudson Rondout Cruises,* 338–6280 (Rondout Belle lunch and dinner cruises in addition to museum tours); *Myles Gordon's Great Hudson Sailing Center,* 338–7313, two-hour sailboat cruises on weekends; *Rip Van Winkle Hudson River Cruises,* 255–6515, excursion boat from Kingston to West Point daily. Most cruises run through October ● *Hudson Valley Wine Village,* Blue Point Road off 9W, Highland, 691–7296. Weekend tours, March to December, 11 A.M. to 5 P.M. Check for current fees. (The Ulster County Public Information Office free brochure gives a complete list of local wineries.)

FOR FURTHER INFORMATION Woodstock Chamber of Commerce, PO Box 36, Woodstock, NY 12498, 679–6234. Ulster County Public Information Office, PO Box 1800, Kingston, NY 12401, 338–5100.

Foliage Watch on the Connecticut River

A cloud of smoke, a cheerful toot of the whistle, and we were off— chugging our way to a rendezvous with the Connecticut River. Outside the windows of the old steam train, the countryside passed in review, dressed in its best fall colors. Marshes and meadows rolled by, an old freight station here, a tiny lace factory there, until at last we spied the sparkling water and two festive riverboats waiting at the dock to provide the second half of one of the region's most unusual foliage tours.

The Valley Railroad has been operating in Essex, Connecticut, since 1970, offering ten-mile excursions into the past aboard the same kind of steam train that Grandpa might have ridden when he was a boy. More than 140,000 people took the ride last year—a nostalgia trip for some, a new adventure for others.

The century-old railroad, abandoned in 1968, is one of more than 90 steam trains flourishing again across the country by giving samples of what travel was like in the not-too-distant past. But this line is unique for its connection with the Connecticut River.

The river completes its 110-mile journey to the sea just a few miles downstream from Essex. Seven nearby towns that call themselves the Gateway Group have taken pains to see that the pristine beauty of the steep riverbanks remains unspoiled. For train passengers who board the double decker riverboats, the stately river still offers only vistas of untouched woodland, with an occasional diversion—a hilltop mansion, the stone turrets of Gillette Castle, or the gingerbread facade of the Goodspeed Opera House—to whip photographers into action. With the coming of autumn foliage, it is a spectacular scene.

After the hour-long cruise, the train returns passengers to the depot, where they can have photos taken in costumes that match the train's vintage, dine in a 1915 grill car, or browse through a shop of memorabilia to warm the hearts of railroad buffs. There are many, according to Valley Railroad officials. Some phone ahead to check whether Engine No. 40 or No. 97 is on duty that day. No. 40, it seems, has a particularly mellow whistle.

On board, conductors oblige railroads fans with a history of the cars in service that day, which may include an open gondola and plush-seated Pullman cars, as well as the standard wicker-seated coaches. In the trainyard there are cabooses, work cars, locomotive cranes, and a unique double-ended snowplow.

When you've had your fill of railroad lore, head for Essex and a second look at the river from one of its most charming landings. The history of Essex, a picture-book town of picket fences and white clapboard Colonial and Federal homes, is inextricably tied to its river. The first wharf at the site of the present Steamboat Dock was in existence in 1656. Essex also thrived as an early shipbuilding center.

The 1878 three-story clapboard Dockhouse with its graceful cupola became a landmark on the river. The Connecticut River Foundation has restored the exterior and a portion of the interior to its warehouse days. It also houses a small but interesting River Museum that tells the story of the waterway with tools, models, and a fascinating model of *The Turtle,* the first submarine, designed in 1776.

There are several river excursion trips offered from the dock; ask about them at the museum.

Pick up a walking tour of Essex at the museum, and you can while away a delightful hour seeing the fine houses lining the winding lanes in town. Watch for the Pratt House on West Avenue above the Congregational Church. It was recently restored by the New England Society for Antiquities, and the Essex Garden Club has planted a lovely Colonial herb garden around the home.

There's also shopping galore on Main Street for antiques, nautical and otherwise, and all the handcrafts, gifts, and gewgaws you'd expect in a town full of strollers. In keeping with the town, however, everything is tasteful.

By car, River Road offers a scenic drive with glimpses of the water and many fine homes.

There is just one inn in Essex, the famous Griswold, which has been open for business on Main Street since 1776. Spring is not too early to reserve a room for fall foliage season, but it's always worth a call in case of last-minute cancellations. The "Gris" is a must, at least for a meal and a visit. The Tap Room, with its busy antique popcorn machine, was once an early Essex schoolhouse; the Steamboat Room simulates the dining salon of an old riverboat, complete with motion from a gently rocking mural at the end of the room; and the Covered Bridge Dining Room, constructed from an abandoned New Hampshire bridge, contains an important collection of Currier & Ives steamboat prints.

No room at the inn? There are plenty of pleasant alternatives nearby. The Copper Beech in Ivoryton has a restaurant that gets raves, the Bishopsgate in East Haddam comes well recommended, and the Inn at Chester is a sophisticated charmer, to name just a few.

Another local attraction requiring reservations many weeks in advance is the Goodspeed Opera House. Musicals of the 1920s and 1930s and new shows aiming for Broadway are served up here in a restored Victorian theater that has been aptly described as a "jewel box." *Annie* and *Man of La Mancha* both debuted at the Goodspeed. The theater is right on the banks of the river, and the Gelston House next door is a scenic spot for before- or after-theater dining and drinks.

A branch of the Goodspeed opened recently in Chester as a showcase for new musicals. The National Theater for the Deaf also performs here. Check at your inn for schedules.

Come Sunday one of the most pleasant afternoon diversions along the river is a picnic at Gillette Castle State Park, where you'll munch your sandwiches with a spectacular cliff-top view. A tour of the castle is a unique experience. It was built by actor William Gillette, a somewhat eccentric gentleman who gained fame and fortune for his portrayal of Sherlock Holmes on stage. The structure cost over a million dollars, quite a pretty penny when it was built in the early 1900s, and was meant to emulate the Rhine Valley castles Gillette had admired in Europe—with turrets, balconies, and the rest.

The interior of the castle is a curiosity. Each of the 24 rooms bears witness to Gillette's eccentricity. No 2 of the 47 doors are alike, and all are fitted with wooden locks operated by hidden springs. A system of mirrors enabled Gillette to observe visitors without being seen, and a secret panel in the study permitted him to escape if he didn't like what he saw.

Gillette also apparently had an aversion to metal. He insisted that no nails or other metal objects be exposed, and even his light switches are made of wood. The interior walls are also made of hand-hewn and carved oak. There is so much wood that Gillette had fire hoses and a sprinkler system installed, safety features that were many years ahead of their time.

After the castle, there are plenty of sights in either direction. A short drive northwest on Route 9 is Middletown, with the art gallery and pleasant campus of Wesleyan College and dining at Town Farms Inn on the river's edge. To the east are Old Saybrook, where you can sample fresh seafood at little outdoor cafés on the harbor, and Old Lyme, a gracious Colonial town with two fine inns and some worthwhile sightseeing. The Florence Griswold House here is a late Georgian mansion that housed one of America's first art colonies; the Lyme Art Association galleries next door show contemporary artists' works.

Or you can end you weekend with a visit to Old Lyme's one-of-a-kind attraction, the Nut Museum, with exhibits that include the world's tallest nutcracker plus nut art, music, and lore, all housed in a Victorian mansion.

Essex Area Code: 203

DRIVING DIRECTIONS New England Thruway (I-95) to exit 69; Route 9 north three miles to Essex (exit 3).
Total Distance: about 100 miles.

PUBLIC TRANSPORTATION Amtrak rail service to Old Saybrook, with Valley Railroad connection to Essex. Check current schedules.

ACCOMMODATIONS *Griswold Inn,* Main Street, Essex, 767–0991, $$ CP ● *Copper Beech Inn,* Main Street, Ivoryton, 767–0330, $$$–$$$$ CP ● *Bishopsgate Inn,* Goodspeed Landing, East Haddam, 873–1677, $$–$$$ CP ● *Inn at Chester,* 318 West Main Street, 526–4961, $$$ ● *Stonecroft Inn,* 17 Main Street, East Haddam, 873–1754, Federal home with pleasant porch in summer, fireplaces in winter, $$$ CP ● *Riverwind,* 46 Main Street, Deep River, 526–3047, small and quaint, part antiques shop, $$–$$$ CP ● *The Fowler House,* Plains Road, Moodus, 873–8906, Victorian, hand carving, and stained glass, $$–$$$ CP.

DINING *Griswold Inn* (see above), dinner entrées $$; Sunday hunt breakfast $ ● *Copper Beech Inn* (see above), dinner entrées $$$ ● *The Gull*, Essex Harbor, 767–0916, $$–$$$ ● *Old Lyme Inn*, 85 Lyme Street, Old Lyme, 434–2600, $$ ● *Bee and Thistle*, 100 Lyme Street, Old Lyme, 434–1667, $$–$$$ ● *Town Farms Inn*, Silver Street, Middletown, 347–7438, $$–$$$ ● *Restaurant du Village*, 59 Main Street, Chester, 526–5058, French bistro, $$$–$$$$ ● *Gelston House*, Goodspeed Landing, East Haddam, 873–9300, Victorian mansion next to opera house, $$–$$$ ● *Fine Bouche*, Main Street, Centerbrook, 767–1277, fine French food, $$$ or prix fixe $$$$.

SIGHTSEEING *Valley Railroad*, Essex, 767–0103. Call for current schedule and rates ● *Connecticut River Museum*, foot of Main Street, Essex, 767–0681. Hours: April to December, Tuesday to Sunday 10 A.M. to 5 P.M. Adults, $1.50; children, $.50 ● *Goodspeed Opera House*, East Haddam, 873–8668, April to November. Phone for current offerings ● *Gillette Castle*, Gillette Castle State Park, Hadlyme, 523–2336. Hours: mid-May to mid-October, daily 11 A.M. to 5 P.M.; October to mid-December, weekends only, 10 A.M. to 4 P.M. Adults, $1; children under 12 free. No fee for visiting park.

Serene Scenes in New Jersey

Frenchtown and Milford are two small villages with much in common. Located a few miles apart on the Delaware River, both are historic pre-Revolutionary War settlements. Once best known as ferryboat crossing points, both villages prospered in early America as sites of mills powered by the river—and today both are ideal candidates for a quiet weekend escape.

Each of these delightful towns offers a special small inn and a few choice shops, and both have far more than their share of fine dining. Combined with excursions to nearby towns like Clinton and Oldwick in the rolling Hunterdon Hills, they provide a serene weekend of scenery, history, and antiquing at their best.

Frenchtown is rapidly becoming known for the four exceptional dining places within its tiny town center. Settle into the Old Hunterdon House, a recently restored three-story Italianate Victorian beauty of a bed-and-breakfast on Bridge Street, and you can have your pick. Right across the street is the Frenchtown Inn, a four-star restaurant in a historic columned brick building. The word is out, so make your reservations well in advance if you want to dine by candlelight amid the bricks and beams on fare such as boneless trout with morels, roasted hen with wild mushrooms, or rack of lamb with a sauce of black trumpet mushrooms, Dijon mustard, and pink peppercorns.

Less formal, but no less appealing, are the innovative cuisine at the Race Street Café and the homemade fare at Rare Essentials, a combination cellar restaurant and gourmet takeout shop. The recently renovated 1851 National Hotel is strong on ambience, a best bet for a drink at its great old bar or for lunch, especially in pleasant weather when you can eat on the upstairs veranda.

As if those weren't enough of a choice, innkeeper Rick Carson at Old Hunterdon House offers guests the opportunity to reserve spaces for the famous six-course dinner served by his partners, Ron Strause and Fred Cresson, at their Evermay Inn, just a few minutes away in Erwinna, on the Pennsylvania side of the Delaware.

You can work off all that good eating by taking the hiking-biking path on the old railroad bed beside the river running from Frenchtown past Bulls Island and all the way to the Prallsville Mills, 15 miles away in Stocktown. If you'd rather be on the river than beside it, take the bridge across to Bucks County and drive downriver a few miles to Point Pleasant Canoe and Tube Rentals.

Frenchtown is still far from a tourist town, but it is blossoming, and you can while away a pleasant hour or two in appealing shops like Blackburn & Yates for antiques, Gem Interiors for country furnishings, and the Antique Hardware Store for nostalgic home fixtures.

Things are even more serene in Milford, where the principal activity is relaxing. Home base here is Chestnut Hill, a Victorian bed-and-breakfast with old-fashioned rockers on the wraparound porch facing the river. Hostess Linda Castagna prides herself on her big breakfasts and homey hospitality. Her hand-drawn map of the area points out where to tube or swim, see the best local scenery, and rent a bike in town.

The favorite Milford dining spot is the Olde Mill Ford Oyster House, a fine choice for seafood, and you'll surely enjoy a pint in the authentic pub atmosphere of the Ship Inn. Another favorite not too far away is the Sergeantsville Inn, serving American cuisine in a cozy, romantic stone house.

The Little Shop in the restored Milford railroad station is a charmer, offering gourmet foods and culinary wares and a florist shop with many unusual plants. The most notable stop in town, however, is The Baker, where a former Le Cirque pastry chef has created a highly successful business selling 18 varieties of home-baked organic whole-grain breads and rolls. These are the same quality baked goods you buy in high-priced metropolitan food shops, but at about half the cost. It's well worth stocking up for the freezer.

If you want more shopping, head downriver to Lambertville, across to Bucks County, or to the big bargain outlets in Flemington.

To discover more small-town charm, just follow Route 78 east to Clinton, one of New Jersey's unsung gems. Just at the point where the south branch of the Raritan River joins Spruce Run Creek, Clinton's main street begins with a waterfall almost 200 feet wide, anchored at either end by an old mill, set against limestone cliffs and a ten-acre park. It's a picture-book setting little changed since the 1700s.

The red mill with the waterwheel is the Clinton Historical Museum. The turning waterwheel is reminiscent of bygone days when grain, flaxseed, limestone, graphite, and talc were processed here. The four floors of exhibits in the mill represent daily rural life in northwestern New Jersey over the past 300 years, and include objects from farm tools and spinning wheels to clothing, china, silver, and glass. The articles are arranged in tableaux depicting the lives of the people who used them. Other buildings house a blacksmith shop, a turn-of-the-century general store and post office, an 1860 schoolhouse, and a log cabin. There are also an herb garden and machinery sheds on the grounds, and in summer, the base of the 150-foot limestone cliff forms a natural amphitheatre for concerts. A Harvest Jubilee is held each year in early October. The park itself makes for a delightful stroll beneath the willows and along the stream, watching ducks and geese paddle by.

The mill across the way, an old stone building with a gambrel roof, was still a working gristmill into the 1950s. Now it's the Hunterdon Art Center, an active community center with changing exhibitions of art and crafts as well as classes, films, and concerts. Many interesting original crafts can be found here in the Sales Gallery.

Clinton's Main Street couldn't be a more charming representation of a nineteenth-century town. But unlike some vintage towns, the shops along the way have not a touristy souvenir among them. The pleasant book shop, the clothing stores, the Clinton Furniture Emporium that sells good used furniture, and the crafts shops are there for the people who live in Clinton and just take pride in keeping up appearances in their hometown.

If you fall in love with the town and want to stay, a modest bed-and-breakfast opened recently in an old home within walking distance of town. At the moment, the best bet for a meal in Clinton is at Weathercock Farms, just outside town. There is a rumor at press time that the historic 1742 Clinton House, a handsome if somewhat rundown local landmark, is going to be redone. Keep an eye on it.

If you want to get out in the autumn air, Spruce Run State Park is just three miles north of Clinton.

A final picturesque stop off Route 78 is the town of Oldwick, a little village that was once known as New Germantown for the Germans who settled it in the 1740s. The entire center of town is a historic district filled with tilty 200-year-old clapboard homes, many of them now antiques shops. If you don't find your heart's desire in town, ask at the shops for the Central New Jersey Antique Trail Guide, which lists some four dozen shops in the general vicinity.

Make a stop at the Magic Shop to feel like a kid again, taking a slide down the rabbit hole past fairy-tale scenes. The shop is a fund-raising venture for a local school for boys and offers toys and music boxes along with its magical slide.

Oldwick makes a perfect lunch stop, whether you choose to sample the rightfully famous onion rings at the quaint Tewksbury Inn or the homemade soups and sandwiches at the General Store. The inn also has a more elegant dining room upstairs for dinner.

Oldwick is surrounded by the hills of Hunterdon County and the Cold Brook Preserve, which encompasses the town and a surrounding area of 298 acres, keeping the rural heritage of Hunterdon safe for future generations. The area includes large numbers of apple and peach orchards and two cider mills, where you can pick up some of the season's favorite beverage.

One of the most scenic drives around begins on King Street, the corner where the inn stands. Follow King across the bridge past Town Farm, where you can detour for cider and apples, and on to Rockaway Road, which takes you beside a rippling brook past picture-book horse farms and distant hilly views to Mountainville, a quaint dot on the map that will surely charm you with its old houses. The Kitchen Caboodle in town offers kitchen wares and excellent homemade lunch and brunch. One of the handful of antiques shops is in the former Old Mountainville Hotel.

If you follow Rockaway Road farther in order to loop back to town, a turnoff on Burrell Road will bring you to Tewksbury Wine Cellars, where you can have a tour of the wine-making process on weekends along with samples of the young winery's products. There is a harvest festival here late in September offering wine, food, music, and crafts. Whenever you come, the setting is great, and you're welcome to use the picnic tables by the pond, sharing the pleasant view of horses in the meadow with the resident ducks and geese.

The unspoiled villages and rolling hills of upper Hunterdon County are at their very best in their fall colors. Remember to bring along a camera—or a canvas.

North Jersey Area Code: 201

DRIVING DIRECTIONS New Jersey Turnpike to exit 14, then take Route 78 west and continue to Route 31 south. From 31, take Route 12 west into Frenchtown. For Milford, take exit 11, Route 614 south (toward Pattenburg), turn left on Route 519, then right onto Bridge Street into town.
Total distance: about 85 miles.

PUBLIC TRANSPORTATION Regular bus service to Frenchtown and Milford; trip from Manhattan is under two hours. Information and schedules available from West Hunterdon Bus Company, Routes 202 and 31, Flemington, NJ 08822, 782–6313, or Port Authority Bus Terminal (212) 564–8484.

ACCOMMODATIONS *Old Hunterdon House*, 12 Bridge Street, Frenchtown, 996–3632, $$$ CP ● *Chestnut Hill*, 63 Church Street, Milford, 995–9761, $$–$$$ CP ● If both inns are full, try two quiet upper Bucks County retreats: *Bridgeton House*, PO Box 167, River Road, Upper Black Eddy, PA, just across the river from Milford. (215) 982–5856, $$–$$$; or the elegant *Evermay*, River Road, Erwinna, PA, across the Delaware and two miles downriver from Frenchtown. (215) 294–9100, $$–$$$ CP ● *Leigh Way*, 55 Leigh Street, Clinton, 735–4311, $–$$ CP, is another alternative.

DINING *Frenchtown Inn*, 7 Bridge Street, Frenchtown, 996–3300, $$$ ● *Race Street Café*, 2 Race Street, Frenchtown, 996–3179, $$–$$$ ● *Rare Essentials*, 10 Bridge Street, Frenchtown, 996–3633, $$ ● *National Hotel*, Race Street, Frenchtown, 996–4871, $$–$$$ ● *Old Milford Oyster House*, Bridge Street, Milford, 995–9411, $$–$$$ ● *Sergeantsville Inn*, Route 523, Sergeantsville, (609) 397–3700, $$$ ● *Weathercock Farms*, Van Syckel's Road, Clinton, 638–6585, $$$ ● *Tewksbury Inn*, Main Street, Oldwick, 439–2641, downstairs dining room, $–$$, country French dinner in handsome upstairs dining room, full dinners $$$–$$$$ ● *General Store*, Main Street, Oldwick, lunches and takeout only, $.

SIGHTSEEING *Clinton Historical Museum*, 56 Main Street, Clinton, 735–4101. Hours: April to October, Monday to Friday 1 P.M. to 4 p.m., Saturday and Sunday noon to 6 p.m. Adults, $2; children 6–12, $1, under 6 free ● *Hunterdon Art Center*, 7 Center Street (off Main), Clinton, 735–8415. Hours: Tuesday to Friday 1 p.m. to 4 p.m., Saturday and Sunday to 5 p.m. Free ● *Tewksbury Wine Cellars*, RD 2, Lebanon, 832–2400. Hours: Saturday and Sunday noon to 5 p.m. Tasting and tour, $2, refunded with purchase.

FOR FURTHER INFORMATION Hunterdon County Chamber of Commerce, Tourism Division, 1 Main Street, Flemington, NJ 08822, 782–5955.

Tailgating and Other Diversions in New Haven

Though some may dispute their claim, it's a matter of pride in New Haven, Connecticut, that football was born here. The first Yale intramural game was played on the village green some 200 years ago, and football has been a welcome fall tradition ever since.

The origins of tailgate picnics are more obscure, but a visit to the Yale Bowl parking lot on a football weekend clearly demonstrates that this diversion, too, has become a local tradition—and one that is observed with style. Hibachis and outdoor grills send out tempting aromas, cocktail shakers clink merrily, folding tables are set with cloths and cutlery, and even the informal picnickers seem to have particularly attractive hampers—or box lunches labeled *Trattoria* or *Brasserie*.

It's a happy custom on a fine fall day—the picnic, the game, the Yale marching band clad in blue blazers putting a bit of wit into its casual halftime show—and if you want to join the fun, you'll find yourself in a town that has a lot to offer both before and after the game.

New Haven has a long history, the largest collection of British art to be found outside Britain, Yale's magnificent Gothic campus for strolling, top museums, some of the best regional theater in the country, and last—but certainly not least—pizza that is unsurpassed. It will take some juggling to fit it all in. One plan might be to do the campus Saturday morning, take in a bit of New Haven history after the game, and reserve Sunday for museums and some autumn leaves in the city's scenic parks.

Begin by visiting the Information Center on the Green, where you can pick up a walking tour map, then head for the Green across the way. One of the nine squares laid out in 1638 in America's first planned city, the Green offers three particularly fine churches, one Gothic, one Federal, and one Georgian in design. The Center Congregational (1813) is considered a masterpiece of American Georgian architecture.

The main entrance to Yale is just off the Green through the William Lyon Phelps Gate on College Street. Free one-hour tours of the campus are offered from the Information Center inside the gate at 10 A.M. and 2 P.M. weekdays and 1:30 P.M. weekends, but you can spend an equally pleasant if less informed hour just roaming through the ivied courtyards and past the Gothic facades of the college. Though Yale is now a university of 11,000 students that spreads over many blocks, the heart of the school still remains the old campus bounded by Chapel, High, Elm, and College streets. Nathan Hale, Noah Webster, and William Howard Taft all studied in Connecticut Hall, the oldest intact building on campus.

The Green and Yale recall New Haven's Colonial and cultural history, but the city also has an important industrial history. Among its prides are New Haven clocks, Winchester rifles, and Gilbert toys, which include that all-time favorite, the erector set. Eli Whitney manufactured his cotton gin here and in 1812 led the way to mass production by turning out rifles with interchangeable parts. New Havenite Charles Goodyear invented vulcanized rubber in this town.

After the game, visit the New Haven Colony Historical Society, where you can see samples of some of these early products, Whitney's cotton gin among them, as well as displays of decorative arts, tableware of New Haven from 1640 to 1840, and antique dolls and toys. Nearby at High and Grove streets, an impressive Egyptian gateway leads to the Grove Street Cemetery, a parklike retreat where Whitney and Goodyear are buried, along with Samuel F. B. Morse and Noah Webster.

New Haven has many excellent restaurants patronized by the many visitors to Yale and by theatergoers in town, including the much lauded Robert Henry, but at dinner hour many make a beeline straight for Wooster Street, the heart of the Italian district. Some of the restaurants here are highly regarded, too, but it is the pizza that makes Wooster Street legendary. It is authentic Italian tomato pie—you have to order mozzarella on top if you want it—and it is delicious. There is a long-standing war between devotees of Pepe's (medium-thick crust) and Sally's (super-thin), but there are enough fans to do justice to both. Come very early, or be prepared for long lines.

Early dinner isn't a bad idea anyway, since you will probably want to get to the theater in the evening. Those who follow theater will need no introduction to Long Wharf, the regional company named for its home in a former food terminal near the water. Long Wharf is a pleasant theatergoing experience, a small and intimate theater-in-the-round with invariably creative staging.

Yale Repertory Theater is another place where you will usually find well-performed experimental theater in New Haven. And recently the old Shubert, home of countless pre-Broadway tryouts in the past, has been renovated and brings in touring companies and concerts, while the new Palace has its own roster of musicals and top-name performers, making for a bounty of evening entertainment in New Haven. Check for current offerings at all.

Another kind of evening entertainment is next door in Milford, where jai alai is played daily through December. The game is fast and the betting furious. If you've never seen it played, here's your chance.

Since museums don't open until afternoon on Sunday, you might sleep late, enjoy brunch, or take a drive to one of New Haven's parks. The city's flat terrain is interrupted by two towering red rock cliffs that are centerpoints for two lovely parks, each with a view of the harbor and Long Island Sound. East Rock Park is also the site of the city's arboretum, Pardee Rose Gardens, a bird sanctuary, and hiking trails at their peak of autumn color. West Rock Park contains a 40-acre zoo.

Your first museum stop should be one of Yale's (and New Haven's) finest attractions, the Yale Center of British Art. This modern structure holds the extensive Paul Mellon collection covering British life and culture from Elizabethan times to the present, with numerous paintings by Turner, Constable, and other noted British artists. There are often concerts and lectures scheduled here on weekends; check the desk for the current offerings.

Across Chapel Street, the Yale University Art Gallery, the nation's oldest college art museum, has a varied collection of American and European art of all periods, American decorative art spanning three centuries, African sculpture, pre-Columbian, Near and Far Eastern art. There is also a sculpture garden.

Another unique attraction is the Yale Collection of Musical Instruments, 850 antique and historical instruments dating from the sixteenth to the nineteenth centuries. The Peabody Museum of Natural History is also an excellent one of its kind, and the Beinecke Library has many rare displays, including a Gutenberg Bible, original Audubon bird prints, and medieval manuscripts.

There is a lot to see—you'll have to pick and choose. And then you'll have the pleasant prospect of picking one of those many fine restaurants in the city to finish off the day.

New Haven Area Code: 203

DRIVING DIRECTIONS Take I-95 or the Hutchinson, Merritt, and Wilbur Cross parkways to downtown New Haven exits.
Total distance: 75 miles.

PUBLIC TRANSPORTATION Metro-North services New Haven as does Amtrak. Some bus transportation is available in town.

ACCOMMODATIONS *Park Plaza Hotel,* 155 Temple Street, 772–1700, $$$ • *Colony Inn,* 1157 Chapel Street, 776–1234, $$$ • *Holiday Inn at Yale,* 30 Whalley Avenue, 777–6221, $$–$$$ • *Howard Johnson's–Long Wharf,* 400 Sargent Drive, 562–1111, $$–$$$.

DINING *Robert Henry's,* 1032 Chapel Street, 789–1010, one of the best in the state, $$$–$$$$ • *Bruxelles,* 20 College Street, 777–7752, upbeat ambience, upscale pizza and rotisserie specialties, $–$$ • *Annie's Firehouse Restaurant,* 19 Edwards Street, 865–4200, American menu in converted firehouse, $$ • *Basels,* 993 State Street, 624–9361, Greek food, music, and dance, $$ • *Fitzwillys,* 338 Elm, 624–9438, sandwiches, quiches, salads—very popular, open till 2 A.M., $–$$ • *Leon's,* 321 Washington Avenue, 777–5366, one of the best Italian restaurants in town, $$–$$$ • *Gentree Ltd.,* 194 York Street, 562–3800, known for ribs, $$ • *Delmonaco's,* 232 Wooster Street, 865–1109, southern Italian food, $$–$$$ • *Old Heidelberg,* 1151 Chapel Street, 777–3639, New Haven's oldest, $$ • *Sally's Pizza,* 237 Wooster Street, 624–5271, $ • *Pepe's,* 157 Wooster Street, 865–5762, $.

SIGHTSEEING *Yale Football,* contact Yale Department of Athletics, PO Box 402A, Yale Station, New Haven, CT 06520, 436–0100, for current schedule and ticket prices • *New Haven Colony Historical Society,* 114 Whitney Avenue, 562–4183. Hours: Tuesday to Friday 10 A.M. to 5 P.M., Saturday and Sunday 2 P.M. to 5 P.M. Free • *Yale University,* guided one-hour walking tours from Phelps Gateway off College Street at New Haven green. Call 432–2300 for current schedule. Free • *Yale Center for British Art,* 1080 Chapel Street, 432–2800. Hours: Tuesday to Saturday 10 A.M. to 5 P.M., Sunday 2 P.M. to 5 P.M. Free • *Yale University Art Gallery,* 1111 Chapel Street, 436–0574. Hours: Tuesday to Saturday 10 A.M. to 5 P.M., Sunday 2 P.M. to 5 P.M. Free • *Peabody Museum of Natural History,* 170 Whitney Avenue, 433–5050. Hours: Monday to Saturday 9 A.M. to 4:45 P.M., Sunday 1 P.M. to 4:45 P.M. Free on Tuesday. Other days: adults, $2; children, $1 ● *East Rock Park,* East Rock Road. Hours: daily during daylight. Free ● *West Rock Park,* Wintergreen Avenue. Hours: zoo open Monday to Saturday 10 A.M. to 4 P.M.; Sunday noon to 4 P.M. Free ● *Long Wharf Theater,* 222 Sargent Drive, 787–4282 ● *Yale Repertory Theater,* Chapel and York streets, 432–1234 ● *The Palace,* 1000 Chapel Street, 624–TIXS ● *Shubert Theater,* 247 College Street, 562–5666 ● *Milford Jai Alai,* 311 Old Gate Lane (I-95, exit 40), (800) 243–9660, in CT, (800) 972–9650. Hours: June to December, Monday to Saturday 7 P.M.; Monday, Wednesday, Saturday 11:45 A.M. General admission, $2; reserved seats, $2.25–$6.

FOR FURTHER INFORMATION Contact New Haven Convention and Visitors' Bureau, Inc., 155 Church, New Haven, CT 06510, 787–8367. Open Monday to Friday 10 A.M. to 4 P.M.

A Vision of the Past in Deerfield

Many consider The Street in Old Deerfield, Massachusetts, the loveliest in all New England—and you'll find it at its very best in autumn.

More than 50 fine Colonial and Federal homes line this mile-long avenue, each one carefully restored to its original condition. In the 12 houses open to the public, visitors can see more than 100 rooms filled with china, glassware, silver, pewter, fabrics, and furniture that are a testament to the good taste of our early settlers.

The difference between Deerfield and other restorations is that this town remains alive and well today. People still live in its historic homes. Even the museum-houses have apartments in the rear for the faculty of Deerfield Academy, the noted boys' school that has stood on The Street since 1797. From the moment you arrive, you will sense the town's continuity with the past.

Seeing this peaceful, elm-shaded village today, it is hard to believe it was once a frontier outpost whose fate was uncertain from day to day. Twice Deerfield was almost destroyed by Indian attacks, in the Bloody Brook massacre of 1675 and the Deerfield Massacre of 1704. Fifty settlers died in the latter battle, and another 111 were taken prisoner and marched off on a brutal midwinter trek to Canada.

But instead of fleeing, the survivors set out to rebuild their town and rework their farms. The town revived and thrived as a center of the wheat industry and an important cattle market. Its more primitive houses were replaced by gracious clapboard homes in the Connecticut Valley tradition. Though rustic compared to homes of this period in Boston or Philadelphia, their very simplicity makes them seem all the more beautiful today.

Deerfield's hard-bitten farmers used the new wealth to bring in the finest furnishings they could buy, particularly the work of the excellent craftsmen and cabinetmakers of their own valley.

By a combination of luck, vision, energy—and money—this era of good taste has been preserved. When the center of farming moved away from New England in the mid-nineteenth century, Deerfield, by then the home of three schools, survived as a center of education. In the next 100 years many local residents began efforts at restoration, but the town's real renaissance was fostered by Mr. and Mrs. Henry Flynt, who came to Deerfield in the 1930s because their son was enrolled at the academy. The Flynts' first move was to buy and restore the white-columned Deerfield Inn in the center of town. They next acquired one of the old houses for themselves, and from then on one house led to another. In 1952 Mr. and Mrs. Flynt founded Historic Deerfield, Inc.

Though Deerfield is only a village, you can't rush through it in an hour or two. Allow at least a full day—or better yet, a weekend.

Start by just strolling The Street, savoring the town's setting among wooded hills and observing the exteriors of the saltbox houses, with their steep-pitched gambrel roofs, weathered clapboard siding, and distinctively carved doorways. Note the academy buildings, the old Brick Church, and the delightful post office, a replica of a 1696 meetinghouse. Then head for the Hall Tavern Information Center, where color photos will help you make the difficult choice of which houses to visit during a limited stay. Each house tour takes from 30 to 45 minutes.

You can begin with Hall Tavern itself, once a hostelry for travelers. One of its seven rooms is an unusual ballroom with gaily stenciled walls.

A must on any tour is Ashley House (circa 1730), the home of Deerfield's Tory minister during the American Revolution. Many may have quarreled with Reverend Jonathan Ashley's politics, but no one could fault his taste. The north parlor, with blue walls setting off red shell-crowned cupboards, a gold satin settee, and rich oriental rugs, has been called one of the most beautiful rooms in America.

Each of the other houses has its own special attractions and a knowledgeable guide to point them out. Many of the guides are longtime

Deerfield residents who have family stories to add to the town's history.

The Sheldon-Hawks House (1743), home of the town's historian, contains fine paneling, a display of sewing equipment, and a memorable bedroom with brilliant flame-stitch bed hangings and red moreen curtains and chairs. The Wells-Thorn House (1717/1751) combines an austere, Colonial exterior with urbane, Federal-period furniture. The Dwight-Barnard House (1750) has an elegant parlor and a doctor's office behind its weathered exterior.

The Asa Stebbins House (1799), the town's first brick edifice, was built by the wealthiest landowner and decorated with French wallpapers and freehand wall drawings. Like many of Deerfield's homes, this one has an excellent collection of early export china.

Mr. Stebbins also built the town's other brick house for his son, Asa, Junior, in 1824. Now called Wright House, it is distinguished for its Chippendale Room, its handsome dining room, and a bedroom hung with crewelwork.

Frary House (1720/1768), a home with a double history, is another highly recommended stop. Its location on the town common made it a refuge for the Frary family in pioneer days and a profitable tavern for the Barnards later on. The house contains a ballroom, many examples of country furniture, and a variety of cooking, spinning, and weaving equipment. There is also a "touch it" room where children and adults may handle some of the tools that are off limits elsewhere.

For a change of pace, step into some of the specialized buildings such as the Wilson Printing House, restored to its original site and used as a printing office and bookbindery, or the Parker and Russell Silver Shop, a farmhouse containing a smith's workshop, a clock collection, and an outstanding display of American and English silver. Both date from around 1815.

Helen Geier Flynt Fabric Hall is a Victorian barn that houses Mrs. Flynt's remarkable collection of American, English, and European needlework, textiles, quilts, bed hangings, and costumes.

Last stop, and a delightful place to stay, is Deerfield Inn, where you can end the day with tea before a roaring fire or stronger refreshments in the tavern room. The inn serves excellent meals in an elegant, candlelit dining room.

With luck you'll be able to get a room at the inn. If not, there are other good inns in the college towns nearby, and wherever you stay, you're in good position on Sunday for a tour of the Pioneer Valley, home of the well-known Five Colleges, haven for craftsmen and antiques dealers, and a bucolic area with more than its share of autumn scenery.

A college tour is a good plan for seeing the sights, and you'll be getting a good cross section of college architecture while you're at it— Amherst with its halls of ivy and picture-book green; the modern University of Massachusetts, a virtual city that actually has a building tall enough for a top-floor restaurant with a view; rustic Hampshire College; and the mix of old and new along the quadrangles of Smith in Northampton and Mount Holyoke in South Hadley. Smith has an excellent and varied art museum with French impressionists, Renaissance sculpture, eighteenth-century English paintings, and—you name it. Amherst's Mead Art Gallery is smaller but does have one curiosity, the Rotherwas Room, dating from 1611 and given to the college by an alumnus who had it brought to America from a British castle. Walnut carved paneling, an ornate mantel, and stained glass windows give the room an authentic baronial flavor.

There's interesting shopping in this area, particularly around Northampton, which has developed into a center for the many crafts artisans in this area. Thornes Market on Main Street and Old School Commons on New South Street are two complexes that offer a good number of intriguing shops. There are many good restaurants in Northampton, as well.

The best-known crafts center in the region is Leverett Craftsmen and Artists in Leverett Center, just northeast of Amherst. It's a cooperative venture of some 100 craftsmen, and their fall and pre-Christmas shows are particularly good ones. There are often artists in residence as well in this converted factory building.

A Western Massachusetts Craft Directory is available if you want to find more shops or visit some of the artists in their studios. There is also a printed guide for antiquers. Ask in the shops or see addresses at the end of this chapter.

For foliage vistas, try Mount Tom on US 5 in Holyoke, where an observation tower is open daily until 8 P.M. On Mount Sugarloaf, off Route 116 in Sunderland near Amherst, another state park with an observation tower offers a sweeping view of the river valley and the flaming hillsides on either side.

Heading home, you may want to make a detour into Springfield, where four free museums for art, fine arts, and natural history are clustered together in a quadrangle downtown. Of more interest to any sports fans along may be the Naismith Memorial Basketball Hall of Fame, which has a replica of the original basketball court dating to 1891, displays on the sport, and free movies.

From Springfield it's an easy drive back on Route 91 and straight back to the city.

Deerfield Area Code: 413

DRIVING DIRECTIONS   Take I-95 or Hutchinson River Parkway and Merritt Parkway to I-91; follow I-91 north to exit 24 and Route 5 into Deerfield center.
   Total distance: 187 miles

PUBLIC TRANSPORTATION   Amtrak trains to Springfield; Peter Pan Bus Lines connects Springfield, Amherst, and Northampton to New York and Boston. Phone (800) 322–8995 in Massachusetts, (800) 322–8995 outside the state.

ACCOMMODATIONS   *Deerfield Inn,* Deerfield, 774–5587, $$$ • *Lord Jeffrey Inn,* Amherst, 253–2576, $$$ • *The Autumn Inn,* 259 Elm Street (Route 9), Northampton, 584–7660, $$ • *Yankee Pedlar Inn,* Route 5, Holyoke, 532–9494, $$ • *Hilton Inn,* Routes 91 and 5, Northampton, 586–1211, the only one of the lot that isn't an inn but a very pleasant lodging of its type, $$ • *The Beeches,* Hampton Terrace, Northampton, 586–9288, former Calvin Coolidge home, $$ CP.

DINING   *Deerfield Inn* (see above), $$–$$$ • *Lord Jeffrey Inn* (see above), $$–$$$ • *Beardsley's,* 140 Main Street, Northampton, 586–2699, French café, $$–$$$ • *Eastside Grill,* 19 Strong Avenue, Northampton, 586–3347, grill and Cajun specialties, $–$$ • *The Depot,* 125A Pleasant Street, Northampton, 586–5366, stylishly renovated train station, varied menu, $–$$$ • *Fitzwilly's,* 23 Main Street, 584-8666, local gathering spot, $–$$ • *India House,* 45 State Street, Northampton, 586–6344, good Indian food, vegetarian, and tandoori specialties, $ • *Panda Garden,* 34 Pleasant Street, Northampton, 584–3858, local favorite for Chinese, $ • *Panda Garden East,* 103 N. Pleasant Street, Amherst, 256–8923, same owners, $ • *The Log Cabin,* Route 141, Easthampton Road, Holyoke, 536–7700, outstanding setting and views, $–$$$ • For a light lunch, try *The Black Sheep Deli,* 79 Main Street, Amherst.

SIGHTSEEING   *Historic Deerfield,* PO Box 321, Deerfield, MA 10342. 774–5581. Hours: Monday to Saturday 9:30 A.M. to 4:30 P.M.; Sunday 11 A.M. to 4:30 P.M. Open until 6 P.M. from July 1 to October 31. Three houses, $4.50; 12 houses, $15; individual houses, $2 to $3 • *Mead Art Gallery,* Amherst College, 542–2335. Hours: weekends 10 A.M. to 5 P.M., weekdays 1 P.M. to 4:30 P.M. Free • *Smith College Museum of Art,* Elm Street, Northampton, 584–2700. Hours: Tuesday to Saturday noon to 5 P.M.; Sunday 2 P.M. to 5 P.M. Free • *Naismith*

Memorial National Basketball Hall of Fame, 1150 W. Columbus Avenue (off I-91 exits 4 and 7), Springfield, 781–6500. Hours: July to Labor Day, daily 9 A.M. to 6 P.M.; after Labor Day, daily 10 A.M. to 5 P.M. Adults, $5; children 9–15, $3; under 9, free.

FOR FURTHER INFORMATION For antiques directory write to Pioneer Valley Antiques Dealers Association, PO Box 62, Westfield, MA 01085. For Western Massachusetts Craft Directory, contact Arts Extension Service, Division of Continuing Education, University of Massachusetts, Amherst, MA 01003, 545–2360. Information: Pioneer Valley Convention and Visitors Bureau, 56 Dwight Street, Springfield Civic Center, Springfield, MA 01103, 787–1548.

A Capital Trip to Albany

How about a ride on the A train, 1940s edition, with wicker seats and ceiling fans—and without graffiti? Or a stroll down Fifth Avenue peeking into the windows at Delmonico's, where the diners are dressed in their 1890s best?

These and much, much more—replicas of a tenement sweatshop, the old port of New York, an old Chinatown store, an antique trading post from the Stock Exchange, the "Sesame Street" TV set, and a 1925 city bus—are among the features of the "The New York Metropolis," the most comprehensive exhibit on the city ever assembled.

But if you want to see it, there's a catch. You'll have to travel 150 miles from Manhattan to the New York State Museum, part of the Empire State Plaza in Albany.

New York's capital rarely used to attract anyone who wasn't forced to make the trip for official state business, but that was before the completion of the Plaza, late Governor Nelson Rockefeller's legacy to the city of Albany. Not everyone agreed with Rockefeller's colossal plan to clear 98 acres of downtown land and dislocate 3,000 people in order to build glass and marble monuments costing a billion dollars of taxpayers' money. But 16 years later, when it was all finished in 1978, there was little doubt that Albany had acquired not only a striking government complex, but a first-rate cultural center, one that has sparked a renaissance in the city.

The futuristic Plaza, built around a landscaped mall of pools and fountains, gardens, and grandiose sculpture, has a huge collection of modern art on display and the largest state museum in the nation. It is definitely worth a visit, particularly in fall when the leafy countryside surrounding Albany is putting on its annual autumn spectacular. Apple picking, hiking, and a look at the fascinating history of the Shaker sect can also be part of the weekend scenario.

Your first stop in Albany should be the Plaza itself, perhaps for a bird's-eye view from the forty-second–floor observation deck of its tallest building, known simply as the Tower. Across the mall four smaller Agency Towers house many state departments. At one end of the mall are the lower-scale structures of the Legislative Office Building and a Justice Building; and at the other end is the handsome Cultural Education Center, which contains the State Museum. The many-tiered steps to the center form a seating area that can accommodate 2,500 people for the free music and entertainment that frequently takes place on the mall.

Next to the Tower is a restaurant, and next to that the most unusual of all the edifices, the Performing Arts Center, universally known as The Egg. The name's origin will be obvious when you see the shape of this flying saucer on stilts.

Having gotten your perspective, you'll be descending underground to the half-mile concourse that connects all the mall buildings. Free guided tours of the Plaza are offered daily from the visitor services headquarters at the north end of the concourse, the same place to make arrangements for a tour of the state capitol. Along the tour you'll be seeing some of the monumental pieces of sculpture standing amid the buildings, most notably a series of painted steel structures by David Smith, and large pieces by Noguchi and Calder.

The entire concourse is a gallery of modern art, some of it highly experimental. The collection indoors and out totals almost 100 pieces. To make sure you don't miss anything, ask at the visitor services desk for a map to help you find works by Frankenthaler, Motherwell, Oldenburg, Kelly, Gottlieb, Nevelson, and many other noted artists.

You'll probably want to return and linger in the State Museum, which has amazing resources for an institution in a city the size of Albany. In addition to the many unique features of the New York metropolis exhibit, there are some interesting special effects in the section called "Adirondack Wilderness," particularly a small dark room where you can hear the awesome sound of a giant tree falling in the forest. Well-made films enhance all of the museum's displays.

When you've had your fill of the Plaza, you might take a walk to the west (behind the agency buildings) to Hamilton Street and Robinson Square, a series of galleries, shops, and restaurants in restored nineteenth-century brownstones. The entire area behind the Plaza known as Center Square, once a slum, is being restored house by house into a totally charming neighborhood well worth the time for a stroll to appreciate the fine Victorian architecture. The area is bounded by Washington and Madison avenues, Lark and South Swan streets.

After lunch on Hamilton or in one of the Plaza restaurants, it's time for a second free tour, this time a look at the ornate state capitol building with its "million-dollar staircase," adorned with carvings, and the beautifully restored Senate and Assembly chambers.

There are several other prize historic homes and churches to visit in Albany. Choice among the houses are Cherry Hill, whose furnishings reflect the changing life-styles of five generations of the Van Rensselaer family, who lived here from 1787 to 1963, and the Schuyler Mansion, home of the prominent early family and a center of activities during the Revolutionary War. George Washington, Benjamin Franklin, and Alexander Hamilton visited this house; Hamilton, in fact, married Elizabeth Schuyler at the mansion. One other important home is the Ten Broeck Mansion, home of a delegate to the Continental Congress and filled with many fine Colonial artifacts.

Among the most notable churches are First Church, whose pulpit, carved in Holland in 1656, is the oldest in America; St. Peters, a Gothic Revival structure containing a silver communion service donated by Queen Anne; the first Episcopal Cathedral in America, with stalls built by monks in 1623 and some of the finest European wood carving in America; and Congregation Beth Emeth, one of the first four reform Jewish congregations in America, with a great folded roof reminiscent of the tent Moses prepared as a desert tabernacle.

As the state capital, Albany is used to visitors, and there are numerous places to stay and dine in the area. If you want to make this a country weekend, you might want to choose one of two inns out a ways from the city, your choice depending perhaps on the direction you plan to take on Sunday. The Greenville Arms, a comfortable Victorian homestead with attractive grounds, is about 28 miles southwest of the city in a peaceful tiny town on the edge of the Catskills. In the other direction, handier to the Shaker Museum, is The Inn at the Shaker Mill Farm, which is indeed an old mill and is furnished in the spare look of the Shakers. It is a little spartan for some tastes, but the setting is superb.

As for evening entertainment, if you are in the city you should find something of interest going on in one of the two arenas of The Egg, which has an ongoing schedule of drama, dance, and music.

Come Sunday, you'll have to pick and choose your destinations. One strong recommendation is to bring along your hiking shoes and make your first stop the John Boyd Thatcher State Park, about 18 miles west of the city on Route 157. The clifftop view here is one of the best around; on a clear day you can see the peaks of the Adirondacks, the

Massachusetts Taconics, and Vermont's Green Mountains, plus the Hudson-Mohawk Valley and the profusion of trees covering the slopes—oaks, elms, red maples, birches, lindens, and white pines—producing a rich palette of fall color.

The hiking shoes are for the half-mile Indian Ladder trail paralleling the Helderberg Escarpment, a cliff of limestone and shale that geologists have declared to be one of the richest fossil-bearing formations in the world. The trail takes about 45 minutes.

If you continue from the park to Route 146 in Altamont, you can pick your own peck of apples at Indian Ladder Farms. If the season is right you may find raspberries ripe for picking as well, and there's always fresh pressed cider for sale as well as fresh grown vegetables.

From here you can choose your direction. If you continue west on Route 20 for perhaps 20 miles you'll come to another natural wonder, Howe Caverns. An 80-minute tour here of the underground caves and subterranean waterways includes an underground boat ride. If you are going to the caverns, bring a jacket; temperatures in the caves are in the chilly fifties.

Another alternative is to drive south. If you have children along you may want to stop at the Catskill Game Farm on Route 32. Otherwise on to Route 23A, the spectacular road to Hunter Mountain, with cliffs and waterfalls along the way and more magnificent foliage vistas. If you take this route, make a detour to Elka Park for Sunday dinner at the Redcoat's Return, a rustic farmhouse whose book-lined dining room is highly recommended in the area.

Or you might choose to make your way back about 20 miles southeast of Albany for a visit to the Shaker Museum on Route 66 in Old Chatham, a complex of eight buildings in a calm and beautiful farm setting showing the enterprise and ingenious simple designs of this industrious sect, who invented such practical aids as the circular saw, the flat broom, and the clothespin. You will see a cabinetmaker's shop; a small chair factory; a smith's shop; galleries of textiles and the looms that produced them; craft shops used by tinsmiths, cobblers, broommakers; the Shaker seed and medicine industries; an herb house adjacent to the herb garden; and nine period rooms and a Shaker schoolroom, all incredibly neat, spare, and functional, with the clean-lined furniture that has inspired so many latter-day craftsmen. If the Shakers interest you, make a note that the third Saturday in September is the annual Crafts Day at the museum, when special demonstrations are scheduled. Also note that the museum store sells reproductions of Shaker furniture and of their handsome oval storage boxes.

If time remains, take a drive through the appealing old towns and the pastoral countryside of the various Chathams and New Lebanon, then drive home via Route 22, where there are some splendid choices for dinner. Two are in Hillsdale, the French L'Hostellerie Bressane and the Swiss Hutte. The third, farther down in Patterson, is a real curiosity. It's an offbeat Mexican restaurant called the Texas Taco where you'll share eating quarters with the most amazing collection of odd memorabilia and animals, including parrots and a monkey. Some people find it so appealing they make a special point of driving home via this route just to stop in again.

Albany Area Code: 518

DRIVING DIRECTIONS New York State Thruway (Route 87) to exit 23. Follow signs to I-787 into Albany, watching for signs to the Empire State Plaza. Elevated traffic loop leads into and under the Empire State Plaza. Parking is available in underground garages and is free after 5 P.M. and on weekends.

Total distance: 150 miles.

PUBLIC TRANSPORTATION Amtrak to Albany is the most scenic route you can take, paralleling the Hudson River almost all the way.

ACCOMMODATIONS *Albany Hilton,* Ten Eyck Plaza, State Street, 462–6611, $$$–$$$$ • *Desmond Americana,* 660 Albany-Shaker Road, 869–8100, indoor pool, $$$$ • *Quality Inn,* 1–3 Watervliet Avenue Extension, 438–8431, $$ • *Susse Chalet,* 44 Wolf Road, Colonie, 459–5670, $ • *Ramada Inn,* 1228 Western Avenue, 489–2981, $$ • *Best Western Inn Town,* 300 Broadway, 434–4111, convenient if you have no car, $$ • *Marriott,* 189 Wolf Road, 458–8444, $$$$ • *Greenville Arms,* Greenville, 966–5219, $$$$–$$$$$ MAP • *Inn at the Shaker Mill Farm,* Canaan, 794–9345, $$$ MAP.

DINING *Yates Street,* 492 Yates Street, 438–2012, Victorian decor, varied menu, $$ • *Café Capriccio,* 49 Grand Street, 465–0439, regional Italian, $–$$$ • *Yono's,* 289 Hamilton Street, 436–7747, Indonesian, $$–$$$ • *Ogden's Restaurant,* Howard Street at Lodge Street, 463–6605, interesting menu, in restored office building, $–$$ • *Chez René,* Route 9, Glenmount, 463–5130, French cuisine in a Colonial home, $$–$$$ • *L'Auberge,* 351 Broadway, 465–1111, French fare in restored steamship ticket office, $$–$$$ • *Jack's Oyster House,* 42 State Street, 465–8854, noisy, old favorite downtown eatery with famous cheesecake, $–$$ • *La Serre,* 14 Green Street, 463–6056, French and fine in a restored factory, $$$ • *Yorkstone Pub,* 79 North

Pearl, 462–9033, hamburgers, soups, sandwiches, $ • *Michael's Restaurant*, 851 Madison, 489–4062, deli with takeout counter if you want a picnic lunch, $ • *Redcoat's Return*, Dale Lane, Elka Park, 589–6379, $$ • *L'Hostellerie Bressane*, off Route 22, Hillsdale, 325–3412, $$–$$$ • *Swiss Hutte*, Route 22, Hillsdale, 325–3333, $$–$$$ • *Texas Taco*, Route 22, Patterson, 878–9665, $.

SIGHTSEEING *Empire State Plaza*, information 474–2418. Tours: daily, hour-long, from visitors services headquarters at north end of the underground concourse, 11 A.M., 1 P.M., and 3 P.M. Observation deck, daily 9 A.M. to 5 P.M. Free • *New York State Museum*, Empire State Plaza, 474–5877. Hours: daily 10 A.M. to 5 P.M. Free • *State Capitol Building*, Empire State Plaza, 474–2418. Tours: on the hour, daily 9 A.M. to 4 P.M. Free • *Cherry Hill*, 523½ Pearl Street, 434–4791. Hours: February to December, Tuesday to Saturday 10 A.M. to 3 P.M.; Sunday 1 P.M. to 3 P.M. Adults, $2; children 6–16, $.75. • *Schuyler Mansion*, 32 Catherine Street, 434–0834. Hours: Wednesday to Saturday 10 A.M. to 5 P.M.; Sunday 1 P.M. to 5 P.M. Free • *Ten Broeck Mansion*, 9 Ten Broeck Place, 436–9826. Hours: March to December, Wednesday to Friday 2 P.M. to 4 P.M.; Saturday and Sunday 1 P.M. to 4 P.M. Free • Churches usually open daytime hours; phone to check; all free: *First Church in Albany*, North Pearl near Clinton, 463–4449; *St. Peter's Church*, 107 State Street, 434–3502; *Cathedral of All Saints*, 62 South Swan Street, 465–1342; *Congregation Beth Emeth*, 100 Academy Road, 436–9761 • *John Boyd Thatcher State Park*, Route 157 off Route 85. Hours: 9 A.M. to 10 P.M. through Labor Day; closes earlier after Labor Day. Free • *Indian Ladder Farms*, Route 156 (two miles west of Voorheesville), Altamont, 765–2956. Hours: Monday to Saturday 9 A.M. to 6 P.M.; Sunday 10 A.M. to 6 P.M. • *The Shaker Museum*, Route 66, Old Chatham, 794–9100. Hours: May 1 to October 21, daily 10 A.M. to 5 P.M. Adults, $4.50; children 8–17, $3; family rate, $12 • *Howe Caverns*, Route 7, Howe Cave. Hours: daily 9 A.M. to 6 P.M. Adults, $7; children 7–12, $3.50; children under 7 free • *Catskill Game Farm*, Route 32, Catskill, 678–9595. Hours: April 15 to October 31, daily 9 A.M. to 6 P.M. Adults, $8; children 4–11, $4.50; children under 3 free.

FOR FURTHER INFORMATION Albany County Convention and Visitors' Bureau, Inc., 52 S. Pearl Street, Albany, NY 12207, 434–1217.

Hounds and Houses in Chester County

For more than 40 years, it has been a ritual. Promptly at 9 A.M. on the first Saturday in October, the huntsman's horn sounds in Chester County, Pennsylvania. It is the signal for the running of horses and hounds for one of the frequent fox hunts in this fabled horse country— and it is the traditional start of the once-a-year celebration known as Chester County Day.

For the rest of the year much of this lush hilly region, roughly midway between Philadelphia and Pennsylvania Dutch country, is somewhat private about its charms, except for the three major sights on the fringe of the county, Longwood Gardens, The Brandywine River Museum, and Valley Forge. But for this one day only, the entire county blows its own horn for the benefit of the local hospital, showing off dozens of its finest residences as well as the covered bridges, old mills, Quaker meetinghouses, gardens, and other historic sites that are all the more appealing just because they aren't widely touted. The day is so special that 6,000 people have been known to attend.

The crowds don't get overwhelming, however, because so many houses are open, everything from Federal-era row houses and columned mansions on the brick-paved streets of West Chester, the county seat, to stone manors and restored barns and carriage houses in the country. So many homeowners take part in the day that two separate day-long itineraries are offered in different areas. Some of the owners also help to make the day more memorable with touches like the aroma of fresh-baked bread from the kitchen and spectacular arrangements of flowers and fruit in the rooms.

One of the particular pleasures of the tour is occasionally meeting some of the hosts whose families have lived in this area for generations. Chester County has been strongly influenced by its Quaker origins. People here don't show off. Their homes and possessions were made to last, and many live quietly every day with family furniture, antiques, and china that would do credit to a museum.

When the owners aren't present, helpful guides will point out some of the treasures.

Because the county covers such a large area, tours alternate locale and emphasis each year. Recent ones have centered on the ironmasters country to the north, the special greenish-tint serpentine stone houses that are unique to this district, and for the area's tricentennial year, the focus was on homes associated with William Penn, who settled the area 300 years ago. Slide-show previews of the homes included are offered on Friday night at Longwood Gardens and the West Chester courthouse to help visitors make the difficult choice of which houses they want to see most. If you can't make these 7, 8, and 9 P.M. showings, early-bird shows are given on Saturday morning at the hospital in West Chester, where bus tours are available for those who prefer not to drive themselves. The slide shows are included in the price of the tour.

A good plan is to write well ahead for a copy of the *County Day* newspaper, which is usually published in August and outlines the year's current tours. The itineraries may influence where you decide to stay for the weekend, but two safe bets any year are West Chester and the Longwood area, both with plenty of accommodations.

The tour will keep you so busy on Saturday you probably won't want to take time for a long lunch. However, a stop at the Marketplace Deli or at the perfectly elegant French Corner takeout shop in West Chester center will equip you with a fine portable meal to be enjoyed along the way. Come dinner time, you can choose from a whole roster of charming country inns.

If you can spare a few minutes on Saturday, do have a look at the small but exceptional Chester County Historical Society Museum in West Chester (closed on Sundays). It is filled with exquisite clocks, furniture, inlaid chests, embroidery, Tucker porcelain, and majolica pottery, the kinds of pieces often featured on the covers of antiques magazines. There are six fine period room settings.

Sunday offers other delightful possibilities. You might want to head for Marshalton to see the annual Triathalon Race beginning at noon, sponsored by the Marshalton Inn. It's a unique and wacky event, competition via canoe, bicycle, and Olympic walk-step. Normally this is a quaint quiet village, but on this day the inn and the nearby Oyster Bar restaurant set up food stands out-of-doors. The place is jumping all afternoon and into the evening, when a Dixieland band holds forth.

If you didn't really see much of the town on Saturday, a walking tour of West Chester is a quieter and quite interesting occupation. The town is a parade of architectural variety—green serpentine stone, brick townhouses, gingerbread porches, porticoed doorways, iron-lace fences, Greek columns. The courthouse, a bank, and a church are massive-columned Greek Revival structures designed by the architect of the nation's capitol, which once caused the little town to be dubbed the Athens of Pennsylvania. The firehouse and public library are Gothic buildings adorned with Tiffany windows. The residential life of the

1800s can be seen in restored houses on Portico Row, Pottery Row, Stone Row, and Wayne Square.

Another special pleasure in the area is the little Dilworthtown Country Store, located south of West Chester on Brinton Bridge Road just off Route 202. It has been at the same stand since 1758, and the original stone walls and low beams add atmosphere to a tantalizing stock of penny candy, country antiques, bolts of calico, hand-fired tools, hand-dipped candles, folk toys, baskets, quilts, and all manner of one-of-a-kind creations from neighborhood craftsmen. The Dilworthtown Inn right next door is one of the best in the area, a good bet for Saturday or Sunday dinner.

Take a drive up Birmingham Road, just past the inn, to see the magnificent gentlemen's farms, a Quaker meetinghouse, an octagonal schoolhouse, and a historic old cemetery.

If the day is fine and you want to enjoy the out-of-doors, take a stroll around the Brandywine Battlefield State Park near Chadds Ford, where you can visit restorations of Washington's and Lafayette's headquarters. Or a half-hour's drive will take you to the 2,200-acre national park at Valley Forge, resplendent in autumn colors. Longwood Gardens and Brandywine River Museum with its Wyeths are other perennial attractions, different with each change of seasons.

Between Longwood and the museum, Route 1 is lined with antiques shops, and a busy flea market is in action every weekend. While you are in Kennett Square, you can also make a stop at the Mushroom Museum and Shop at Phillips Place. The giant mushrooms for sale here in the town that calls itself the world's mushroom capital will make the ones in your local supermarket look like miniatures.

On the less-traveled roads to the north you can visit a former elegant spa at Yellow Springs, now an arts and crafts center, or St. Peters Village, a restored Victorian settlement of stores and crafts shops near another state park along French Creek.

North or south, the back roads of Chester County don't get a lot of attention compared to those in nearby Bucks or Lancaster counties, yet they are full of unexpected discoveries—historic, scenic, and just plain fun. You'll find that whatever direction you choose to explore, it's almost impossible to make a wrong turn.

Chester County Area Code: 215

DRIVING DIRECTIONS Take the New Jersey Turnpike south to exit 6, Pennsylvania Turnpike, then west to exit 24, Schuylkill Expressway (Route 76), then south to Route 202 to West Chester. Continue on 202 to Route 1 south to Longwood Gardens.

Total distance: 120 miles.

ACCOMMODATIONS *Duling-Kurtz House,* S. Whitford Road, Exton, 524–1830, charming inn, $$$–$$$$ CP ● *Fairville Inn,* Route 52, Mendenhall, 388–5900, country antiques, canopy beds, $$–$$$$ CP and afternoon tea ● *Sweetwater Farm,* Box 86, Glen Mills, 459–4711, a warm and gracious country retreat, $$$–$$$$ CP ● The other choices are motels: *West Chester Inn,* Route 202, West Chester, 692–1900, motel, but a nice one, $$; *Chadds Ford Ramada Inn,* Routes 1 and 202, Glen Mills, 358–1700, $$; *Mendenhall Inn,* Kennett Pike (Route 52), Mendenhall, 388–1181, $–$$; *Longwood Inn,* Route 1, Kennett Square, 444–3515, $–$$.

DINING All of the following are attractive old country inns; pick one that is convenient and phone for exact driving directions ● *Chadds Ford Inn,* Route 1, Chadds Ford, 388–7361, $$ ● *Mendenhall Inn* (see above), $$–$$$ ● *Coventry Forge Inn,* Route 23, Coventryville, 469–6222, worth a drive for classic French food in a pre-Revolutionary house, $$$–$$$$, prix fixe Saturdays, $$$$ ● *Historic Dilworthtown Inn,* Old Wilmington Pike and Brinton Bridge Road, Dilworthtown (south of West Chester), 399–1390, $$–$$$ ● *Historic General Warren Inne,* Old Lancaster Avenue, Malvern, 296–3637, $$$ ● *Marshalton Inn,* 1300 West Strasburg Road (Route 162), Marshalton, 692–4367, $$–$$$ ● Other choices: *La Cocotte,* 124 West Gay Street, West Chester, 436–6722, French local favorite, $$; *Pace One,* Thornton-Concord Road, Thornton, 459–9784, restored barn, good for Sunday brunch, $; dinner, $$–$$$; *Vickers,* Welch Pool Road and Gordon Drive, Lionville, 363–7998, gourmet dining in a former underground railroad station, $$–$$$.

SIGHTSEEING *Chester County Day,* tickets, $12 (no children under 12); bus tours from Chester County Hospital beginning at 9 A.M. (first two buses depart for the hunt), $17; tickets include slide show previews. For information, tickets, copy of *Chester County Day* advance newspaper, write *Chester County Day,* PO Box 1, West Chester, PA 19280 ● *Longwood Gardens,* US 1, Kennett Square, 388–6741. Hours: April to October, daily 9 A.M. to 6 P.M.; rest of year to 5 P.M.; conservatories 10 A.M. to 5 P.M. Adults, $5; children 6–14, $1 ● *Brandywine River Museum,* US 1, Chadds Ford, 388–7601. Hours: daily 9:30 A.M. to 4:30 P.M. Adults, $3; children 7–12, $1.50 ● *Brandywine Battlefield Park,* US 1, Chadds Ford, 459–3342.

Hours: Tuesday to Saturday 9 A.M. to 5 P.M.; Sunday noon to 5 P.M. Adults, $1; children, $.50 ● *Phillips Mushroom Place,* US 1, Kennett Square, 388–6082. Hours: daily 10 A.M. to 6 P.M. Free ● *Valley Forge National Historical Park,* near Pennsylvania Turnpike, exit 24, 783–7700. Hours: daily 8:30 A.M. to 5 P.M. Park is free, fee for guided bus tours ● *Chester County Historical Society,* 225 North High Street, 692–4800. Hours: Tuesday, Thursday, Friday, and Saturday, 10 A.M. to 4 P.M.; Wednesday, 1 P.M. to 8 P.M. Adults, $2; children, $.50.

FOR FURTHER INFORMATION Chester County Tourist Promotion Bureau, 117 West Gay Street, West Chester, PA 19380, 431–6365.

Fairs, Festivals, and Big Apples in the Nutmeg State

There was music coming from a carousel on the midway, an oxen draw scheduled at one, a corn-husking contest at two, and a wild west show about to begin.

But for one towheaded four-year-old named Billy, it was all an anticlimax. The highlight of his day had been a new acquaintance named Elsie. She was the first cow he had ever seen outside a storybook.

From July to October country fairs are in high gear all over the state of Connecticut, a harvest ritual that gives farmers a showcase for their crops and livestock, homemakers a place to exhibit their prize baking and canning, and everyone the opportunity for some old-fashioned fun.

For many a suburban or city parent, however, the best show of all is watching youngsters like Billy wide-eyed at their first sight of real, live farm animals.

A self-addressed stamped envelope will get you a full listing of current dates and times of fairs in the Nutmeg State from the Association of Connecticut Fairs.

Often the last fairs of the season offer a bonus since they are strategically located in scenic central and northwestern parts of the state that offer fine foliage as well as other special fall pleasures—hayrides, harvest festivals, apple picking, and a dazzling display of thousands of chrysanthemums in bloom.

Fairs are usually scheduled in late September and early October for the towns of Durham, Berlin, Harwinton, and Riverton. Each one offers its own attractions. Durham may present arts and crafts and antiques along with top-name country music acts. There will probably be nail-driving, wood-chopping, and corn-husking contests; a frog jump; and a turtle race in Berlin. Harwinton has featured an early America display with demonstrations of old-time crafts and a country store, while Riverton, the smallest of the fairs, offers competitions in sawing and chopping as well as a pie-eating contest. Exact events may change, but the general pattern does not.

Whichever fair you choose you'll see fine specimens of sheep, goats, poultry, rabbits, pigs, and other livestock competing for blue ribbons, as well as prize crops, cooking, and baking, and such down-home competitions as horse, oxen, and tractor pulls. All the fairs offer entertainment as well.

And wherever you attend, you'll be within a short drive of Bristol, where there are some prime attractions. Bristol Nurseries, which has been described as the Disneyworld of the plant world, puts on an eye-boggling show each year during chrysanthemum season, with more than 80,000 specimens of mums, button-size to giant pompons, in an autumn rainbow of golds, bronzes, yellows, whites, and purples of every hue. Bring plenty of color film.

The whole town gets into the spirit of things with a chrysanthemum festival in late September, featuring an art show, a parade, and a Mum Ball crowning each season's queen.

While you're in Bristol have a look at the American Clock and Watch Museum, one of the few of its kind in the country. There are more than 1,600 timekeeping exhibits, some dating as far back as 1680, many of the pieces manufactured in Connecticut.

Not far away in Terryville, you can sample another kind of fall country tradition, a hayride. Just climb aboard with Ken Wood of Wood Acres, and you'll go lumbering off for an hour's drive through the woods, ensconced in a wagon piled high with sweet-smelling hay and pulled by a picture-book pair of giant dapple gray Percheron horses.

A few miles farther west is Litchfield, one of the state's oldest and loveliest towns, with a wide stately main street of 1700s Colonial mansions that rightfully ranks as one of the region's most beautiful. It's at its best in fall dress and definitely rates a detour. Here you can also visit the nation's first law school, the Tapping Reeve House.

If the Riverton Fair is your destination, be sure to stop at the Hitchcock Museum to see examples of the famous nineteenth-century chairs. The present Hitchcock factory here maintains many of the old handmade procedures and has a showroom and gift shop open to the public. Note that museum and factory are both closed on Sundays after October. There's also a Seth Thomas clock outlet store here, and other pleasant shops.

Fair or not, foliage watchers will want to head to Riverton for a drive through the People's State Forest nearby, a ride made even more beautiful by the reflected colors in the sparkling reservoir running beside the road. There are several scenic stop-offs on the forest road, many of them with picnic areas.

Finally, if your outing includes the first two weeks of October, you'll find the annual Apple Harvest Festival in full swing around the village green in Southington, an easy stop-off on your way home.

Pie-eating contests and apple-bobbing competitions are the order of the day along with a "Just Mutts" dog show, and an old-time parade, and all kinds of races, including the wild and wooly "bed race," in which cribs, four-posters, and brass bedsteads come careening down-hill to the delight of cheering spectators.

All through the festival an arts and crafts fair is open, and food stands offer pies, fritters, fried apple rings, caramel apples, cider, and just about everything having to do with fall's favorite crop. There's another way to get a lofty perspective of the festival and the fall foliage in Southington, via New England Hot Air Balloons. They'll take you up early morning or late afternoon any day when the wind is right. Phone ahead if you are interested.

If all the festivities inspire you to want to do some apple picking on your own, there are orchards where you are invited to do just that: in Cheshire, not far south on Route 10; in Wallingford, off Route 91; and in Middlefield, north of Durham on Route 157. A call ahead to the orchards is advisable, just to make sure the pick-them-yourself policy is still in effect.

As for the apple festival, it's all authentic small-town Americana, unsophisticated fun for everyone, and as traditional as—you guessed it—apple pie.

Connecticut Area Code: 203

DRIVING DIRECTIONS Take I-95, New England Thruway. For Durham, get off at exit 48, take the I-91 connection at New Haven then follow I-91 to exit 15, Route 68 east. For Berlin, from I-91 take Routes 5 and 15, Berlin Turnpike, at Meriden. For Harwinton and Riverton, get off I-95 at Route 8 (exit 27), just past Bridgeport. Harwinton is east of Route 8 on Route 118; Riverton is farther north and also east on Route 20.

Total distance: about 110 miles.

ACCOMMODATIONS *Yale Inn,* 900 East Main Street, Meriden (at junction of Route 15 and I-91; I-91 exit 16 or 17), 238–1211, convenient for Durham or Southington, $$ ● *Hawthorne Motor Inn,* 2387 Wilbur Cross Highway (Route 15), Berlin, 828–4181, $$ ● *Old Riverton Inn,* Route 20, Riverton, 379–8678, $$ with breakfast ● *Yankee Pedlar Inn,* 93 Main Street, Torrington (off Route 8), 489–9226, convenient for Harwinton, $$ ● *Chimney Crest Manor,* 5 Founders Drive, Bristol, 582–4219, a bed-and-breakfast that is truly a baronial manor, $$ CP ● *Highland Farm,* Highland Avenue, New Hartford, 379–6029, pretty Victorian in the country, $$–$$$ CP ● *Cobble Hill Farm Inn,* Steele Road, New Hartford, a real charmer on 22 acres with a pond, 379–0057, $$$ CP (with a big farm breakfast).

DINING *Yankee Pedlar Inn* (see above), $–$$ ● *Old Riverton Inn* (see above), $–$$ ● *Hawthorne Motor Inn* (see above), $–$$ ● *The Tributary,* 19 Rowley Street, Winsted, 379–7679, pleasant and unpretentious, $$ (See also Litchfield and inns at Lake Waramaug, page 67.)

SIGHTSEEING *Country Fairs.* For free listing of fairs, dates, events, and admission fees, call the Connecticut Department of Economic Development, toll-free (800) 243–1685, for the current address of the Association of Connecticut Fairs (the chairman changes annually). Enclose a self-addressed stamped legal-size envelope when you write to the Association ● *American Clock and Watch Museum,* 100 Maple Street, off Route 6, Bristol, 583–6070. Hours: April to October, daily 11 A.M. to 5 P.M. Adults, $2.50; children 8–15, $1.25; under 8 free ● *Tapping Reeve House and Law School,* South Street (Route 63), Litchfield, 567–8919. Hours: mid-May to mid-October, Tuesday to Saturday 11 A.M. to 5 P.M. Adults, $1; children free ● *Hitchcock Museum,* Route 20, Riverton, 379–1003. Hours: June to October, Wednesday to Saturday 11 A.M. to 4 P.M., Sunday 1 P.M. to 4 P.M.; November through May, Saturdays only ● *Hayrides,* Ken Wood, Wood Acres, Terryville, 583–8670. Phone in advance for rates, reservations, and driving directions ● *Apple Orchards.* Phone to confirm information before you go: Drazen Orchards, 241 Wallingford Road, Cheshire, 272–7985; Hickory Hill Orchard, 351 South Meriden Road, Cheshire, 272–3824; Lyman Farms, junction of Routes 147 and 157, Middlefield, 349–9337; Young and Sons, Inc., 22 South Branford Road, Wallingford, 269–3865 ● *Southington Apple Harvest Fes-*

tival. Contact Greater Southington Chamber of Commerce, 7 North Main Street, Southington, CT 06489, 628–8036, for current festival information and dates ● *New England Hot Air Balloons*, PO Box 706, Southington, 621–6061 ● *Bristol Chrysanthemum Festival*, call 589–4111 for information and dates.

Family Foliage Parade to West Point and Museum Village

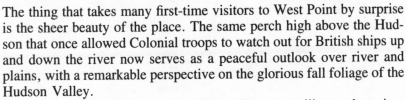

The thing that takes many first-time visitors to West Point by surprise is the sheer beauty of the place. The same perch high above the Hudson that once allowed Colonial troops to watch out for British ships up and down the river now serves as a peaceful outlook over river and plains, with a remarkable perspective on the glorious fall foliage of the Hudson Valley.

For many who don't consider themselves pro-military, there is a second surprise in the impressiveness of the stone buildings and the contagious pride you sense in the young cadets who are continuing the "long gray line" of patriots who marched here before them.

As a result, lots of parents who come to the U.S. Military Academy primarily for the kids wind up loving the place themselves, particularly if they are able to make it on a football weekend, when the cadets are out for a full-dress parade.

Football or not, a day at West Point, combined with a Sunday visit to the old-time craftsmen at Orange County's excellent Museum Village at Monroe, is an ideal itinerary for fall family foliage watching— maximum scenery for the front seat, with minimum driving to inspire complaints from the back.

A phone call to the Academy Information Center of Public Affairs office will give you an up-to-date schedule of games, ticket information, and news of any other special events around the time you plan to visit. Even if you are able to get tickets to a game, you may have trouble finding a motel room nearby. But since the drive is short and scenic, it is easy enough to start from home Saturday morning and move out of the area for the night. You can see the cadet parade whether you see the game or not, and if you bring along a picnic lunch, the day at West Point won't cost you a cent. All the sites are free to visitors.

First stop at the Academy is the Visitor Information Office just inside Thayer Gate. A movie on West Point is shown here hourly, and they'll give you a self-guided tour map, schedule of the day, and any other data you might like before you set out.

The tour takes you toward Michie (pronounced *my*-key) Stadium and the parking fields nearest Fort Putnam. It's an uphill path to the fort, so wear your best walking shoes. The fortress includes a small museum and gives you some idea of a soldier's living conditions during the time of the American Revolution, as well as a splendid view of West Point and the river.

Mill Road leads on past the magnificent Gothic Cadet Chapel, which has outstanding stained-glass windows and the largest church organ in the world (18,000 pipes), and farther on past the gracious nineteenth-century homes of the superintendent and the commandant, facing the parade grounds known as The Plain.

Among the roster of cadets who have marched here are Presidents Ulysses S. Grant and Dwight D. Eisenhower; Jefferson Davis; General George Armstrong Custer; and Edward White, the first astronaut to walk in space. Major General George W. Goethals, who designed the Panama Canal, was another West Point alumnus, as was Abner Doubleday, a Union commander in the Civil War who is far better known as the inventor of baseball.

A tip: If you plan to see a parade, arrive at The Plain early for good viewing and for a parking space in the lots nearby.

Trophy Point is a special favorite spot for most young children, who love clambering over the cannons. Among the many relics on display at the point overlooking the river are links from the giant chain that was once stretched across the Hudson from West Point to Constitution Island to block the progress of the British fleet. The links weigh 300 pounds apiece.

A statue of the Polish soldier, Thaddeus Kosciuszko, who masterminded this blockade strategy, is elsewhere on the grounds. The battle monument at Trophy Point is dedicated to the men who were killed in the Civil War.

The West Point Museum in Thayer Academic Hall is one of the largest collections of military history in the Western hemisphere. It is a two-story panorama of the art of war from prehistory through Vietnam, and includes models of famous battles and a re-creation of the Civil War Shenandoah Valley campaign of 1862, spearheaded by another West Point graduate, Thomas J. "Stonewall" Jackson.

There's even more to see at the Academy. In the Post Cemetery is the Old Cadet Chapel, with walls lined with battle flags, and marble shields commemorating the American generals of the Revolutionary War. One shield bears only a date and no name; it belonged to Benedict Arnold, who tried to betray the fort to the British when he was in command of his post in 1780. Some other remaining sights are the Chapel of the Most Holy Trinity, a Catholic church in Norman Gothic style patterned after an abbey church in England, and Fort Clinton, another Revolutionary War station. And you might enjoy dropping into Grant Hall, where the cadets gather in their free time.

There are designated picnic sites overlooking the river, just north of the public dock where the Hudson Dayliner pulls in. Recently the Dayliner and other cruise lines have been offering mini-cruises from West Point, a fine way to get a river's-eye view of the foliage.

The only other place to eat on the grounds is the Hotel Thayer, which is used by visiting families of cadets. It's a fine place to stay if you can get in, as well as a reasonable choice for a family dinner. If you want fast food establishments or an ice cream parlor, you'll find them in Highland Falls outside the gate, and there are also places here that will prepare a picnic for you if you haven't brought one from home.

If you can't get a room at the Thayer or in Highland Falls, the pleasant rustic Bear Mountain Inn is just a few miles away. And there are a few winning small inns in Cold Spring, a burgeoning antiquer's mecca just across the Hudson. Otherwise your best bet is Newburgh, which itself is a historic town with many Revolutionary War sites. Two of the principal ones are the Jonathan Hasbrouck house on Liberty Street, Washington's final headquarters during the war, and the New Windsor Cantonment off Route 32, a reconstruction of the last American encampment, which also has the only surviving log structure actually built by the troops.

Sunday drive farther south on Route 87 and turn west on Route 17 to exit 129 and the Museum Village of Orange County. This is one of the country's largest outdoor museums, with more than 30 buildings telling the story of the making of crafts in nineteenth-century America, from handwork to the beginnings of modern technology. It offers an interesting and entertaining bit of history with demonstrations of pottery and broom-making, weaving, blacksmithing, printing, and other trades and crafts. Among the buildings you can tour are a one-room school, a general store, a blacksmith's shop, an apothecary, and a log cabin. On October weekends you'll see special demonstrations of "putting by for winter," autumn chores such as grinding and drying corn, preserving, cidering, and other typical activities on a farm in the fall season 150 years ago. There is a snack bar on the museum grounds and, once again, picnic facilities.

From here it's a short drive to county Route 12 and Sugar Loaf, a village full of crafts shops where you can watch latter-day artisans at work and possibly pick up an original souvenir of your trip.

Sugar Loaf makes for a pleasant transition back to the present, and you may still have enough light to get in some last foliage watching as you connect back to Route 17 and an easy drive home.

West Point Area Code: 914

DRIVING DIRECTIONS George Washington Bridge to Palisades Interstate Parkway to Bear Mountain Circle (end of parkway); then Route 9W north, following signs to Highland Falls and West Point. *Total distance:* 50 miles.

ACCOMMODATIONS *Hotel Thayer,* U.S. Military Academy grounds, West Point, 446–4731, $–$$ • *Palisades Motel,* Route 218 off 9W, Highland Falls, 446–9400, $ • *West Point Motel,* 361 Main Street, Highland Falls, 446–8726, $–$$ • *Howard Johnson's Motor Lodge,* Route 17K at Thruway, Newburgh, 564–4000, $$–$$$ • *Holiday Inn,* Route 17K at Thruway, Newburgh, 565–2100, $$ • *Bear Mountain Inn,* Bear Mountain State Park, 786–2731, $$ • *Hudson House,* 2 Main Street, Cold Spring, 265–9355, country inn near the river, $$$ • *Pig Hill Bed & Breakfast,* 73 Main Street, Cold Spring, 265–9247, charming B&B/antiques shop—if you like your furniture, you can buy it! $$$–$$$$ • *Plumbush,* Route 9D, Cold Spring, 265–2633, Victorian estate, $$$–$$$$.

DINING *Hotel Thayer* (see above), $–$$ • *Bear Mountain Inn* (see above), $$–$$$; Sunday buffet, $$ • *Banta's Steak & Stein,* Union Avenue, New Windsor, 564–7678, salad bar, children's plates, $–$$$ • *Brewster House,* 1762 Temple Hill Road, New Windsor, 561–1762, $ • *Chianti Restaurant,* 362 Broadway, Newburgh, 561–3103, $–$$ • *Painter's Tavern,* Route 218 on the village square, Cornwall-on-Hudson, 534–2109, $–$$ • *Gasho of Japan,* Route 32, Central Valley (near Monroe), 928–2277, cooking at your table, $$ • *Barnsider Tavern,* Kings Highway, Sugar Loaf, 469–9810, warm, rustic, $ • The following are well recommended dining places on the east side of the Hudson; note that a couple may be pricey for family dining: *Hudson House* (see above), $$–$$$; *Plumbush* (see above), $$$–$$$$; *Xavier's,* Highlands Country Club, Route 9D, Garrison, 424–4228, elegant, $$$; *Dutchess Manor,* Route 9D, Beacon, 831–3650, Hudson views, continental menu, $$–$$$

SIGHTSEEING *U.S. Military Academy.* Information center just inside Thayer Gate, 938–2638. Hours: daily 8:30 A.M. to 4:15 P.M.

Phone for parade schedules and other information. *West Point Museum*, daily 10:30 A.M. to 4:15 P.M.; *Chapel*, daily 8:30 A.M. to 4:15 P.M. except Sunday from 1 P.M.; *Fort Putnam*, late May to early November, daily 10:30 A.M. to 4 P.M. All free ● *Museum Village in Orange County*, Museum Village Road, NY 17M, US 6 (New York 17, exit 129). Hours: April 15 to October, daily 10 A.M. to 5 P.M. Adults, $4.75; children 6–15, $2.75 ● *Hasbrouck House Washington's Headquarters State Historic Site*, 84 Liberty Street, Newburgh, 562–2295. Hours: April to December, Wednesday to Saturday 10 A.M. to 5 P.M., Sunday from 1 P.M. Free ● *New Windsor Cantonment State Historic Site*, Temple Hill Road, Newburgh, 561–1765. Hours: April to late October, Wednesday to Saturday 10 A.M. to 5 P.M., Sunday from 1 P.M. Free ● Hudson River Cruise information: Dayliner (212) 279–5151; Hudson Highlands Cruises, 446–7171; Rip Van Winkle Cruises, 255–6515.

A Taste for History in the Tobacco Valley

The oldest house in the oldest town in Connecticut has a colorful gallery of ghosts in its past—and a guide who delights in telling about them.

"Here's the happy couple," she began, pointing to dour-faced portraits of Lieutenant and Mrs. Fyler, the home's original owners. "And here's the cupboard where they hid the brooze when the parson came to call."

The woman's lively commentary proved an appropriate introduction to Windsor and Connecticut's "Tobacco Valley," an area that seems to relish its history. Named for its best-known farm crop, this area just north of Hartford has the look of old New England and more than its share of sightseeing variety. In the peaceful little towns within the valley you can prowl the passages of a notorious underground prison or have a look at aviation history. The nearby Farmington River Valley adds some appealing lodging and good dining to the agenda. A bonus is a ride through the scenic woodlands of the state-maintained People's Forest.

A good place to begin your tour is Windsor, a town that was already 140 years old when the Declaration of Independence was signed in 1776. Windsor's historic district still boasts its village green, a 1630 white-steepled church, the original town burying ground, and about three dozen houses built before the Revolutionary War. Six of the houses date to the 1600s. Almost all are still occupied.

Open to visitors is the Oliver Ellsworth Homestead, the elegant Colonial home of the nation's third chief justice. Fyler House, the oldest of the houses, has been meticulously cared for and filled with furnishings that reflect its rich history as a home, a shop, and the town post office. Adjacent Wilson Museum displays more mementos of the town's past. If you're lucky you'll get the guide who'll fill you in on the juicier details.

Windsor is also the heart of the tobacco-farming area that gave the valley its name. Connecticut Shade Grown Tobacco was known through the world as the finest wrapper leaves available for fine cigars. Many of the farms are disappearing as the land gives way to development, but so far, at Kendrick Brothers Farm off Poquonock Road, you can still see the tobacco growing under netting on a family-run farm that has been in continuous operation since 1635.

Head north on Palisado Avenue, Windsor's main street, and you'll get yourself right back to US 91. Head north and take the exit for Route 20 to East Granby, where you'll come upon one of the most unusual of our national historic landmarks, the Old New Gate Prison and Copper Mine. First chartered as a mine in 1707, it was converted into a prison in 1773, designated as a place of confinement for burglars, horse thieves, robbers, and counterfeiters. During the Revolution it was used for Tories and prisoners of war. During its 42-year history as a prison, more than 800 prisoners were committed to New Gate's underground cells.

Today you can go down into the mine for a well-lit, self-guided tour of the winding passages where the prisoners lived in total darkness. Bring a sweater—mine temperatures can be in the mid-forties even on a sunny day.

Plane buffs will want to detour here on Route 75 near Bradley Airport in Windsor Locks, where the New England Air Museum displays some 75 historic aircraft, including a 1911 Bleriot, a World War II "Warbird," and the actual plane used in Clark Gable's 1938 movie, *Test Pilot*. You can also try out an authentic training cockpit simulator and see the prizewinning film, *To Fly*.

Continue from here south on Route 202 to Simsbury, in the Farmington River Valley, where some of the earliest coins minted in the original Granby mines are on display at Massacoh Plantation. This 22-acre site traces 3 centuries of Simsbury history. On the grounds are a Victorian carriage house, manufacturing exhibits, a sleigh shed, a one-room schoolhouse, an icehouse, and a seventeenth-century meetinghouse. One of the favorite exhibits is a Yankee peddler's wagon, loaded with gewgaws and knickknacks.

Massacoh's Phelps House is one of the finest remaining examples of an old Connecticut tavern. Be sure to note the narrow lighted cupboard over the mantel. It is a rarity that is believed to have been built by a retired shipwright since it is reminiscent of a sailing ship's forecastle. Look carefully and you'll see that the paneling in the tavern room includes witches' crosses meant to keep evil spirits away while the men enjoyed their liquid spirits.

Simsbury, with its wide, tree-shaded main street, is one of the valley's most charming villages, and has the area's loveliest inn. It's also an ideal place for browsing. Simsburytown Shops is a complex of boutiques featuring everything from cookery to Indian jewelry to homemade pâté. The Ellsworth Art Gallery at Massacoh Plantation has contemporary art of high quality.

The Gallery on the Green in nearby Canton, operated by the local Artists' Guild, is another good place to see changing art exhibits in two galleries. Canton offers a cache of antiques shops as well.

A few miles south in Avon, the Farmington Valley Arts Center on Route 44 is also a pleasant browsing spot, a collection of artists' studios and a gallery housed in a historic stone building that was once an explosives plant.

Finally, for fall foliage watching, take Route 44 west out of Avon, turn right at Route 318 past New Hartford, and watch for the road that takes you through the People's State Forest and eventually to Riverton. It's a drive made even more beautiful by the reflections in the sparkling reservoir that runs beside the road, and there are several scenic stopoffs along the way to let you enjoy the view, many with picnic areas.

To end the day with a last look at the colorful Connecticut hills, take Route 20 west out of Riverton and connect with Route 8 south. You'll enjoy panoramic vistas almost all the way back to the junction of Merritt Parkway before Bridgeport.

Connecticut Area Code: 203

DRIVING DIRECTIONS Hutchinson River Parkway to the Merritt Parkway to I-91. Take exit 37, Route 305, to Windsor. Bear left onto Route 159 across the Farmington River into the historic district.
Total distance: About 123 miles.

ACCOMMODATIONS *Sheraton Tobacco Valley Inn,* 450 Bloomfield Avenue (at I-91, exit 37, Route 305), Windsor, 688–5221, motel, $$–$$$, weekend packages available • *Simsbury House*, 731 Hopmeadow Street, Simsbury, 658–7658, beautifully restored, elegant 1820 Colonial, $$$–$$$$ CP • *Executive Inn*, 969 Hopmeadow Street, Simsbury, motel, 658–2216, $$ • *Avon Old Farms Hotel*, Routes 44 and 10, Avon, 677–1651, five Colonial rooms in 1757 inn, another 44 in motel units, $$–$$$.

DINING   *Dunfey's Tavern*, Sheraton Tobacco Valley Inn (see above), Colonial style, new but with charm, $$–$$$ • *Simsbury House* (see above), really fine continental fare, $$$ • *Hop Brook*, 77 West Street, Simsbury, 651–1118, gristmill overlooking pond, $$–$$$ • *Chart House*, 4 Hartford Road, Simsbury, 658–1118, former 1780 tavern, $$–$$$ • *Avon Old Farms Inn* (see above), 677–2818, $$–$$$.

SIGHTSEEING   *New England Air Museum*, Route 75 at Bradley International Airport, Windsor Locks, 623–3305. Hours: daily 10 AM. to 5 P.M. Adults, $5; children 6–11, $2 • *Fyler House and Wilson Museum*, 96 Palisado Avenue, Windsor, 688–3813. Hours: April to November, Tuesday to Saturday 10 A.M. to noon and 1 P.M. to 4 P.M. Adults, $1; children under 12 free • *Oliver Ellsworth Homestead*, 778 Palisado Avenue, Windsor, 688–8717. Hours: May to October, Tuesday to Saturday 1 P.M. to 5 P.M. Adults, $2; children under 12 free • *Old New Gate Prison*, Newgate Road, East Granby, 566–3005. Hours: mid-May to October, daily 10 A.M. to 4:30 P.M. Adults, $1.75; children 6–17, $.75; under 6 free • *Massacoh Plantation*, 800 Hopmeadow Street, Simsbury, 658–2500. Hours: May to October, daily 1 P.M. to 4 P.M. Adults, $3; children under 17, $1.50.

Year-round Color in Pennsylvania Dutch Country

It may be at its scenic best against a backdrop of autumn foliage, but there's plenty of color left even after the leaves fall in Pennsylvania Dutch country.

Picture-book farms, bright hex signs, windmills, and covered bridges dot the landscape. You'll still find yourself sharing the roads with black-frocked men and bonneted women driving shiny horse-and-buggy rigs into town. And the auctions, the farmer's markets, and the colorful shops await anytime you visit this unique corner of America.

The large number of people who do want to visit, however, have spawned a bit of a paradox. While the area is filled with touristy gift shops and tourist-oriented re-creations of Amish villages and farms, the most interesting sights by far are the real thing. Don't waste your time, which will seem short enough anyway; pick the most authentic of the attractions vying for your attention.

A good start might be a reservation for a room on a Mennonite farm. Or you might pick your lodging according to the location, since some of the towns are much more appealing and less touristy than others. One very pleasant stop is Lititz (accent on the first syllable), seven miles north of Lancaster, one of the most carefully preserved towns in Lancaster County and one with a special flavor from its Moravian origins. A walk down Main Street in Lititz takes you past more than a dozen homes dating to the mid-1700s, and the brick and stucco buildings of the Moravian Church Square, which include the church itself and the old Brethren's and Sister's Houses.

At 221 Main Street you can visit the Pretzel House, where owner Julius Sturgis made the first commercial pretzels in the United States in an adjoining bakery. (You'll have a chance to try your own hand at fancy twisting.) The Museum-House of Johannes Mueller at 137 Main is virtually unchanged since Mr. Mueller lived there in 1792.

The delicious aroma that hangs over Lititz is from Wilbur's Chocolate Factory, where you are invited in to see displays of historical candymaking equipment.

Having savored the peaceful small-town flavor of Lititz, move on to the city of Lancaster and one of its famous farmer's markets. Awaiting you there are potpourris of fresh fruit and vegetables; savory homemade bologna, sausage, and scrapple; and home-baked pies, cakes, and cookies, as delicious to the eye and nose as to the tummy.

Lancaster, America's largest inland Colonial town, could easily fill up a day on its own. Among the many things to do and see in town are the historic walking tour led by costumed guides; Wheatland, the beautifully preserved home of President James Buchanan; the Heritage Center of Lancaster County in the Old City Hall; Rock Ford and the Kaufman Museum (home of a Revolutionary War commander and a barn containing collections of rifles and folk artifacts); and the Community Art Gallery. Nearby, too, are the largest collection of timepieces anywhere at the National Association of Watch and Clock Collectors Museum in Columbia, and a Railroad Museum plus rides on a huffy-puffy old-fashioned steam train at the Strasburg Railroad.

Strasburg is another special little town, a railroading mecca with a selection of lodgings, including the chance to spend the night in a comfortably rigged-out caboose.

But if you have just a two-day weekend, you might do better to settle for the market and concentrate on the small towns and the countryside that are the real heart of Pennsylvania Dutch country.

Begin at the Visitors' Bureau outside Lancaster on Route 30, where you can arm yourself with maps and information and see a 27-minute film to prepare you for the sights ahead. You'll learn that the people of the region are not Dutch but German (*Deutsch* became *Dutch* to the American ear), and that the Amish are only one sect among the "Plain People."

The bearded men you'll spot along the road are all Amish married men, obliged to mark their status by this very visible sign.

It is a firm belief among the "Old Order" of the Amish that duty to God means living simply and tilling the soil. Cars, phones, and electricity are forbidden, not because they are considered evil in themselves, but because they are temptations to a more worldly life. A more liberal sect, called "Church Amish" because they hold services in a church rather than at home, does allow electricity and cars, but only plain black sedans. Mennonites are similar to the Old Order; you can spot their buggies because they are flat-roofed and black, while the Amish vehicles have rounded roofs and are painted gray.

In spite of warnings about some of those tourist attractions, you may well want to make time at this point for one, the Amish Farm and House, a bit farther east on Route 30, simply because it is a chance you might not get otherwise to see the inside of a typical Amish home and a close-up look at a working farm in operation. You'll discover that while their clothes and furnishings are plain, the Amish show their love of beauty indoors through the artistic decorations on the old dower chests, the gaily painted china, and the embroidered towels inside the home.

Finally it's time to get out into the real countryside again, following busy Route 30 through Paradise and wandering along any of the lush, peaceful back roads between Routes 30 and 340 to see the farms. You'll recognize the Amish homesteads by their windmills and lack of electric wires; note also the distinctive additions on some of the farms. Known as "Gross Dawdis," they are an Amish solution to the generation gap. When a farmer reaches retirement age, an annex to the main house is built, allowing him to enjoy the fruits of his labor and still be part of the family group without getting in the way of the younger generation coming up. Sometimes you'll see double additions, marking a three-generation home.

Continue back west on 340 through Intercourse and Bird-in-Hand.

You'll need no guide on any of the main roads to find shops full of hex signs and fudge and every gift imaginable with Pennsylvania Dutch motifs. Some more interesting stops, however, are clustered around Intercourse. The People's Place is a center for Amish and Mennonite arts and crafts. The Quilt Room in the Old Country Store on Main Street has quilts made by local craftswomen, and one-of-a-kind handmade furniture is still turned out at Ebersol's Chair Shop.

There is a regular Saturday Farmer's Market in Bird-in-Hand, and with luck you could also find yourself here for one of the auctions that take place on some Saturdays behind Zimmerman's store. One of the special pleasures of an auction is the possibility of seeing the Amish at close range and hearing their quaint dialects; another is the chance to garner one of those decorated dower chests. Don't expect huge bargains, but you may well pay less than you would outside this area. Auction dates change, so ask at your farm or inn or motel to find out where you are likely to find one in action during your visit.

One last attraction well worth a stop is the excellent state-operated Farm Museum of Landis Valley outside Lancaster. More than 30 buildings here filled with 250,000 items show rural life and the role of agriculture in Pennsylvania history. Four of the buildings are period homes of 150 years ago; others are shops, farms, a school, and a tavern. The annual Harvest Days held here the first weekend of October portray old-fashioned crafts and activities of the season such as apple drying, apple-butter making, and drying and grinding corn.

On Sunday wend your way through the countryside west on Route 772 to 272 to Mennonite country and one of its most interesting settlements, the Cloister, a restored community of a monastic sect founded in 1730. You'll have to duck your head to enter the low doorways (a reminder of humility) and go single-file down the narrow halls (symbols of the straight and narrow path) to see where these dedicated people lived and the narrow wooden ledges where they slept—with eight-inch wooden blocks for pillows. There are eight surviving buildings, evoking an unusually vivid sense of the austere way of life practiced here.

If you choose to stay in this quieter region, Ephrata offers three prime inn choices. From Ephrata, drive north toward Reading, well known for its dozens of outlet stores, and you're on your way to Gay Dutch country, famous for its enormous banked barns decorated with giant versions of those brightly painted geometrical designs known as hex signs. Contrary to the name, the signs have nothing to do with warding off evil and are there only for their color and beauty, or as the Pennsylvania Dutch say, "chust for nice." These are so delightful you may be inspired to buy some miniatures as souvenirs.

Old Route 22, which parallels Route 78, is known as Hex Highway for the large number of barns it passes by. Route 183 from Reading to Bernville and Shartlesville has a few barns along the way, and Shartlesville is your last chance for a real Pennsylvania Dutch meal at Haag's Hotel, which has been serving up groaning tables to tourists for four generations.

An average meal here includes chicken, ham, and beef (all you can eat), lima beans, ceci (chick-peas), dried corn, garden peas, the Pennsylvania Dutch "seven sweets and seven sours," which might include pickled beets, pepper cabbage, olives, pickles, piccalilli, applesauce, dried apricots, and all manner of desserts including home-baked pies such as lemon sponge and that molasses-flavored local delicacy, shoofly pie. If it isn't the best meal you've ever had, it will certainly be one of the biggest.

Continuing west on the Hex Highway to Lenhartsville, you can turn south on 143 and watch for the covered bridge on the left, then make a right to one side road boasting nine barns. If you drive north on 143 you'll come to a bird- and nature-lover's special retreat, Hawk Mountain, the only designated sanctuary for birds of prey, a place to spy eagles and hawks on their migratory patterns in the fall as well as get spectacular views of the entire area spread below.

From either direction you can connect with Route 78 and a direct drive back to New York—which may suddenly seem much farther than a three-hour drive away from the spirit of Pennsylvania Dutch country.

Lancaster Area Code: 717
Reading Area Code: 215

DRIVING DIRECTIONS New Jersey Turnpike to Pennsylvania Turnpike to Route 222, then south to Route 30 into Lancaster; Lititz is seven miles north on Route 501.
Total distance: 159 miles.

ACCOMMODATIONS *General Sutter Inn,* 14 East Main Street, Lititz, 636–2115, small, pleasant, hotel-inn, $$ ● *Historic Strasburg Inn,* Route 896, Strasburg, 687–7691, new despite the name and more motel than inn, but pleasant, $$ ● *Strasburg Village Inn,* 1 West Main Street, Strasburg, 687–0900, restored B&B inn, $$$ CP ● *Red Caboose Motel,* Route 741, Paradise Lane, Strasburg, 687–6646, cute cabooses with surprises such as a TV in the potbellied stove, $ ● *Cameron Estate Inn,* RD 1 Donegal Springs Road, Mount Joy, 653–2048, restored Victorian mansion, one of the area's most elegant lodgings, $$–$$$$ CP • *Donegal Mills Plantation,* Trout Run Road, Mount Joy, 653–2168, rooms in the mansion of a restored mill village, $$–$$$$ CP • *Witmer's Tavern,* 2014 Old Philadelphia Pike, Lancaster, 299–5305, restored 1725 inn, $$ CP • *The Guesthouse at Doneckers,* 322–324 N. State Street, Ephrata, 733–8696, stylishly decorated, $$$–$$$$ CP • *Smithton Inn,* 900 West Main Street, Ephrata, 733–6094, charmer with poster beds, fireplaces, $$–$$$ CP • *Covered Bridge Inn,* 990 Rettew Mill Road, Ephrata, 733–1592, cozy 1814 home, $ CP • Two area resorts with indoor pools, tennis, golf: *Host Farm,* Lincoln Highway East, Lancaster, 299–5500, $$$–$$$$$ MAP (less after October 31), and *Willow Valley Resort,* 2416 Willow Street Pike, Lancaster, 464–2711, $$$. For an extensive list of area motels and farms that accept guests, contact the Pennsylvania Dutch Visitor's Bureau. For a listing of Mennonite farms accepting guests, write to Mennonite Information Center, 2209 Millstream Road, Lancaster, PA 17602, 299–0954.

DINING *General Sutter Inn* (see above), $$ • *Cameron Estate Inn* (see above), $$ • *Groff's Farm,* Pinkerton Road, Mount Joy, 653–2048, noted Pennsylvania Dutch specialties in a farmhouse, $$–$$$ • *Brownstown Restaurant,* Brownstown, 656–9077, authentic Pennsylvania Dutch, $–$$ • *Lemon Tree,* 1766 Columbia Avenue, Lancaster, 394–0441, elegant and excellent, $$–$$$ • *Jethro's,* First and Ruby streets, Lancaster, 299–1700, simple setting, sophisticated menu, $$–$$$ • *Washington House,* Historic Strasburg Inn (see above), $$–$$$ • *Log Cabin,* 11 Lehoy Forest Drive, Leola, 626–1181, delightful wooded setting through a covered bridge, but call for driving instructions! $$–$$$ • *Joe's,* 450 South Seventh Street, Reading, 373–6794, worth a detour into town for this famous wild mushroom cookery, $$$ • *Haag's Hotel,* Main Street, Shartlesville, 488–6692, $.

SIGHTSEEING *Farmer's Markets:* Central Market, Penn Square, Lancaster. Hours: Tuesday and Friday, 6 A.M. to 2 P.M., and Saturday 6 A.M. to 3 P.M. • *Meadowbrook Market,* Route 23, Leola. Hours: Friday 9 A.M. to 8 P.M., Saturday 8 A.M. to 4 P.M. • *Pennsylvania Farm Museum of Landis Valley,* 2451 Kissel Hill Road (off Route 272), Lancaster, 569–0401. Hours: Tuesday to Saturday 9 A.M. to 5 P.M., May to October; Sunday noon to 5 P.M., to 4:30 P.M. in winter. Adults, $3; children 6–18, $1; children under 6 free • *Amish Farm and House,* Route 30 east of Lancaster, 394–6185. Hours: daily 8:30 A.M. to 6 P.M., spring and fall to 5 P.M., winter to 4 P.M. Adults, $3.90; children 6–11, $1.90 • *Sturgis Pretzel House,* 219 East Main, Lititz,

626–4354. Hours: Monday to Saturday 9 A.M. to 5 P.M. Adults, $.75; children 4–12, $.50 ● *Ephrata Cloister,* 632 West Main Street, Ephrata, 733–6600. Hours: April to November, Monday to Saturday 9 A.M. to 5 P.M., Sunday noon to 5 P.M.; rest of year closed Monday. Adults, $2.50; children 6–17, $1; under 6 free ● *Hawk Mountain Sanctuary,* Route 2, Kempton (approach via Route 143), 756–6961. Hours: daily 8 A.M. to 5 P.M. Adults, $2.50; children 6–12, $1.

FOR FURTHER INFORMATION Contact the Pennsylvania Dutch Visitors' Bureau, 501 Greenfield Road, Lancaster, PA 17601, 299–8901.

Winter

Uncovering the Past
in Hartford

At the turn of the century, when upper-middle-class women were expected to stick close to their elegant hearths and homes, Theodate Pope Riddle of Farmington, Connecticut, would have none of it.

The daughter of a multimillionaire industrialist and wife of an ambassador to Russia and Argentina, Ms. Riddle was a trailblazer, studying to become one of the first licensed women architects in the country. She designed several Connecticut schools, but her most notable achievement came at the precocious age of 16 when she helped Stanford White design a home for her parents, a mansion unique because it was deliberately planned to show off the collection of Impressionist art that astute Alfred Atmore Pope acquired before the rest of the world had recognized such talents as Manet, Degas, and Monet.

Twenty major works of art were all that Mr. Pope had room for amid the Empire sofas and four-poster beds, the porcelains, bronzes, and etchings that filled his home; and he made his choices wisely, including two of Monet's haystack paintings, Degas's famous *Dancers* and *Jockeys,* and portraits by James Whistler and Mary Cassatt.

Hill-Stead, as the Mount Vernon–like hilltop mansion was called, is now a public museum, one of the few places where museum-quality art can be seen in a gracious residential setting. This little-heralded art treasure in a Hartford suburb is one of many surprises awaiting visitors to Connecticut's state capital. The nation's oldest statehouse, its first free public art museum, the flamboyant Victorian home of Mark Twain, and the priceless firearms collection of Sam Colt are among many unexpected finds in and around Hartford, hidden from passersby on the whizzing turnpike by the glass-sided mini-skyscrapers that mark America's insurance center.

The first inkling that Hartford is more than insurance companies comes with your very first stop Saturday, at the Old State House housing the city's information center. The 1796 Federal-style masterpiece by Charles Bullfinch sits smack in the middle of those new office towers; it was scheduled for demolition to make way for a parking lot when Hartford's aroused citizens refused to give up this memento of the city's historic past. In the late 1970s they raised $850,000 to give their grande dame a much needed facelift, and another million to ensure its future as a museum. The landscaping was accomplished by cleverly reviving an old Colonial era "viewing tax," a tax on windows that produces an annual voluntary levy of over $8,000 from the businesses surrounding the Old State House, with their total of 2,753 windows.

Now the courtroom and original Senate and House chambers are restored to their former splendor, and visitors to Hartford can tour the architectural landmark where seven former U.S. presidents from Adams to Grant also once paid their respects.

At the visitors' center in the Old State House, you can pick up maps and booklets on the city as well as a self-guided walking tour that offers a quick and easy overview.

First stop, however, should be the Museum of Connecticut History, since it closes for the weekend at 1 P.M. on Saturday. The Colt collection of guns here is recognized as one of the finest collections of firearms anywhere. The 1,000 guns tell the long history of the company that Sam Colt founded in 1836 and moved to his native Hartford in 1847. By 1855 he had the world's largest private armory, and Colt revolvers were known the world over. The guns on display range from Wyatt Earp's six-shooter, to Colt's then-revolutionary Gatling machine guns, to the M2 and M3 aircraft guns. In a curious way the guns are markers of the nation's history.

The fascinating small museum also has a fine collection of timepieces by early Connecticut clockmakers; much early industrial memorabilia such as the 1877 Selden, one of the earliest automobiles; and many historical documents, including the charter once hidden in the state's fabled Charter Oak.

Across the street, on a knoll dominating the city's 41-acre Bushnell Park, is the gold-domed state capitol building. Its Moorish interior is open to the public only on weekdays, but the exterior deserves more than a passing glance. The complex architectural style offers everything from Gothic spires to classical arcades, and many fine statues decorate the facade, depicting allegorical figures as well as some of the state's early heroes.

Bushnell Park's other pride is its meticulously restored 1914 carousel, a favorite of Hartford youngsters in the summertime.

With the state museum taken care of and your walking tour firmly in hand, you're now prepared to explore the curious mix of old and new that marks downtown Hartford. You'll see, for example, the white steeple of Center Church, circa 1807, reflected in the gold-mirrored walls of the Bushnell Tower, designed by I. M. Pei in 1969. View one of the earliest successful urban renewal efforts at Constitution Plaza, as well as one of the city's oldest homes at 396 Main Street. The 1782 Butler-McCook Homestead is well worth a stop, particularly interesting because it was occupied by one family for four generations until 1971. Their furnishings reflect the changes in style from Windsor and Queen Anne through Empire and Victorian.

Another special stop is the Wadsworth Atheneum on Main Street. America's first free public art museum, established in 1842, is now four buildings and a sculpture court and includes major work from every period, including modern paintings by Picasso, Monet, Andrew Wyeth, and Hartford-born Frederick Church. Outside the museum, Alexander Calder's soaring stabile *Stegosaurus* straddles Burr Mall.

A more controversial outdoor sculpture is the Stone Field on Gold Street, 36 glacial boulders ranging in weight from 1,000 pounds to 11 tons. Sculptor Carl Andre received $87,000 for this rock collection, which may or may not be a work of art, depending on whom you ask.

Two other major sights of the city are Union Place, renovated by ambitious shopkeepers and the city, which helped recycle the century-old train station; and the Hartford Civic Center, a combination shopping mall, hotel, convention center, and coliseum.

Come Saturday night, you may want to visit the Hartford Stage Company, a first-rate regional theater, see the Hartford Whalers, the city's National Hockey League entry, or take in the action at jai alai. You could also check the newspaper for concerts or special events at Bushnell Auditorium or on the campus of Trinity College. Some of the local spots for jazz, rock, and country music include 36 Lewis Street, The Russian Lady, and Sean Patrick's.

Sleep late on Sunday, fortify yourself with a hearty brunch, and head for Hartford's major literary landmark, Nook Farm. This Victorian enclave, settled during the second half of the nineteenth century, was a colony populated by prominent actors, editors, and celebrities of the day. Among them were Harriet Beecher Stowe and Samuel Clemens, better known as Mark Twain. Their restored homes and two former carriage houses preserve an important portion of this unusual neighborhood. The Stowe House is a simple cottage furnished with many of its original pieces and decorated with the delicate watercolors the author produced between books.

The Clemens household, however, is quite a different affair, built in 1874 for the then-princely sum of $130,000. It is a showplace with its carved mantels, goldleaf wallpapers, inlaid mahogany furniture, and decorative work by the likes of Louis Comfort Tiffany. The Twain humor is evident, however, in touches like the optical illusion fireplace, and the cigar, pipe, and billiard cue ceiling decor of the third-floor study. The story goes that Clemens gave up his second-floor study because his children were too noisy to suit him, and retired upstairs, where he wrote his masterpieces with a billard table at his side.

The billiard room leads to two balconies, one of which Clemens called the Texas Deck because it reminded him of the uppermost deck of a riverboat steamer. Clemens himself once described his home as part steamboat, part medieval stronghold, and park cuckoo clock.

From Nook Farm, continue west down Farmington Avenue and you'll soon arrive at Farmington. This town contains more than 100 houses built prior to 1835, and most of the original village is a state historic district. You may want to make your first stop a look at the Stanley Whitman House, a gracious seventeenth-century New England home full of furnishings and other artifacts of earlier days. Then you've saved the best for last, a visit to Ms. Riddle's regal Hill-Stead. The last tour begins at 4 P.M.

Hartford Area Code: 203

DRIVING DIRECTIONS The quickest way is to follow the New England Thruway (I-95) into Connecticut to New Haven, then connect with I-91 straight to Hartford. The more scenic route follows the Hutchinson River Parkway into the Merritt Parkway, making the I-91 connection just before Wallingford. In daylight, the Merritt is well worth an extra few minutes. Take the Hartford exit marked CAPITAL DISTRICT.

Total distance: 113 miles.

PUBLIC TRANSPORTATION Amtrak serves Hartford from New York's Penn Station. Most of the city sights are walkable from downtown hotels in decent weather. Take a cab to reach Nook Farm.

ACCOMMODATIONS Plenty of center-city hotels and motels; take your pick. ● *Ramada Inn,* 440 Asylum Street, 246–6591, $$ ● *Holiday Inn—Downtown,* 50 Morgan Street, 549–2400, $$$–$$$$ ● *Hotel Summit,* 5 Constitution Plaza, 278–2000, $$$–$$$$ ● *Sheraton Hartford,* Trumbull Street at Civic Center Plaza (connected to Civic Center), 728–5151, $$$–$$$$ ● *Farmington Motor Inn,* 827 Farmington Avenue, 677–2871, $$–$$$ CP ● *Susse Chalet Motel,* 185 Brainard Road (I-91 exit 27), 525–9306, $ ● *Barney House,* 11 Mountain Spring Road, Farmington, 677–9735, handsome old home, $$–$$$.

DINING *Carbone's Ristorante,* 588 Franklin Avenue, 249–9646, Italian restaurant popular with politicos, $$–$$$ ● *Gaetano's,* Hartford Civic Center, second level, 249–1629, excellent French and

Italian, $$ ● *36 Lewis Street,* at the same address, 247–2300, popular spot on historic street, $$ ● *L'Americain,* 2 Hartford Square, 522–6500, truly fine French, $$$ ● *Apricots,* 1593 Farmington Avenue, Farmington, 673–5405, French, river setting, $$–$$$ ● *Reading Room,* Mill Lane, Farmington, 677–7997, old gristmill, $$$.

SIGHTSEEING *Old State House,* 800 Main Street, 522–6766. Hours: Monday to Saturday 10 A.M. to 5 P.M., Sunday noon to 5 P.M. Free ● *Capitol Building,* 210 Capitol Avenue, 240–0222. Hours: Monday to Friday 8:30 A.M. to 4 P.M.; free tours 9:15 A.M. to 2:45 P.M., except mid-November to February, July and August; closed weekends ● *Museum of Connecticut History,* 231 Capitol Avenue, 566–3056. Hours: Monday to Friday 9 A.M. to 4:45 P.M.; Saturday 9 A.M. to 1 P.M. Free ● *Butler-McCook Homestead,* 396 Main Street, 522–1806. Hours: May 15 to October 15, Tuesday, Thursday, and Sunday noon to 4 P.M. Special Christmas displays in December. Adults, $2; senior citizens, $1; children, $.50 ● *Nook Farm,* Farmington Avenue at 77 Forest Street (I-84, exit 46), 525–9317. Tours: June to August, Tuesday to Saturday 9:30 A.M. to 4:30 P.M., from 9:30 A.M. to 4 P.M. the rest of the year; Sunday 1 P.M. to 4 P.M. Combined tour Twain and Stowe houses: adults, $6; children under 16, $2.75. Single home: adults, Twain $3.75, Stowe $3; children under 16, $1.50 and $1.25 ● *Hill-Stead Museum,* 35 Mountain Road, 677–4787. Hours: Wednesday to Sunday 2 P.M. to 5 P.M. Adults, $3; children over 11, $2; children under 11, $1 ● *Stanley Whitman House,* 37 High Street off Route 4, 677–9222. Hours: March, April, November, and December, Sunday 1 P.M. to 4 P.M.; May to October, Tuesday to Sunday 1 P.M. to 4 P.M.; closed January and February. Adults, $2; children 6–14, $1 ● *Wadsworth Atheneum,* 600 Main Street, 278–2670. Hours: Tuesday to Sunday 11 A.M. to 5 P.M., first-floor galleries to 7 P.M. Adults, $3; children, $1.50; children under 13 free. Free to all on Thursday and Saturday, 11 A.M. to 1 P.M.

FOR FURTHER INFORMATION Contact the Greater Hartford Convention and Visitors' Bureau, 1 Civic Center Plaza, Hartford, CT 06103, 728–6789.

Christmas Cheer at Bear Mountain

One of the younger natives was getting restless.

She had oohed at the lighting of the 40-foot Christmas tree, listened happily to the first of the carols. But now, with frosty puffs punctuating her words in the wintry night air, she could be heard plaintively asking her Dad, "When's he coming?"

Almost as if on cue, the choral group broke into "Here Comes Santa Claus," and there was the great man himself, making a grand entrance in a flurry of "Ho, ho, ho's," singing a few carols in a belly-deep baritone, and inviting everyone to come to call in a few minutes as soon as he was settled in his quarters downstairs in the Bear Mountain Inn.

The youngster's grin was ear to ear once again.

Santa's arrival on the second Friday in December annually marks the start of the season for the kids as well as the opening of the traditional Bear Mountain Christmas Festival, a regular event since 1968 under the sponsorship of the Palisades Interstate Park Commission and the Bear Mountain Inn.

For three weeks, through the start of the New Year, the bottom floor of the inn is transformed into a world of handmade crafts and special holiday displays meant for nearby families as well as visitors from afar. With Santa in residence until he is called away on Christmas Eve, warm hospitality at the inn, plus a setting that would do credit to a Christmas card, there are few better weekends jaunts for getting into the spirit of the season.

The Bear Mountain Festival is neither huge nor slick, but it has a pleasant down-home flavor and features handmade crafts and folk art. The community is invited to get involved, by lending crafts and creations such as gingerbread villages and candy cottages. The major displays change from year to year. Recently they have ranged from Early American quilts and antique toys to Hümmel figurines and decorated Ukrainian eggs. Working toy-train layouts are perennial favorites, as are the Christmas trees decorated in original motifs.

Santa welcomes children to his workshop, off in a wing of its own, where they find him surrounded by a retinue of bigger-than-life animated friends, including a toy soldier, a Raggedy Ann doll, a panda bear, a snowman, and a group of mechanical carolers. The kids love it.

Bear Mountain Inn is a rustic fieldstone and timber affair with big beams and a giant fireplace that stretches from floor to ceiling. Out the windows, brightly garbed families can be seen ice skating against a backdrop of mountains and evergreens. At night, when the rink is lit and a dozen trees around the perimeter also light up along with the giant tree and a 40-foot star on the mountaintop, it's fairyland time.

You can choose from rooms in the inn building or the newer Overlook Lodge, or opt for four smaller lodges on the opposite side of the lake—pleasant accommodations that surround a central lobby with a fireplace. There's dancing in the inn on Friday and Saturday nights, as well as a smorgasbord dinner including shrimp and top round. Children eat half-price at the Sunday buffet, which features a salad bar and your choice of five main dishes.

When the weather cooperates, the days fly by, filled with skating, sledding, and playful snowball fights. Should you seek further diversion, West Point is just north on Route 9W, or you can cross the bridge and head a few miles north on Route 9 to Cold Spring. Pick up a walking tour brochure in one of the shops and see the historic sights of the picturesque village; then if the kids will cooperate, you can visit some of the 50-plus antiques shops that crowd each other in a 3-block stretch of Main Street, which runs down to a bandstand on a little spit out into the Hudson.

Late in the day, head back south on 9 to Garrison, where you can enjoy another area holiday tradition, a candlelight tour at Boscobel. This beautiful nineteenth-century mansion with its columns and porticos is an outstanding example of New York Federal architecture, and its period furnishings take on a special elegance in the candleglow. Musicians are on hand to enhance the mood, and the house smells invitingly of the warm cinnamon-flavored cider refreshments waiting at the end of the tour.

Like Cold Spring, incidentally, Garrison has an overlook with a splendid Hudson view.

Treat yourself to a special dinner in Garrison in front of the fireplace in the low-ceilinged, atmospheric dining room of the Bird and Bottle Inn, a restored eighteenth-century tavern. An even more elegant (and more expensive) dinner choice farther north in Stormville is Harralds, a five-star selection with dining room where the glow from the fireplace and the candlelight make for an ambience as pleasing as the food.

To end the weekend on a final traditional note, head home via Route 9 and stop in at the Sleepy Hollow Restorations. Each of the three buildings has a different offering: Van Cortlandt Manor in Croton-on-Hudson presents the traditional decorations of St. Nicholas Day; Sunnyside in Tarrytown displays the ways that Washington Irving entertained his family and friends at Christmas; and Philipsburg Manor in north Tarrytown is filled with the traditional trimmings for Twelfth Night or Old Christmas. Each building also offers candlelight tours; check the schedules to see if they coincide with your own.

Bear Mountain Area Code: 914

DRIVING DIRECTIONS Across George Washington Bridge to Palisades Interstate Parkway to Bear Mountain Park.
Total distance: About 50 miles.

ACCOMMODATIONS *Bear Mountain Inn,* Bear Mountain, NY 10911, 786–2731, $$. See also Cold Spring and West Point, page 174.

DINING *Bird and Bottle Inn,* just off Route 9, Garrison, 424–3000, prix-fixe dinner, $$$$ ● *Harralds,* Route 52, Stormville, 878–6595, prix-fixe dinner, $$$$$ ● *Bear Mountain Inn* (see above), $$–$$$; Sunday buffet, $$ ● *Breakneck Lodge,* Route 9D, Cold Spring, good for families, 265–9669, $$. See also Cold Spring and West Point, page 174.

SIGHTSEEING *Bear Mountain Christmas Festival,* Bear Mountain Inn, 786–2731. Hours: mid-December to January 1, 10 A.M. to 9 P.M.; Santa's arrival (with tree lighting, caroling, and lighting of yule log), second Friday in December, usually beginning at 6 P.M.; visits with Santa around 7:15 P.M.; Santa's house to December 24; exterior light displays to January 1. Call for current hours and events ● *Boscobel,* Route 9D, Garrison, 265–3638. Hours: April to October, 9:30 A.M. to 5 P.M.; March, November, and December, 9:30 A.M. to 4 P.M. Phone for current schedule and fees for tours ● *Sleepy Hollow Restorations,* 150 White Plains Road, Tarrytown, NY 10591, 631–8200. Phone or write for holiday exhibits, tour dates, and hours. Adults, $5; children and senior citizens, $3.

FOR FURTHER INFORMATION Contact Palisades Interstate Park Commission, Bear Mountain, NY 10911, 786–2701.

Catching the Brandywine Spirit

The ghost of Christmas past is alive and well in the Brandywine Valley.

Teddy bears and toys that delighted children a century ago, trees festooned with nature's own ornaments, a New England winter scene populated by antique dolls, the foods and feasts of early America, Victorian garlands and wreaths, candlelight, carols, and cascades of red poinsettias light up this rural area where Delaware and Pennsylvania meet, creating a contagious, noncommercial spirit that even old Ebenezer Scrooge would have found hard to resist. If you're feeling a bit cynical about the season, there's no better antidote than a dose of Brandywine cheer.

All the hotels in Wilmington are decked out for the season and offer special weekend package rates that make them ideal holiday headquarters. Planning an itinerary is more of a challenge, since the list of annual events runs into the dozens. One practical approach is to work around the major attractions, starting with the ones closest to Wilmington.

The Delaware Art Museum delights visitors young and old with its old-fashioned displays. One special recent favorite was the antique toys of Pennsylvania collector Richard Wright. Called "Remembrances of Holidays Past: Dolls, Toys, and Teddy Bears," the exhibit included European and American dolls in porcelain, wood, wax, cloth, china, and bisque; early Disney characters and Steiff bears; miniature furniture and a choice dollhouse.

The Museum's Christmas crèche is another area favorite, an elaborate eighteenth-century Nativity scene with more than 40 hand-carved and amazingly lifelike figures.

Children love the downstairs White Whale gallery, where participatory exhibits allow them to express their own creativity. Parents, meanwhile, will be free to visit the museum shop, with its array of unusual gifts, and the gallery where contemporary art is for sale.

The works of Howard Pyle, the Wyeths, and other noted American artists remain on display during the Christmas season.

Rockwood, the second Wilmington high spot, is a total change of scene, a rural Gothic home and garden with Victorian decorations to match the decor in its period rooms and conservatory. A recent added display of miniature rooms was so popular it seems destined to become a regular feature for the holidays. The settings varied from a tiny rendition of Santa's workshop to a perfect replica of Winterthur's famous Readbourne Parlor.

Follow Route 52 out of town to Winterthur itself, and you'll find that the antiques-filled rooms of one of the nation's greatest collections of early American furnishings have been filled for the season with holiday fare that might have been appropriate for each room's period. Dessert parties, musicales, punch parties, Yuletide balls, and a Pennsylvania-German supper, with foods ranging from suckling pigs to syllabub to homemade cakes and cookies, are all so lifelike you'll want to dig right in. All are based on documented evidence of early Yuletide customs. Christmas trees, a conservatory banked with poinsettias, and a formal boxwood-edged garden room are part of the tour.

If it leaves you feeling starved, there are lunch stops nearby on Route 52. Greenery Too in Greenville Center has excellent salads, hot sandwiches, and a local favorite, oyster stew. Ristorante Amalfi offers Italian specialties.

Hagley Museum, situated right on the Brandywine River, was created to show how the river's water power built early industries that helped industrialize the nation, including du Pont's black powder mills. The exhibits tracing industry from the 1600s into this century are interesting, as are the restored mills and shops; but at this time of year it's the 1803 Georgian home of E. I. du Pont, Eleutherian Mills, that is a tribute to the season. It is decorated upstairs and down with original creations using fruit and greenery and other natural materials that may well give you lots of new ideas for your own home holiday decor. A little booklet on sale at the museum shop will teach you how to make the apple and pineapple door fans, pine ropes, ivy wreaths, cranberry trees, and Victorian natural tree ornaments that make this house so full of good cheer.

If you've chosen the second weekend of December for your visit, you'll want to get back in time to attend the annual candlelight house tour in Colonial New Castle, six miles south of Wilmington on Route 9. Time seems to have stood still in Delaware's onetime capital, leaving the red-brick Georgian and Federal homes of the town looking much as they did in the 1700s. They are a real delight decked out for the holidays, with candles in every window and along the paths outside, and carolers adding even more atmosphere with their songs of the season.

Other evening Christmas festivities can be found at the Grand Opera House on Wilmington's Market Street Mall, where Christmas concerts and all kinds of seasonal entertainment are among the attractions scheduled each December.

On Sunday, head across the Pennsylvania border for two of the valley's prime attractions. It's hard to imagine a cheerier scene than the Brandywine River Museum, where tiny fingers can be seen pointing in all directions as children urge parents to "look, look" at the wondrous sights. The December features have become a local tradition, repeated year after year, and are always eagerly anticipated. In one section of this museum, which displays so many works by the Wyeth family, Ann Wyeth McCoy offers an annual gift to the children of the community, an exhibit featuring her magnificent collection of antique porcelian dolls. A doll's Christmas tree is one of the scenes put together by Mrs. McCoy and her artist husband, John, and each year there is a special scene such as a winter landscape of dolls congregating in front of a New England church, each quite literally "dolled up" in Victorian finery. It's so realistic that there's even a crying youngster who slipped trying to cut across the frozen river.

Another gallery here whizzes and hums with five toy trains winding their way along thousands of feet of track, through mountains and valleys, past houses and factories, on their way to a huge railroad yard. Grown-ups love it just as much as the small fry. The model O-gauge railroad is a serious year-round interest of the museum, which employs a special full-time "engineer" to restore and maintain the antiques and other toy trains and the extensive scenery.

Other museum galleries, as always, feature the artistic efforts of Brandywine artists, including the Wyeths and Howard Pyle, but they take second place in December to the five giant trees in the hallway, festooned with munchkins, mice, beguiling angels, and other totally wonderful whimsical "critters" made by museum volunteers each year from natural materials found in abundance in the woods outside. Once again a little booklet is available to show you how to make these tiny treasures for your own tree, and there are other unique gift ideas in the shop, as well as Wyeth prints.

Things become even merrier in the museum when choral groups appear during the day to put the festivities to music. Outside the rustic converted mill, vendors in the courtyard offer roasted chestnuts and handmade gifts—dolls, quilts, and tree ornaments among them.

It's hard to leave the good cheer at the Brandywine, but you'll find ample compensation when you proceed on Route 1 to Kennett Square and Longwood Gardens. Santa's figure in an antique sleigh pulled by sparkling reindeer greets you from the main terrace, and inside the conservatory is resplendent with thousands of poinsettias, begonias, primroses, coleus, and spring bulbs, a breathtaking red and white holiday display.

Prizewinning trees decorated by local garden clubs are just a prelude for Longwood's own 16-foot beauty, and to put you further in a Christmas mood, organ recitals and choral concerts are offered in the adjacent ballroom at 2, 4, and 7 P.M. on weekends.

Visit the Reception Suite beneath the conservatory, where a model home will give you further ideas for decorating your own quarters, and if you stay until the sun goes down, 3,500 lights will twinkle outside, bedecking dozens of trees near the parking area and the walkways.

And these are just the major sights in the valley. Every weekend there are more—open houses in historic homes, traditional Swedish and Colonial celebrations, tree displays, fairs featuring homemade gifts and fresh baked goodies, more candlelight tours, caroling, tree-trimming parties, and many other classic holiday delights. And as a bonus along the way, the winter landscape of the valley is a typical Andrew Wyeth scene come to life.

It's an extraordinary Christmas celebration here in the Brandywine Valley—one you may well decide to make a tradition of your own.

Delaware Area Code: 302
Eastern Pennsylvania Area Code: 215

DRIVING DIRECTIONS Take the New Jersey Turnpike to its end and cross the Delaware Memorial Bridge, pick up 295 to I-95 north into Wilmington.

Total distance: 121 miles.

ACCOMMODATIONS *Hotel du Pont,* 11th and Market streets, Wilmington, 656–8121, $$$–$$$$ ● *Hotel Raddisson,* 700 King Street, Wilmington, 655–0400, $$$ ● *Christina House,* 707 King Street, Wilmington, 656–9300, $$$$. Ask about weekend packages. See also page 34.

DINING See page 34.

SIGHTSEEING *Delaware Art Museum,* 2301 Kentmere Parkway, Wilmington, 571–9590. Hours: Tuesday to Saturday 10 A.M. to 5 P.M., 9 P.M. on Tuesdays; Sunday noon to 5 P.M. Free ● *Hagley Museum,* Route 141, Greenville, 658–2400. Hours: daily 9:30 A.M. to 4:30 P.M. Adults, $5; children 6–14, $2.50; children under 6 free. Call for fees and schedules of candlelight tours ● *Rockwood Museum,* Shipley Road, Wilmington, 571–7776. Hours: Tuesday to Saturday 11 A.M. to 3 P.M. Adults, $3; children 5–16, $1 ● *Winterthur Museum,* Route 52, Winterthur, 654–1548. Tours: one-hour Yuletide tours by reservation only, Tuesday to Saturday. Call for current hours. Tickets:

adults, $8 days, $11 evenings; children under 17, $4 days, $5.50 evenings ● *Brandywine River Museum,* Route 1, Chadds Ford, Pennsylvania, 459–1900. Hours: daily 9:30 A.M. to 4:30 P.M. Adults, $3; children, $1.50 ● *Longwood Gardens,* Route 1, Kennett Square, Pennsylvania, 388–6741. Hours: daily 10 A.M. to 5 P.M. Adults, $5; children, $1; under 6 free ● *Historic New Castle Candlelight Tour.* For current dates and fees, phone 322–8411.

FOR FURTHER INFORMATION   Contact Greater Wilmington Convention and Visitors' Bureau, PO Box 111, Wilmington, DE 19800, (800) 422–1181, or Delaware Tourism Office, 99 Kings Highway, PO Box 1401, Dover, DE 19003, 736–4271, toll-free (800) 441–8846, for a complete listing of Brandywine Valley Christmas activities.

All Aboard for a Connecticut Christmas

The conductor looks familiar. There's something about the pudgy build, the bright red suit. And why is he handing out goodies instead of punching tickets?

The reason, of course, is that Santa Claus himself presides aboard Connecticut's North Pole Express, a huffing, puffing steam train that rides the rails every season between the towns of Essex and Chester.

The Express is one of the many happy traditions that make Christmas special for children in Connecticut. Take a weekend off with the family, and you can share that ride with Santa, visit with his reindeer and toymakers, mail your cards from a picture-postcard village called Bethlehem, go caroling or sleigh riding, see a magnificent eighteenth-century Italian crèche, load down the trunk with one-of-a-kind gifts, and maybe even head home with a tree you've chosen and chopped down yourself.

This is a rambling trip, but it isn't difficult since no two points in this compact state are more than two hours apart. And there are so many interesting stops along the way, it's doubtful whether you'll hear many complaints coming from the backseat.

For your first stop, drive north past New Milford, past gracious white clapboard homes and kids skating on ponds, to a unique shop where the children may actually let you get some shopping done because they'll be so intrigued with the giant tree that is a holiday tradition at The Silo. This converted stable, silo, and barn are chock-full of gifts made by local craftspeople—everything from baskets and batiks to quilts and statues. Even the ornaments on the eye-boggling 18-foot tree are handmade. The gingerbread, dough, blown-glass, and stained glass creations can be purchased right off the tree.

From New Milford, drive east on 109 through the handsome Colonial village of Washington, continuing on to Route 61, then south to Bethlehem, where the post office on intersecting Route 132 will not only postmark your cards but will offer an assortment of 24 rubber stamps dating back over the years to personalize your envelopes. It's a good idea to bring extra paper for the kids, most of whom seem determined to try out every stamp design at least twice.

As you might expect in a little town of Bethlehem, there is a super Christmas shop—the state's largest—located at 18 East Street and full of imported ornaments and toys.

Bethlehem also holds an annual Christmas Festival, usually the second weekend in December, with dozens of artisans and craftspersons on hand with a bounty of original gifts, food stalls on the green, strolling carolers, and Santa himself to say hello to the crowd. He does get around this time of year.

About a mile south of Bethlehem village green, in a weathered barn on the grounds of the Regina Laudis Priory, is an eighteenth-century Neopolitan crèche of museum quality. It is, in fact, the gift of a wealthy collector of religious art whose other endowments now rest with New York's Metropolitan Museum.

The crèche is 16 feet long by 4 feet high by 5 feet deep. The setting is a blend of a scene from an eighteenth-century Italian hillside village and a classical nativity, and the detail in the 60 carved figures is fascinating. All the clothes are of silks, satins, and brocades in rich muted shades; each figure is a lifelike re-creation of the townsperson going about his or her daily tasks. It is a rare work of art in a remarkable rural setting.

Continuing north to Torrington, you'll find another kind of creation, the town's annual Christmas Village. Santa Claus has been in residence here the week before Christmas for more than 30 years, receiving young guests in a comfortable, oak-beamed living room with logs crackling in the fireplace. After a chat and a small gift from Santa, the children can go across the corridor to the toy shop, where local "elves" are busily working on toys for youngsters in the town hospital.

On the grounds near the rear of the building is a Nativity scene with almost life-size figures. And nearby is Santa's sleigh, a favorite spot for photographers with pint-size models along. Eight reindeer are waiting in a pen close at hand, as is Rudolph, a red-nosed reindeer with his own gingerbread house. There's also Snowflake, a baby deer who's a favorite with the youngest visitors. There is no admission charge to the village and nothing is for sale here. It's a Christmas gift from Torrington residents for the enjoyment of children.

If you want to add an old-fashioned sleigh ride to your agenda, make arrangements ahead with Ken Wood in Terryville, located about midway between Bethlehem and Torrington.

You can stay the night in Torrington if you've had enough driving for one day, but it's worth trying for the less-than-an-hour's trip to Hartford via 202 and 44 eastbound and the annual Festival of Lights in that city's Constitution Plaza. In the midst of the 250,000-bulb spectacular are sculptured angels with brass trumpets, reindeer, a Nativity scene, a 75-foot Christmas tree decked with hundreds of tiny lights and a 6-foot starburst, the South Plaza Fountain, a cascade of shimmering light.

Check the papers to see if the Hartford Ballet is doing its holiday run of *The Nutcracker*, just in case you couldn't get tickets at Lincoln Center.

Sunday morning you'll set out on I-91 to Route 9 for Essex, but if the dates are right, you may want to make a shopping stop along the way at Wesleyan Potters. The work of more than 200 fine craftsmen is for sale here from late November through mid-December—pottery, jewelry, weaving, wood, leather, glass, and pewter—all one of a kind and all high quality.

The North Pole Express leaves the Essex depot afternoons and evenings on Friday, Saturday, and Sunday in December. The cars are lit with toy-shaped Christmas lights, the caroling begins as soon as the train whistle blows, and the Connecticut countryside outside the window is bedecked with special Christmas lights and decorations supplied by friendly residents along the train's route. The ride has a special charm at night when the decorations are aglow.

Since the first train rides of the day aren't until noon, you'll have time to take a stroll through Essex, a lovely old seaport town whose beautifully preserved homes are a delight any time of year, but especially with Christmas decorations decking the doors and windows. After a snowfall, Essex is a Christmas card come true.

Have your lunch—or the big late Sunday hunt breakfast—or at least a look inside the Griswold Inn on Main Street. A village landmark since 1776, the inn is a must, not only for its Colonial ambience but also for the many collections that make it almost a mini-museum of nautical lore.

After you ride the train, you can head east on I-95 to Mystic Seaport, which is transformed every December into a nineteenth-century celebration of Christmas. Evergreens sprout from the masts of historic ships, doorways are festooned, homes are decorated for the holiday, and carolers stroll the grounds, inviting visitors to join in the chorus. Costumed guides lead groups to selected exhibits of Christmas past, and lanternlight tours are held late in the afternoon. There are also special hands-on activities for children kindergarten through third-grade age, reliving pastimes of the nineteenth century—roasting chestnuts, making pomanders, and decorating a shell tree. Advance reservations are needed for tours and children's festivities.

You may want to stay for the romantic lanternlight strolls or the wassail and plum pudding that are available at the Seaman's Inne. Or you may want to get an earlier start back onto 95, where any of several easy detours will bring you to farms where you can pick out your Christmas tree and chop it down yourself. Just don't forget to come prepared with enough rope to anchor the tree to the car roof.

Properly laden with memories and your tree, you should be set to keep up the holiday spirit after you get home.

Connecticut Area Code: 203

DRIVING DIRECTIONS Take the Hutchinson Parkway to I-684 to I-84 east. Take exit 4, US 202 to Brookfield and New Milford; then 202 north, 109 east, 61 south to Bethlehem. Then 61 north to Litchfield and 202 north to Torrington, 202 and 44 west into Hartford. Middletown and Essex are on Route 9 east of Hartford. Mystic is east on Route 95.

Total distance: to Torrington, 109 miles; to Hartford, 113 miles; to Essex about 100 miles.

ACCOMMODATIONS *Yankee Pedlar Inn,* 93 Main Street, Torrington, 489–9226, $$ ● *Griswold Inn,* Main Street, Essex, 767–0991, $$–$$$ CP ● For numerous hotel-motels in Hartford, see page 190; for more on Essex, see page 142; for Mystic seaport, see page 29 ● *Eastover Farm Bed & Breakfast,* Guilds Hollow Road, Bethlehem, 266–5740, Colonial home on 70 acres, $$ CP.

DINING *Yankee Pedlar Inn* (see above), $$ ● *Griswold Inn* (see above) $$; Sunday hunt breakfast, $.

SIGHTSEEING *Valley Railroad,* Essex, 767–0103; phone for current Christmas schedule and rates ● *Bethlehem Post Office.* Hours: weekdays 8 A.M. to 6 P.M., weekends to 5 P.M., December 1 to 23.

Free • *Abbey of Regina Laudis,* Flanders Road off Route 61, Bethlehem, 266–7637. Hours: throughout the holiday season and to mid-
January, weather permitting, daily 10:30 A.M. to 4:30 P.M. Free •
Christmas Village, Alvord Memorial Playground, Church Street, Torrington, 489–2274. Hours: mid-December to Christmas eve, 1:30 P.M.
to 4:30 P.M. and 6:30 P.M. to 8:30 P.M. Free • *Sleigh Rides,* Ken
Wood, Wood Acres, Griffen Road, Terryville, 583–8670.

FOR FURTHER INFORMATION For a complete schedule of
Christmas events in Connecticut, contact Tourism Division, Depart-
ment of Economic Development, 210 Washington Street, Hartford,
CT 06106, 800-243–1685 (in Connecticut, 800-842–7492).

Winter Pleasures
Around Williamstown

He's a die-hard skier, one of the first on the slopes no matter what the
weather.

She's ambivalent. If the sun isn't bright, the snow isn't powdery,
and the temperature isn't above 20 degrees, she'd just as soon be inside
a good museum.

Can they find happiness together on a winter weekend?

If there is any area equipped to handle both athletes and aesthetes, it
is the northern Berkshires of Massachusetts. For skiers there is a
choice of Brodie Mountain, Jiminy Peak, or Bousquet, which are chal-
lenging enough for all but the most expert, and Vermont areas like
Haystack and Bromley are within an hour's drive for the really
determined.

This is also good territory for cross-country skiers. A new center
opened recently at Brodie, with 5 miles of packed trails and 50 acres of
rolling fields, plus a network of 25 miles of unplowed roads adjacent to
the magnificent 11,000 acres of Mt. Greylock State Reservation.

But for those who want no part of wintry winds, here's an area with
more sophisticated pleasures than most destinations farther north, beginning with one of the most inviting and impressive small museums to
be found anywhere, Williamstown's Sterling and Francine Clark Art
Institute.

Sterling Clark had the good fortune to be heir to the fortune his
grandfather amassed as a partner to Isaac Singer, the sewing maching
king. Clark began using his inheritance to collect fine art around 1912,

beginning with works of the Old Masters. But with the encouragement of his French-born wife, he shifted emphasis in the 1920s and 1930s to concentrate on nineteenth-century French painting, with some attention also to American artists like Sargent, Remington, and Winslow Homer, who is represented by seven choice oils.

In the 1950s, when the Clarks decided to build a structure to house their collection, they chose Williamstown for the beauty of its pastoral setting and had a building designed to make the most of it. Tall windows in the corridors look out on natural scenes that are works of art in themselves and that add to the pleasure of visiting the museum.

The fact that the galleries are done to drawing-room scale and furnished in many cases with fine antiques also makes a visit to the museum more rewarding.

You'll see excellent examples of some of the world's greatest painters here, dating from the Renaissance and later, including Van Ruisdael, Hals, Gainsborough, Tiepolo, Goya, Turner, and Mary Cassatt. There is also a remarkable silver collection, five centuries of the most exquisite pieces of the silversmith's art.

The French works include Géricault, Courbet, Daumier, Corot, and Millet, but the real heart of the museum, the paintings that may remain in your mind's eye long after you've left the galleries, are the exceptional works by Rubens, Monet, Degas, and Renoir. Among the most memorable pieces are Monet's "Tulip Fields at Sassenheim" and one of his Rouen Cathedral series, and Renoir's "At the Concert" and "Sleeping Girl with Cat."

One of the most interesting exhibits is Degas's "The Ballet Dancer." This sculpture has so fascinated viewers who cannot resist touching the skirt's net hem that the costume has shortened considerably from wear over the years.

There are grander and more famous museums than the Clark Art Institute, but few that offer a more satisfying visual experience.

All of Williamstown, in fact, is a visual delight. It is a beautiful old New England town with a college dating to 1793 at its center. Williams is so much a part of its hometown that it is hard to distinguish where the campus begins and ends, and it offers other interesting places to visit. The Chapin Library on the second floor of Stetson Hall has an extensive collection of rare books—some 17,000 of them—and changing exhibits on English and American literature. The Williams Art Museum has a notable collection of art, with sculpture and painting dating from ancient Egypt to the present. There is a whole room of Spanish art and a section of Early American paintings and furnishings.

If you've absorbed your artistic limit for the day, walk over to Water Street (Route 43) and poke through half a dozen shops that include custom leather goods; gold and silver jewlery; two gift shops with a mix of wares; and The Potter's Wheel, a gallery of high-quality stoneware, glass, metal sculpture, and jewelry. The view of the frozen brook behind the gallery is one of its prize exhibits.

The most elegant lodging in Williamstown is The Orchards, which is not Colonial from the outside, but most definitely is within, done in handsome period decor. One of many nice touches here is the owner's collection of silver coffeepots, which are used at dinner. The Williams Inn is disappointing for such a special town—comfortable enough and with an indoor pool, but lacking any warmth and charm. Other alternatives are the Berkshire Hilton in Pittsfield, the many inns in Lenox, 20 miles to the south, or the very cozy alpine style Milhof, just across the New York state line, about 12 miles from Williamstown.

If the weather remains willful on Sunday, some driving is required to see the remaining sights in the area. About 20 minutes to the north is Bennington, Vermont. Old Bennington with its green, monument, Colonial homes, and church is worth quite a few snapshots, and you can stop in at Bennington Potters to see (and buy) some of the well-known stoneware produced here. Hawkins House in nearby Shaftsbury is another crafts gallery of working studios and shops set in a landmark Colonial home and barns on the property. Quilts, carvings, glass and pottery, sculpture, wrought-iron pieces, jewelry in gold and silver, candles, and drawings are some of the works you'll find being turned out in the studios.

Back in Massachusetts, Pittsfield has the Berkshire Museum, a place to see paintings from Old Masters to the Hudson River School. And if you are a lover of Herman Melville and *Moby Dick,* phone ahead for an appointment to visit Arrowhead, where Melville lived while he wrote his epic. The home is now headquarters of the Berkshire County Historical Society.

If there is still time to spare while one partner is up on the slopes, there is West Stockbridge, with another dozen shops and galleries to explore. Or you'll find the lodge at Brodie a very congenial place to pass the time—Irish decor, good company, and good Irish coffee.

By now you should be back together again and ready to enjoy dinner in one of the many good Berkshire inns farther south on your way home, a happy ending to an exhilarating winter weekend.

Williamstown Area Code: 413

DRIVING DIRECTIONS   Saw Mill River Parkway north to the Taconic Parkway to the New York Thruway, Berkshire spur (Route 90);

east to exit 2, then follow Route 102 to US 20 past Lenox and Pittsfield into Route 7 and Williamstown.
Total distance: 175 miles.

ACCOMMODATIONS *The Orchards,* 222 Adams Road, Williamstown, 458–9611, best in town, $$$–$$$$$ (ask about weekend packages) ● *Williams Inn,* on the green, Williamstown, 458–9371, $$$–$$$$ ● *Berkshire Hilton Inn,* Berkshire Common at West Street on Route 7, Pittsfield, 499–2000, $$$ ● *Milhof Inn,* Route 43, Stephentown, New York, (518) 733–5606, $$ CP ● *1896 Motel,* Route 7, Williamstown, 458–8125, $$ with continental breakfast. For Lenox accommodations and dining, see page 91.

DINING *Le Jardin Inn,* Route 7 and Cold Spring Road, Williamstown, 458–8032, converted estate, French menu, $$–$$$ ● *River House,* Water Street (Route 43), Williamstown, 458–4820, varied menu, also lunch and late-night snacks, $–$$ ● *The Orchards* (see above), $$–$$$ ● *1896 House* (see 1896 Motel above), $$–$$$ ● For lunch and light fare almost any time, a best bet is the *Erasmus Café at the College Bookstore,* 76 Spring Street, Williamstown, open Monday to Saturday, 9 A.M. to 10 P.M.

SKIING *Jiminy Peak,* Corey Road, Hancock, 738–5500 or 445–5500; daily and night skiing. Phone for current rates ● *Brodie,* Route 7, New Ashford, 443–4752, daily and night skiing ● *Bousquet Ski Area,* Tamarack Road, Pittsfield, 442–8316, daily and night skiing. For winter brochure with details on vertical drops, number of trails, lift ticket prices, and special ski packages available at local lodgings, write to Berkshire Visitors' Bureau.

SIGHTSEEING *Sterling and Francine Clark Art Institute,* South Street, Williamstown, 458–9545. Hours: daily except Monday 10 A.M. to 5 P.M. Free ● *Williams College Art Museum,* 1846 Lawrence Hall, 597–2429. Hours: Monday to Saturday 10 A.M. to 5 P.M.; Sunday 1 P.M. to 5 P.M. Free ● *Chapin Library,* Stetson Hall, 597–2462. Hours: Monday to Friday 9 A.M. to noon, and 1 P.M. to 5 P.M.; closed on weekends. Free ● *Berkshire Museum,* 39 South Street (Route 7), Pittsfield, 443–7171. Hours: Tuesday to Saturday 10 A.M. to 5 P.M.; Sunday 1 P.M. to 5 P.M.; open Monday July and August. Donation ● *Arrowhead,* 780 Holmes Road, Pittsfield, 442–1793. Phone for appointment in winter. Summer hours: Memorial Day to October 31, Monday to Saturday 10 A.M. to 4:30 P.M.; Sunday 11 A.M. to 3:30 P.M. Adults, $3; children 6–16, $1.50.

FOR FURTHER INFORMATION Contact Berkshire Visitors' Bureau, The Common, Pittsfield, MA 01201, 800-BERKSHR (except in Massachusetts) or 443–9186.

Philadelphia for All Seasons

The old joke was always a laugh: First prize, one week in Philadelphia. Second prize, two weeks in Philadelphia.

But things have changed drastically in the City of Brotherly Love. The town once known mostly for its dullness has done a remarkable turnaround in the past two decades, returning by its tricentennial in 1982 to what it was in the first place—a vibrant, varied, and interesting city.

Staid William Penn still presides atop the block-square City Hall at Broad and Market streets, but he has been joined by Claes Oldenberg's giant "Clothespin" across the way, one of the visible symbols of the new contemporary beat throughout the city.

It all begin in the late 1960s when the National Park Service rescued beautiful Independence Hall and the rest of the city's pre-Revolution buildings, razing the warehouses and urban blight that had all but hidden them and transforming the area into a handsome historic urban park.

While the park was taking form, neighboring Society Hill also began to revive with restorations of its cobbled streets and charming red-brick Colonial town houses. NewMarket, a lively modern complex of shops and restaurants, grew up between Society Hill and the Delaware River. The waterfront itself was refurbished for the 1976 Bicentennial, old piers and ramshackle buildings giving way to a park and sculpture garden with a floating nautical museum of three permanently moored historic ships at the pier.

And good things just keep happening. More than 500 restaurants have opened in Philadelphia since 1976—and a thriving new local restaurant school produces fine chefs to serve them. Gleaming new office buildings and high-rise hotels have transformed the city's skyline. Even Philadelphia's sports teams suddenly came to life, and a new sports complex was built to house their happy fans.

With all of the new, plus the best of the old—more than 100 museums, the fine Philadelphia Orchestra, the bustling Italian market and historic Germantown, the cheese-steak shops and pretzel vendors, the world's largest city park—a weekend is hardly enough time to take it all in. But a winter weekend, when many of the better hotels offer tempting bargain packages, is a perfect time to begin to get acquainted.

The logical place to start is where our nation started—in the recently created Independence National Historical Park. Make a first stop at the city's excellent midtown Visitor's Center at 16th Street and JFK Boulevard for free walking tours and maps, then either a pleasant 15-minute walk or the Market Street bus will take you to the oldest part of the city.

There are few places that can re-create so vividly the charged atmosphere of a new colony daring to challenge the powerful English crown. A film at the park Visitor's Center sets the stage, and the enthusiastic park guides help to make the past events come alive with colorful stories about the eventful days that saw the nation declare its independence. In Independence Hall you'll stand in the room where it all happened, just a few strides from the chair where Benjamin Franklin sat and the rostrum where John Hancock presided over the signing of the Declaration of Independence. This room is also where the Constitutional Convention met. The square just outside is where the Declaration was first read to the citizens of Philadelphia—and to the world.

The many visitors who take the 25-minute tour of Independence Hall and only glance at the other buildings making up the park are missing out on interesting sights. Flanking Independence Hall are Congress Hall, where the first American Congress met, and the Old City Hall, which housed the first Supreme Court. In Congress Hall you'll learn that the Senate became known as the Upper House quite literally because it was quartered on the second floor.

Carpenter's Hall has been restored to the way it was when the First Continental Congress met there, the Second National Bank has become a portrait gallery of the nation's founders, and down the block is the house where Dolley Payne lived when she met her future husband, James Madison, a delegate to the Constitutional Convention.

Don't overlook Franklin Court, tucked away in an alleyway between 3rd and 4th streets off Market. Only a steel frame remains as a symbol of Franklin's home, but the museum underground would almost certainly have pleased the ingenious Mr. Franklin. The entry is history, disco-style—a mirrored hall with flashing signs citing Franklin's many roles as statesman, inventor, wit, and much more. There is a bank of telephones and a listing of numbers to dial to talk to people like John Adams, George Washington, and John F. Kennedy about Franklin's importance to the country. A dial-it computer produces Franklin witticisms on almost any subject, his many inventions (including library steps hidden in a chair and the first pair of bifocals) are on display, and a changing marionette gallery depicts his adventures as ambassador for his country. It's an altogether delightful way to learn about a remarkable man.

And then, of course, there is the Liberty Bell, housed in a glass pavilion, accessible to the throngs who want to gaze at the famous crack and touch the bell for luck. The bell, you'll learn, was actually ordered in 1751, the fiftieth anniversary of the democratic constitution granted by William Penn to his colony, but its motto, "Proclaim Liberty," became prophetic for a new nation. It had been recast before, but the final crack that put it out of service came in 1835 as the bell tolled the death of Chief Justice John Marshall, according to local lore.

If you do it justice, Independence Park will take the entire morning, finishing just in time for a historic lunch in the 1773 City Tavern, once called "the most genteel tavern in America" by John Adams. The menu still includes old English favorites, and your waitress will be dressed as she might have been in Adams's day.

After lunch there are many nearby sights for exploring. Society Hill, south of the park, roughly between South and Spruce and 2nd and 7th streets, has become a prototype for urban restoration with its many blocks of Colonial town houses lovingly restored within the past two decades. A walk through the area also takes you past several historic churches, all clearly labeled with informative signs, and past some intriguing shopping areas to get you out of the cold, including Head House Square, a red-brick restored marketplace, and NewMarket and South Street, a mix of funky shops and nightlife a bit reminiscent of Greenwich Village.

Another quite elegant shopping complex nearer to Independence Park is the Bourse, once a Victorian merchants' exchange, now a series of couturier boutiques and other lavish shops and eateries around a ten-story atrium. While you're in the neighborhood, look into the Curtis Publishing Company building, which houses the Norman Rockwell Museum, including many of the artist's famous *Saturday Evening Post* covers, as well as an unexpected art treasure in the lobby, a magnificent wall-to-wall Tiffany glass tile mosaic called *The Dream Garden*, the only one of its kind in this country.

North of Market Street is the Old City, the old commercial district that is still a bit run down. Do walk over, however, to see Elfreth Alley, the perfectly charming cobbled avenue lined with 33 houses built between 1713 and 1811, the oldest continually occupied street in America. Not far away is historic Christ Church, where Washington and many members of the Continental Congress worshiped, and the tiny Betsy Ross House where the nation's first flag was made.

If the weather is conducive and there is time, you may also want to tour the tall ships and the submarine at Penn's Landing.

When it comes to dinner, the choices are endless. Le Bec Fin is considered the city's finest—and most expensive—restaurant. Both Bookbinder restaurants are landmarks and full of atmosphere. And there are more than 100 restaurants in the area around NewMarket and South Street.

As for city nightlife, there are piano bars at Frog and at the Borgia Café; Memphis and Polo Bay are "in" discos at the moment; and at the Middle East you'll find belly dancers gyrating downstairs and a lineup of comedians hoping to be discovered upstairs at the Comedy Works.

If you want to hear the Philadelphia Orchestra at bargain prices and you don't mind sitting in the peanut gallery, join the long line of locals waiting for the gallery tickets that go on sale before each performance at the Academy of Music.

For Sunday brunch, recommended spots are the Four Seasons Hotel for elegance and Carolina's for an inventive menu. If you want to sample a cheese steak, try Jim's Steaks at 4th and South streets.

Sunday is the day to board the Victorian trolley that leaves the tourist center for tours through Fairmount Park. It will take you past lush meadowland and rustic trails, restored mansions, outdoor theaters, a zoo, and even a Japanese teahouse. In spring and summer regattas are a regular sight on the river adjoining the park, rowing out from the boathouses along the edge.

During the warmer seasons the trolley runs every 20 minutes all day and you can make unlimited stop-offs along the 90-minute tour, just catching up with the next bus that comes along. In winter they sometimes eliminate stops since so many attractions are closed, making it a warm motor tour with one stop to see whichever mansion may still be open to the public.

Philadelphia's best-known museums, located at the entry to Fairmount Park on broad Benjamin Franklin Parkway, know no seasons. The Philadelphia Museum of Art takes you anywhere from an Amish farmhouse to a Peking palace. The art collections are large, the American wing outstanding, the Oriental section is a knockout, with a Buddhist temple, a palace reception room, a Chinese scholar's study, and many magnificent pieces of rosewood furniture from the Ming dynasty. If you climb the banks of steps outside that *Rocky* made famous, you'll be rewarded with a striking vista of the city.

Across the parkway in the Rodin Museum is one of the largest collection of the sculptor's works to be found outside France, including such masterpieces as "The Thinker," "The Burghers of Calais," and "Gates of Hell," all a gift to his fellow citizens from a little-known Philadelphian named Jules E. Mastbaum.

The Franklin Institute Science Museum on the other side of the boulevard is a change of pace and one of the most innovative institutions of its kind, with participatory exhibits that let you pilot a plane, steer a ship, ride a 350-ton locomotive, and walk through a giant human heart.

With the park and the museums, the day will be gone before you know it and you still won't have been to Germantown or the Italian Market or the Mummer's Museum, or seen the excellent American art collection at the Pennsylvania Academy of the Fine Arts or the famous Mummy Room at the University Museum, which has shared many archaeological expeditions with the British Museum. And then there are the U.S. Mint and the "Please Touch" Museums and the gardens . . . and later in the year the outdoor activity at NewMarket and in Fairmount Park . . . and the antiques stores on Pine Street . . . and on and on.

W. C. Fields might not have enjoyed spending time in the native city he used to joke about, but nowadays most first-time visitors to Philadelphia leave town calculating how soon they can come back.

Philadelphia Area Code: 215

DRIVING DIRECTIONS Take the New Jersey Turnpike to exit 7. Follow signs to Route 206 southbound. Continue to Route 295, then to exit 34, Route 70 west, which leads to Route 30 west and the Benjamin Franklin Bridge into the city.
Total distance: 98 miles.

PUBLIC TRANSPORTATION Amtrak has frequent service to Philadelphia, and the city's sights are easily accessible on foot or via public transportation.

ACCOMMODATIONS Many Philadelphia hotels, including the most elegant, offer excellent weekend package deals. The Convention and Visitors' Bureau has a complete current list. The hotels that follow are just a small sampling of the dozens available in the city • *Latham Hotel,* 17th at Walnut, L03–7474, small, elegant, European, $$$$ • *Four Seasons,* 1 Logan Square, 963–1500, luxurious, tops in the city, $$$$ • *The Palace,* 18th at Benjamin Franklin Parkway, 963–2222, another luxury contender, $$$$ • *Holiday Inn–Independence Mall,* 4th and Arch, 923–8660, $$$ • *Barclay Hotel,* Rittenhouse Square, 545–0300, old standby, $$$$ • *Quality Inn–Center City,* 22nd at Benjamin Franklin Parkway, 568–8300, convenient for museums, $–$$ •

Warwick Hotel, 1701 Locust Street, 735–6000, super-elegant small hotel, $$$–$$$$ • *Sheraton Society Hill,* 1 Dock Street, 238–6000, great location in historic district, $$$$. Also note the bed-and-breakfast listing for local registries.

DINING Literally hundreds of possibilities. A few suggestions • *Le Bec Fin,* 1523 Walnut Street, 567–1000, splurge at the city's best, prix-fixe dinner, $70 • *Café Royal,* The Palace (see above), $$$$ • *Deux Cheminées,* 251 S. Camac, 985–0367, more fine French, $$$$ • *Alouette,* 334 Bainbridge Street, 629–1126, French, romantic, $$$ • *Raymond Haldeman Restaurant,* 110–112 South Front Street, 925–9888, cosmopolitan cuisine, contemporary setting, $$–$$$ • *La Truffe,* 10 South Front Street, 925–5062, French, both traditional and nouvelle, $$$–$$$$ • *Carolina's,* 261 South 20th Street, 545–1000, American fare, jazz on weekends, $$ • *Apropos,* 211 South Broad Street, at Walnut, 546–4424, bistro atmosphere, imaginative menu, $–$$$ • *Marabella's,* 1420 Locust Street, trendy, seafood, burgers, pasta, $ • *DiLullo Centro,* 1407 Locust Street, 546–2000, elegant decor, fine Italian food, $$–$$$ • *Il Gallo Nero,* 254 S. 15th Street, 546–8065, another Italian favorite, $$–$$$ • *Dante's & Luigi's,* 762 10th Street, 925–7000, modest old-timer near the Italian market, $–$$ • *Strolli's,* 1528 Dickinson Street, 336–3390, no decor, south Philly Italian bargain, make reservations, $ • *The Commissary,* 1710 Sansom, 569–2240, "in" spot includes Southwest and Cajun at *USA Café,* $–$$, self-service at *"Downstairs,"* $, hot sandwiches at the *Piano Bar,* $ • *DiNardo's Famous Crabs,* 312 Race Street, 925–5115, the name says it, $–$$ • *The Fish Market,* 18th and Sansom, 567–3559, well prepared seafood, $$–$$$ • *Bookbinder's Old Original,* 125 Walnut Street, 925–7027, an old city landmark, $$–$$$ • *City Tavern,* 2nd and Walnut, 923–6059, Revolutionary history, good choice for lunch, dinner, $$–$$$, lunch, $ • *Dickens Inn,* 421 South 2nd Street, 928–9307, pub atmosphere, roast beef, Yorkshire pudding, $$–$$$.

SIGHTSEEING *Independence National Historical Park,* 3rd and Chestnut, 597–8974. Hours: daily 9 A.M. to 5 P.M. Free • *Betsy Ross House,* 239 Arch Street, 627–5343. Hours: daily 9 A.M. to 5 P.M. Free • *Christ Church,* 2nd Street above Market Street, 922–1695. Hours: Monday to Saturday 9 A.M. to 5 P.M., from 11 A.M. in winter; Sunday 1 P.M. to 5 P.M. Free • *Fairmount Park Trolley Bus,* from Visitors Center, 16th Street and JFK Boulevard, 636–1666. Check for current rates and schedules • *Franklin Institute Science Museum,* 20th Street and Benjamin Franklin Parkway, 564–3375. Hours: Monday to Saturday 10 A.M. to 5 P.M.; Sunday noon to 5 P.M. Adults, $4.50; children 4–12, $3.50 ● *Norman Rockwell Museum,* Curtis Building, 6th and Walnut, 922–4345. Hours: daily 10 A.M. to 4 P.M. Adults, $1.50; children under 12 free. (No charge to see mosaic in building lobby.) ● *Rodin Museum,* 22nd and Benjamin Franklin Parkway, 736–8100. Hours: Tuesday to Sunday 10 A.M. to 5 P.M. Donation ● *Philadelphia Museum of Art,* 26th and Benjamin Franklin Parkway, 763–8100. Hours: Wednesday to Sunday 10 A.M. to 5 P.M. Adults, $4; children under 18, $2. Free on Sunday until 1 P.M.

FOR FURTHER INFORMATION Write or phone Philadelphia Convention and Visitors Bureau, 1515 Market Street, Philadelphia, PA 19102, 636–330. Philadelphia Visitors Center, 16th Street and JFK Boulevard, 636–1666, is open daily 9 A.M. to 5 P.M. For information packet, call toll-free (800) 523–2004.

Snow and Snuggling in the Litchfield Hills

It's just as the song pictures it. Outside, there's a sleigh waiting to jingle you through the snow. Unless, of course, you'd rather skate on the pond, or practice your cross-country strides, or head for a ski area where snowmaking guarantees that 95 percent of the slopes are always ready for action.

If it's too cold or too warm for all that, how about antiquing or sightseeing, or snapping photos of white-steepled churches and picture-book village greens? Or you could always just join that contented tabby cuddled in front of the inn fireplace.

Weekends are all but weatherproof in the Litchfield Hills of Connecticut, where winter sports share billing with New England villages, interesting shops, and old-fashioned inns where hospitality is warm, whatever the weather.

For skiers, the major attraction here is Mohawk Mountain, Connecticut's largest, a small, friendly area with many of the amenities of a bigger complex. Mohawk is unusually attractive, set in the middle of a state forest, reached via an arching bridge over a surrounding brook, with lakes that are sometimes used for ice skating. The chalet-style cedar lodge has a wall-size picture window and a large deck for enjoying the view. And this is one of the few lodges that worries about creating inviting indoor atmosphere, with potted trees and green plants, rafters hung with sleighs, wagon wheels, and old wooden skis, and even a wall of books next to the fireplace for those who aren't skiing for the day.

Mohawk is an ideal place to learn to ski. There are special day rates for novices and even a separate, slower chairlift for beginners. Cross-country lessons and rentals are also available, and there are miles of beautiful trails in the adjacent Mohawk State Forest. If Mohawk's 24 downhill trails are not as steep as those farther north in Vermont, there's the compensation of lift lines that seldom call for more than 5 to 10 minutes' wait.

At day's end welcoming fires and refreshments await in a number of inns in the area. A few are particularly noteworthy, making for a pleasant winter weekend with or without skiing.

For a small, secluded spot away from it all, head for the Under Mountain Inn, north of Mohawk in the charming village of Salisbury. Each of the seven rooms is decorated differently, many with reproductions of Early American wallpapers. The British owner-chef prepares tasty fare like fish and chips, Scottish salmon, or steak and kidney pie as well as continental specialties to be enjoyed in the fireplace-warmed dining room, and you can be sure of a proper pot of English tea, kept warm in its own cozy. From this inn, you can cross-country ski on quiet country lanes right down the road.

Another Salisbury landmark is the venerable White Hart on the village green. The dining rooms are cozy, and the fire in the tap room is warming, though the rooms are ordinary. Stop by for a drink or a meal.

Just below Salisbury in Lakeville, the home of the prestigious Hotchkiss School, Interlaken Inn is an attractive modern complex, with an exercise room and sauna indoors, ice skating on neighboring ponds, and plenty of cross-country skiing territory nearby. A couple of period homes on the property have been redecorated for those who prefer inn atmosphere.

Both Salisbury and Lakeville offer antiquing and some interesting small shops.

About 15 miles east in the picture-book town of Norfolk, Beth Denis of Horse & Carriage Livery offers sleigh rides through the countryside followed with hot mulled cider, the perfect way to snuggle and admire the wintry landscape. If there's no fluffy coating of snow to accommodate the sled, you can settle for a carriage ride instead.

Three appealing inns beckon in Norfolk. Mountain View is a homey Victorian, while Manor House is an elegant turn-of-the-century showplace with carved stairs and Tiffany windows. They'll pamper you here with breakfast in bed, and the big front bedroom has a warming fireplace of its own. Greenwoods Gate is a 1797 Colonial bed-and-breakfast home whose stylishly decorated bedrooms could easily wind up on a magazine page.

About 20 minutes below Mohawk Mountain, near New Preston, two inns around Lake Waramaug are also tempting choices. The Inn at Lake Waramaug, housed in a 1791 Colonial, offers an indoor pool and sauna, Ping Pong and a pool table for the kids, and plenty of room to ice skate or cross-country ski over the snow-covered lake. Twenty modern units on the property come with canopy beds and fireplaces.

The Boulders is a gracious inn in a rustic 1800s stone building with an antiques-filled living room that offers an unbeatable view of lake and hills from its big picture window. You can choose from handsome period rooms upstairs or cottage rooms on the grounds with working fireplaces.

From Lake Waramaug, it's just a few miles to Litchfield, one of the area's most historic and photogenic towns. In Litchfield, drive to Bantam Lake off Route 209 and you can watch ice boaters in action on winter afternoons.

Or you may decide to forget it all and return to the most traditional winter activity in northwest Connecticut—sitting by the fire alongside that contented cat.

Litchfield Hills Area Code: 203

DRIVING DIRECTIONS For New Preston, take I-684 north to exit 9E, I-84 east to exit 7, US 202 north. From New Preston follow signs and lakeside road to Inn at Lake Waramaug. For Salisbury use above route but continue on I-684 north to the end (it becomes NY 22), then take US 44 east. Continue east on Route 44 for Norfolk, or head north via the Hutchinson River Parkway to the Merritt Parkway and take Route 8 north, then 44 west to Norfolk. For Lakeville, follow 41 south from Salisbury. For Mohawk Mountain, follow Route 7 north to Route 4 east at Cornwall Bridge and follow signs.

Total distance: to New Preston, 83 miles; Salisbury, 115; Lakeville, 113; Norfolk, 130.

ACCOMMODATIONS (Ask about weekend and ski packages) ●
Under Mountain Inn, Undermountain Road (Route 41), Salisbury, 435–0242, $$$$ MAP ● *Yesterday's Yankee,* Route 44, Salisbury, 435–9539, Cape Cod cottage B&B, $$ CP ● *Interlaken Inn,* Route 122, Lakeville, 435–9878, $$$–$$$$ ● *Mountain View Inn,* Route 272, Norfolk, 542–5595, $$–$$$ CP ● *Manor House,* PO Box 701, Maple Avenue, Norfolk, 542–5690 $$–$$$$ CP ● *Greenwoods Gate,*

Greenwoods Road East, Norfolk, 542–5439, $$$$ CP ● *Inn at Lake Waramaug,* Lake Waramaug Road, New Preston, 868–0563, $$$$–$$$$$ MAP ● *Boulders Inn,* Route 45, New Preston, 868–7918, $$$$ MAP.

DINING *Under Mountain Inn* (see above), $$–$$$ ● *White Hart Inn,* Main Street at Routes 41 and 44, Salisbury, 435–2372, $$–$$$ ● *Mountain View Inn* (see above), $$–$$$ ● *Interlaken Inn* (see above), $$–$$$ ● *Woodlands,* Route 41, Lakeville, 435–0578, $–$$ ● *Holley House,* Pocketknife Square, Lakeville, 435–2727, restored factory, varied menu, $$–$$$ ● *The Inn at Lake Waramaug* (see above), $$–$$$ ● *Boulders Inn* (see above), $$–$$$ ● *Le Bon Coin,* Route 202, New Preston, 868–7763, French in a country house, $$–$$$.

SLEIGH RIDES *Horse & Carriage Livery,* PO Box 264, Loon Meadow Drive, Norfolk, 542–6085.

SKIING *Mohawk Mountain Ski Area,* Cornwall, 672–6464. Call for current prices.

FOR FURTHER INFORMATION Litchfield Hills Travel Council, PO Box 1776, Marbledale, CT 06777, 868–2214.

Yankee Winter Weekends in Sturbridge

Open fires and roasting chestnuts set the scene. Your welcoming drink is a steaming eighteenth-century concoction. The hostesses are in Yankee costumes, and Friday dinner is served to the tunes of a strolling minstrel singing Colonial songs. Another Yankee winter weekend is under way.

The weekends, held throughout January, February, and March, were initiated by the Publick House Inn, no doubt as a way to drum up winter business, but they've proven so popular that they are now a tradition, looked forward to and carried out in grand style each year in cooperation with Old Sturbridge Village. The notion is to revive Early American winter pleasures to make our twentieth-century winters a little more bearable, concentrating on the many facilities at Sturbridge Village and a luscious menu that was obviously devised in less calorie-conscious times.

Saturday, for example, begins with a breakfast of fried corn mush, sausages, and hot deep-dish apple pie. To work it off, you bundle up and take a stroll around Old Sturbridge Village, the 40-building reconstruction of a typical Colonial town. Even if you've been here before, the village takes on a new dimension in the winter as it concentrates on cold weather activities of its time. After lunch you'll even get to see how they used to make maple sugar candy by hardening the syrup in the snow.

The usual crafts demonstrations—weaving, printing, tinsmithing, and the like—are also in order in the winter, and you finally may have time to take a look at some of the indoor exhibits that usually are forgotten in the summer. There are seven galleries to be seen, filled with firearms, clocks, lighting devices, folk art, textiles, blown and molded glass, mirrors, scientific instruments, hand-sewn and knitted garments, weaving and quilts, and much more.

A buffet lunch and hot mulled cider are served at the Village Tavern, and after you watch the maple candy in the making, you'll be treated to a rollicking sleigh ride through the snow.

Wild boar pâté and roast venison are the kinds of things you can expect on the dinner menu; afterward it's back to Sturbridge Village for an evening of nineteenth-century entertainment at the tavern.

All the meals are served at the village or at the Publick House Inn, no matter where you are staying. The inn itself is most people's first choice for lodging as well (the price for the weekend is standard whether you are in an inn or motel). It is a onetime coaching tavern opened in 1771, and the atmosphere probably hasn't changed a lot since then. Period furniture, low ceilings, and tilty floors and doorframes remain, though the carpeting and TV sets upstairs are strictly twentieth century.

One equally appealing alternative is the Ebenezer Crafts Inn, under the same management, a restored 1786 Colonial home with ten airy bedrooms furnished in Colonial style and with sweeping views of the snow-covered hills from the windows. Other accommodations are at the Inn's Motor Lodge, or the Chamberlain House, a nearby residence.

Wherever you stay, you'll be back to the inn on Sunday for yet another glorious breakfast—hearty portions of homemade sausage and country eggs with pumpkin and blueberry muffins, porridge with maple syrup and cream, and hot apple pandowdy. Figuring that half the guests can't move anyway, the rest of the day is unplanned. You can return to Sturbridge or visit some of the area shops on Route 20 such as Sturbridge Yankee Workshop or the Seraph for reproductions of Early American furniture, or Basketville, or the Quilter's Quarters, or a variety of other shops, any of which can supply excellent souvenirs of the weekend.

One other possibility is to take the less than half an hour's drive farther east on 86 to Route 90 and discover a surprising New England town. Worcester, Massachusetts, is mainly thought of (and accurately) as a factory town, but it is much more. New England's second largest city, it has a Colonial heritage that dates to 1673, an attractive hilly terrain, and lovely residential areas. It is the home of twelve colleges and two fine museums.

The most special of the two is the New England Science Center, where the building's self-sufficient energy system is actually displayed for the public's edification in an exhibit. There are some clever demonstrations of scientific principles—a push-pull device to show how a fulcrum works, a hot air compressor that shows what makes balloons go up—as well as more traditional natural science exhibits, including a giant stuffed Indian tiger. The live animals outside feature a couple particularly appropriate for winter visitors—Ursa Major and Ursa Minor, a polar bear pair known affectionately as the Major and Ursa, and their cub, Kenda. A special window lets you watch them swimming underwater.

Worcester's Art Museum may surprise you. The traditional stone building contains some fine exhibits, including a thirteenth-century French chapel rebuilt here stone by stone. The brochure describes the collection as "the development of man as seen through 50 centuries of his art," and they've shown just that through displays from Greek and Roman vases to Persian and Indian miniatures to Rembrandts, Goyas, Matisses, and Picassos. The painting galleries are separated by schools, including Dutch, French, Spanish, and Italian.

The two Worcester museums are easy to find, as signs are posted pointing the way no matter how you enter the city. The contrasting exhibits make for a rewarding afternoon, and when you're done you'll discover that some of those dull factories associated with the city are now converted into very lively places for food and drink. One good choice right around the corner from the art museum is Northworks on Grove Street—casual, congenial, and inexpensive with a menu of burgers, fried zucchini, and other light foods that may be welcome after all that Colonial feasting in Sturbridge.

If you have a more elegant dinner in mind there's Maxwell Silverman's Tool House. And Worcester now has a Legal Sea Foods and other new spots in a transformed police station–firehouse complex.

If you're ever in Worcester on a day other than Sunday, by the way, keep in mind that the Town Center, a shopping mall, contains a large, bargain-packed, and uncrowded edition of Filene's basement, inexplicably located on the second floor. The Worcester Crafts Center also has beautiful original pieces for sale.

Reliving the past and discovering a promising small city of the present—it's a winning combination for a winter weekend.

Worcester Area Code: 617
Sturbridge Area Code After July 16, 1988: 508

DRIVING DIRECTIONS Hutchinson River and Merritt parkways or I-95 north to I-91 to Hartford; from Hartford take I-84 toward Boston. Sturbridge is exit 3. The Publick House Inn is on Route 131 in the center of Sturbridge, south of Route 20.
Total distance: 160 miles.

ACCOMMODATIONS *Sturbridge Yankee Winter Weekends.* Lodging, two dinners, two breakfasts, Saturday lunch, and all admissions, $175–$185 per person, double occupancy. Weekends run January through March. Choice of accommodations: Publick House Inn, Chamberlain House, Ebenezer Crafts Inn, or Publick House Country Motor Lodge. For information, contact Publick House Inn, Sturbridge, MA 01566, 347–3313.

DINING *Northworks,* 106 Grove Street, Worcester, 755–9657, $ • *Maxwell Silverman's Tool House,* 25 Union Street, Worcester, 755–1200, $$–$$$ • *Legal Sea Foods,* Exchange Place, Exchange and Walden streets, Worcester, 792–1600, $–$$$. For more area dining, see page 124, Brimfield.

SIGHTSEEING *Worcester Art Museum,* 55 Salisbury Street, 799–4406. Hours: Tuesday to Friday 10 A.M. to 4 P.M.; Saturday to 5 P.M.; Sunday 2 P.M. to 5 P.M. Free • *New England Science Center,* 222 Harrington Way, 791–9211. Hours: Monday to Saturday 10 A.M. to 5 P.M.; Sunday 1 P.M. to 5 P.M. Adults, $3.50; senior citizens and children 3–15, $2.75.

Snowtime in the Poconos

Invigorating days out-of-doors and a welcoming fire at a cozy inn at day's end: For many people that's the perfect formula for a winter weekend. But it's not an easy order to fill in Pennsylvania's Pocono Mountains. Though there is plenty of scenery and an abundance of outdoor activity in this area so easy to reach from the city, Poconos lodgings run to large resorts, honeymoon havens, or bland motels. Until you get to Canadensis, that is.

Remember that name, Canadensis. This tiny town—hardly more than a crossroads, really—has two of the choicest country inns in the Poconos. And once you've found them you've found the best of both worlds. You can be snug and secluded when you want, but when you don't feel like sitting home by the fire, not only are the major ski areas at your disposal but also the facilities at many of those big resort hotels as well. Many of them are ideal if you are a cross-country skier or even just beginning at downhill.

First then, pick an inn. The most sophisticated is Overlook Inn, which you might guess when you note that the chairs in the living room bear family college seals from Williams and Harvard. The Tuppers are one of those couples who decided to get away from it all by establishing a warm and welcoming inn, and they've done a fine job with this century-old home. Walk past the wide, railed porch into the entry and you'll find a comfortable living room with the obligatory fireplace on the right, a book-lined, paneled, and inviting library–game room–den on the left. Afternoon tea is served every day.

Upstairs the rooms are furnished simply with old-fashioned pieces—iron bedsteads, Victorian chests, and the like.

Dinner at the Overlook is fine—home-baked bread, tender filet de boeuf, fresh-caught brook trout, moist rice pilaf, vegetables cooked just right to retain their crunch.

Pine Knob, which has been accommodating visitors since the 1880s, is more like a visit to Grandma's house. Redoing the old house was another labor of love, this time by Jim and June Belfie, expatriate suburban Philadelphians. It has a homey touches, like hobnail bedspreads, sheer ruffled curtains, and African violets on the bedside tables. The living room parlor is Victorian, dominated by a grand piano, an immense breakfront, and an ancient stone fireplace. Cotton chintz tablecloths, bentwood chairs, and arrangements of evergreens and dried flowers brighten the dining room, which is also highly recommended in the area. Hot corn muffins or popovers, homemade soups and chowders, and deserts such as praline cheesecake keep people coming back for more.

One more possibility north of Canadensis in South Sterling is the Sterling Inn, a larger complex where you can cross-country ski, ice skate, or sled right on the premises. Rooms here are comfortable country. Choicest are the suites in the newer Nearbrook building, with fireplaces and decks overlooking the brook.

Now, having made your choice, enjoyed your breakfast, and resisted the lure of the fire, you have the pleasant prospect of planning an outdoors day in the Poconos. Skiing is gentle here, but there are compensations since even Camelback, the closest and largest of the ski areas, is able to offer snowmaking over the entire mountain. There is also night skiing, if you are so inclined. Between Camelback and other areas such as Big Boulder, Jack Frost, or Shawnee, there should be enough to suit all but the really expert skier. Write ahead to the Pocono Mountains Vacation Bureau, and they'll send you a free guide to all the areas so you can choose your slope in advance.

If you are a beginner, you may be happier heading for Buck Hill, a resort that is even closer to Canadensis and where the two slopes and J-lifts are open to the public for a fee. Fifteen miles of cross-country trails are also available at no charge if you have your own skis, but they do ask that skiers register at the desk prior to setting out. And if you want to try out a snowmobile, you can rent one by the half hour or the hour, with the Buck Hills golf course at hand to provide plenty of room for safe maneuvering.

Pocono Manor also allows skiing on its trails and baby slopes, which are served by a J- and T-bar. This is also where you will find the Rossignol Nordic Touring Center, with rentals and lessons and 40 miles of groomed and marked trails for all abilities.

Buck Hill and the Manor are two of the grand old timber and stone mountaintop hotels that were once the pride of the Poconos, with 6,000 and 3,000 acres of spectacular grounds, respectively. Their locations, views, and grounds are as grand as ever, though the hotels themselves are struggling to maintain themselves in a new resort era. If they're not quite what they used to be, they're still quite something and you should see them while you're in the area. If you like to do winter hiking, trails at either hotel are simply magnificent.

Skytop is the one grand manor that has retained its elegance, and it is worth a drive to see its fine building and setting. You can visit or dine if you like, but you won't be invited to use the facilities.

At Mount Airy, however, a far livelier and much different kind of resort, you'll find not only downhill, cross-country, and snowmobile trails available to you, but guaranteed snow for all three. They actually make snow for the cross-country and snowmobile trails, taking no chances on disappointing their guests. If the weather is hopeless, you can also use Mount Airy's Indoor Sports Palace for a fee, complete with tennis, ice skating, a health club, heated pool, and basketball and handball courts.

The Poconos area is not one for quaint villages, but if shopping is your favorite sport, there is enough to keep you occupied for a pleasant couple of hours.

At the Pocono Mineral and Gem Company in Colony Village, just south of Canadensis, you'll see a magnificent display of natural gems and have the chance to buy your own gem jewelry at reasonable prices. Christmas in Mountainhome offers mementos such as Swiss music boxes and unusual ornaments for your Christmas tree. The Other Woman in Mountainhome and Kellys in Swiftwater are havens for antiquers.

Several Poconos shops give you a show with your shopping. Callie's Candy Kitchen in Mountainhome has chocolate-covered everything—from strawberries to potato chips—plus a laugh-a-minute chocolate-making demonstration from the colorful Mister Callie. Thirty-seven kinds of yummy soft pretzels are the offerings at Callie's Pretzel Factory, where you're invited to taste samples, watch the "pretzel bender" in action, and try bending one of your own. A few miles north in LoAnna, you can watch the making of pottery and china giftware at Holley Ross Pottery.

Memorytown, U.S.A. is another only-in-the-Poconos shopping experience, a group of 1800s buildings made over into seven unusual shops. If you want a souvenir of your trip, have a photo taken in fancy Victorian dress and top hat here at Lucky Ned Pepper's Picture Parlor.

While you are out driving, take the scenic drive up through Big Pocono State Park to the top of Camelback Mountain for mountain vistas. There are tables here for a picnic with a view or you can have lunch at the Cameltop restaurant atop the mountain.

Two other crafts shops to visit on Route 611 are Stoney Hollow Potters in Tannersville and The Woodworker in Bartonsville, where you'll find unusual handmade furniture.

One other kind of recreation widely available in the Poconos is horseback riding. A number of stables offer horses and/or guided trail rides, and on the right day there's really nothing like the beauty of moving past untouched snow through the winter stillness.

"Pocono People Love Winter" is the slogan from the local vacation bureau, and considering the many ways they have to enjoy the season, it's no wonder.

Poconos Area Code: 717

DRIVING DIRECTIONS Take the George Washington Bridge to I-80 west to exit 52 in Pennsylvania. Follow 447 north to Canadensis. Ask your inn for more specific directions to its door.

Total distance: 109 miles.

ACCOMMODATIONS AND DINING *Overlook Inn,* Dutch Hill Road, Canadensis, 595–7519, $$$$ MAP ● *Pine Knob Inn,* Route 447, Canadensis, 595–2532, $$$$ MAP ● *The Sterling Inn,* Route 191, South Sterling, 676–3311, $$$$–$$$$$ MAP ● *Pump House Inn,* Skytop Road, Route 390, Canadensis, 595–7501, if you eat away from your inn, this is the area's best, $$–$$$. There are also a few rooms available upstairs, $$ CP.

SKIING For information and prices for all Pocono ski resorts, plus the "Ski the Poconos" brochure, write Pocono Mountains Vacation Bureau, 1004 Main Street, Stroudsburg, PA 18360, 421–5791.

Ringing Sleigh Bells in Southbury

A one-horse sleigh may sound like fun, but Glen Morris says a pair of horses is even better.

Morris is one of a handful of Connecticut traditionalists devoted to preserving the old-fashioned pleasures of a sleigh ride through the snow, jingling bells and all—a treat he will provide for you any weekend when Mother Nature cooperates with the necessary white ground cover.

He has been dashing off across the scenic golf course behind Harrison Inn in Southbury for more than a decade now in a bright red antique sleigh. Half-hour rides are available any weekend when snow is on the ground, but advance reservations are a must.

A schoolteacher by profession, Morris uses the proceeds he brings in from winter sleigh rides and fall and spring hayrides to help support the Morgan horses he breeds and trains. He'll tell you fondly about his two-time Morgan national champion, Townsend Challenge, as well as about the father-mother-son trio that sometimes forms a three-horse hitch for his sleigh. That family was raised and trained by another father, mother, and son, he notes with pride, referring to his own family.

The Morrises also own two antique sleighs that they show at winter sleigh rallies, an almost vanished tradition that has managed to survive in this part of Connecticut. Rallies are a Currier & Ives scene come to life. Judging categories go from teams of ponies to giant draft horses like Percherons, and driver categories range from juniors and ladies to old-timers over age 64. The final judging, the Currier & Ives class, is the one that brings out the gleaming antiques and passengers swathed in Victorian cloaks and greatcoats, bonnets and muffs and stovepipe hats. These unusual events are held regularly during the winter and are listed in local newspapers, but they are never widely promoted outside the immediate area since they are usually held on a local farmer's land with no facilities for large crowds of spectators. One regular event open to the public is sponsored by the Newtown Parks and Recreation Department in mid-February. Rallies, like sleigh rides, are subject to the whims of the weather.

Morris is not the only person who offers sleigh rides (see Norfolk, page 216), but he's a safe driver to aim for since you could spend a happy winter weekend in this area even if there's a snow drought.

The Harrison Inn itself is an excellent choice for lodging. It's an unusual building for this locale, a contemporary complex of rough-hewn wood with super-modern rooms, but the welcome is no less warm for its modern architecture. There are wide stone fireplaces aglow downstairs, a billiards room, a sauna and whirlpools for the guests, a busy bar, a lavish Sunday brunch and—adjoining the inn—a multilevel shopping complex where you can while away the hours without ever having to go outdoors.

If Colonial is more your style, drive north on US 6 to Woodbury, a typical New England town of white-steepled churches and a Main Street lined with antiques shops. Curtis Inn here is the oldest hostelry in the state. It's an unpretentious place, moderately priced, where you can sleep in a canopy bed and dine in authentic Early American atmosphere.

Another Colonial-style inn in one of prettiest New England villages in this or any other state is the Mayflower Inn in Washington. Here is a picture-perfect green, dominated by the tall-spired Congregational church and surrounded with magnificent white clapboard homes set off with dark shutters. This is a very private town—old wealth, old homes, two prestigious prep schools—but it still offers pleasures for visitors. The Hickory Stick Bookstore makes for perfect browsing on a cold winter's day; the Gunn Historical Museum is small but packed with interesting mementos of the past; and the Washington Art Association is an attractive gallery with an interesting schedule of shows.

A more unusual place to visit is the American Indian Archaeological Institute, dedicated to showing the life of the first inhabitants of the northeastern woodlands. The exhibits include a reconstructed long-house, a mammoth mastodon, and other artifacts portraying 12,000 years of Indian history. In addition to the baskets and crafts on display, there are special collector's pieces for sale in the museum shop.

The Mayflower Inn is a handsome building set on 32 acres, but it has changed owners and chefs in the past couple of years so it's difficult to know how you'll find it at the present.

Any one of these inns is convenient to the Woodbury Ski and Racquet Club, where you can make your own tracks in the snow. This small, uncrowded slope is an ideal place for learning or practicing downhill skiing, and the 50-mile network of cross-country trails offers challenge for every level of skill. Lessons and rentals are available for both kinds of skiers. Woodbury makes its own snow for downhillers, but should the weather prove totally uncooperative, there are indoor tennis and paddle tennis facilities.

A mix of a morning of antiquing, a ride through the snow, an afternoon in Washington, and a Sunday out-of-doors makes for a near-perfect winter weekend recipe. And if you can manage to end things with a visit to an old-time sleigh rally, you'll have Currier & Ives icing for dessert.

Southbury Area Code: 203

DRIVING DIRECTIONS Hutchinson River Parkway to I-684 north to exit 9E, I-84 east to exit 15, US 6 north to Southbury. Follow Route 6 north to Woodbury, then 47 northwest to Washington.

Total distance: about 100 miles.

ACCOMMODATIONS Ask about weekend and winter packages ● *Harrison Inn,* Village Green, Heritage Village, Southbury, 264–8200, $$$–$$$$ ● *Curtis Inn,* Main Street, Woodbury, 263–2101, $–$$ CP; dinner, $$–$$$ ● *Mayflower Inn,* Route 47, Washington, 868–0515, $$–$$$ CP; dinner, $$–$$$.

DINING All of the above, plus: ● *The Bistro,* 107 Main Street North, Woodbury, 263–0466, continental café, $$–$$$ ● *Portofino,* 10 Sherman Hill Road, Woodbury, 263–2371, northern Italian, $$ ● *Jonathan's,* Route 47, Washington Depot, 868–0509, American menu, $$; also a good bet for brunch.

SIGHTSEEING For a sleigh rides listing and up-to-date information about rallies, write Connecticut Department of Economic Development, 210 Washington Street, CT 06106, or call toll-free, (800) 243–1685 ● *Sleigh Rides:* Write or phone Glen Morris, Poverty Road, Southbury, CT 06106, 264–6196, for reservations, current rates, and driving directions to stables ● *Newtown Sleigh Rally,* Newtown Parks and Recreation Department, phone 426–8131 for dates ● *Woodbury*

Ski and Racquet Club, Route 47 north of town, Woodbury, 263–2203. Phone for current rates • *American Indian Archaeological Institute,* off Route 199, Washington, 868–0518. Hours: Monday to Saturday 10 A.M. to 4:30 P.M.; Sunday noon to 4:30 P.M. Adults, $2, children $1 • *Gunn Historical Museum,* on the green (Route 47), Washington, 868–7756. Hours: Tuesday, Thursday, 1 to 4 P.M.; Saturday noon to 3 P.M. Free.

FOR FURTHER INFORMATION Litchfield Hills Travel Council, Box 1776, Marbledale CT 06777, 868–2214.

Newport: Snug Harbor in the Off Season

The winter waves were whipping against the cliff. A couple, knitted hats pulled down against the wind, arms wound around each other's ski parkas, were standing on the Cliff Walk, mesmerized by the sight.

Newport, Rhode Island, summer haven for the socialite, the sailor, and the sightseer, has a fascination of its own in the winter's chill. The Ocean Drive looking out to sea is even more spectacular, the Cliff Walk along the bluffs more dramatic, and the harbor takes on a special serenity in its unaccustomed stillness.

The boats and crowds may have taken cover until spring, but with the fabled mansions still receiving visitors, the sights still worth seeing, and dozens of shops and restaurants still open for business, Newport remains a snug harbor for a weekend by the sea. To make things even nicer, rates at the inns go way down in winter.

Top choice for a romantic outlook is the Inn at Castle Hill on Ocean Drive. The old Victorian House with huge rooms has an unmatched view of rocky coast and a crackling fire downstairs to ward off winter chills. The Inntowne Inn, an elegant Colonial on a block of equally stylish renovations, lacks a view but offers charming decor and a fine afternoon tea. Two other resort standards in town are the Sheraton Islander Inn (with indoor pool), a five-minute drive away on Goat Island, and the Treadway Inn in the middle of the action at the wharf area.

There are also many appealing guest houses in Newport's historic district. Two of the nicest are tucked away on quiet Clarke Street, just a block from all the action in town. Melville House is a cozy and welcoming 1750 Colonial with antiques in the living room, fresh fruit and flowers in the snug bedrooms upstairs. Right next door, the Admiral Farragut House is a real charmer, filled with handmade Shaker furniture and painted chests, and with delightful original murals in the halls and whimsical surprises like drawings in the closets.

The latter is owned by the Admiral Benbow, another choice lodging, an elegant and antiques-filled 1855 home with spacious bedrooms.

To get a sense of the city, begin by taking the well-marked 10-mile Ocean Drive past all the mansions and out along the bluffs looking out to sea. If the weather is kind, stop off along Bellevue Avenue and follow some of the 3½-mile Cliff Walk, a path along the bluffs giving you views of lawns and mansions on one side and an eagle's-eye ocean view on the other.

To warm up you can take a tour of the mansions. If you think we had no royalty in this country, you may well change your mind when you see the massive scale, the marble floors, chandeliers, the ballrooms, and priceless brocades of these summer "cottages" of America's nineteenth-century industrial magnates, some with as many as 70 rooms. Three of the homes are open weekends during the winter: Marble House, designed by Richard Morris Hunt for William K. Vanderbilt and named for the many kinds of colors of marble used in its construction and decoration; the Elms, a summer residence of Philadelphia coal magnate Edward Berwind, modeled after the Château d'Asnieres near Paris; and Château-sur-Mer, one of the most lavish examples of Victorian architecture in America and the site of Newport's first French ballroom. Less opulent but also interesting is Hunter House, a mansion that once served as headquarters for the French naval forces during the Revolution. It is open in winter by appointment. Also open are the Newport Historical Society, the Newport Art Museum, and two historic homes: the Edward King House and the Old Colony House.

Back in town everything centers around the harbor. Sailboats and yachts have replaced the clipper ships that once dropped anchor here with treasures from around the world. The first American Navy was established in Newport in 1775 to protect against the British H.M.S. *Rose*. As a result the town was burned by the British not only during the Revolutionary War but again during the War of 1812.

Newport kept her Navy ties and was home to a large fleet of ships up until 1973. It was after the Navy destroyers moved out that the yachts and America's Cuppers moved in, and shops began to spring up along the restored wharf areas. The two principal centers are Bowen's and Bannister's wharves right on the waterfront and the Brick Market Place across the way.

Along the wharves, in old restored warehouses and new structures with Colonial-modern lines, you'll find shops with wares from around the world, original gold and silver jewelry designs, handcrafted leather goods, children's clothing and toys, and a candy store noted for its homemade fudge.

The Brick Market Place is a cobbled maze of condominiums and 30 shops with a wide variety of goods—crafts and art, Irish fabrics and hand-knits, and Scandinavian imports, to name a few.

Nostalgia Factory contains every kind of collectible that has to do with old advertising, from movie posters to Coca-Cola signs as well as old political campaign buttons and early postcards. At Kitchen Pot Pourri you'll find rack upon rack of utensils and gourmet cookbooks and tea balls in the shapes of spoons, bells, and miniature teapots. Fortify yourself for more shopping here with a hot cup of the house blend or special-of-the-day coffee, or a choice of teas and pastries.

If antiquing is your goal, you'll find shops on the lower Thames, on parallel Spring Street, and on many of the side streets tucked in between. Note that Newport shop hours can be irregular in the off season, but most are open sometime over the weekend. If you miss one or two, there are plenty to take their place.

On Sunday you can sample some of the city's other numerous and varied attractions. Drive or walk the narrow streets near the town center, where scores of seventeenth-century Colonial homes have been lovingly restored, painted rainbow hues, and occupied by proud residents. Stop at the lovely Colonial-style Touro Synagogue, the nation's oldest, and the Trinity Church designed by Christopher Wren. The Tennis Hall of Fame on Bellevue Avenue offers aficionados a look at early racquets and quaint costumes. Come back in summer and you can play on their grass courts by the hour or have a round of croquet on the lawn. There are changing exhibits at the Newport Art Museum, housed in a fine 1862 building designed by Richard Morris Hunt, and Belcourt Castle, an 1891 Hunt mansion designed in the style of Versailles, is another look at the lavish world of yesterday. Hammersmith Farm, the girlhood home of Jacqueline Kennedy Onassis, is a fascinating house filled with Kennedy memories. Off season, it is open weekends only in March and November; fit it in if you can.

There are more than enough things to do in Newport. But who could blame you if you were to decide to forget them all and just return to the Cliff Walk to memorize that mesmerizing vista of the wintry sea?

Newport Area Code: 401

DRIVING DIRECTIONS Take I-95 east to exit 3 in Rhode Island, then Route 138 east to Newport.

Total distance: about 185 miles.

PUBLIC TRANSPORTATION   Amtrak to Providence or Boston; Bonanza Bus service from Providence and from Boston's Logan Airport. Much of the town is walkable.

ACCOMMODATIONS   Rates listed are for high season weekends; all are less in winter, some even less on weekdays. Call for current offerings ● *Inn at Castle Hill,* Ocean Drive, 849–3800, $$$–$$$$$ CP ● *Inntowne,* 6 Mary Street, 846–9200, $$$–$$$$ ● *Sheraton Islander Inn,* Goat Island, 849–2600, $$$$–$$$$$ ● *Treadway Inn,* America's Cup Avenue, 847–9000, $$$$–$$$$$ ● *Mill Street Inn,* 75 Mill Street, 849–9500, modern suites in a restored mill, $$$$–$$$$$ CP ● *Melville House,* 39 Clarke Street, 847–1811, $$–$$$ CP (closed January and February) ● *Admiral Farragut Inn,* 31 Clarke Street, 849–0006, $$–$$$ CP ● *Admiral Benbow Inn,* 93 Pelham Street, 846–4256, $$–$$$ CP ● Some other appealing small guest houses: *Brinley Victorian,* 23 Brinley Street, warm and cheerful, $$–$$$ CP; *The Pilgrim House,* 123 Spring Street, 846–0040, friendly hosts and a fine harbor view from the deck, $$$ CP ● *Wayside,* Bellevue Avenue, 847–0302, is a different lodging, an imposing home on mansion row, large on space, small on warmth, but fairly priced, $$–$$$ CP. (Two more suggestions if you come back in season: *Cliffside Inn,* 2 Seaview Avenue, 847–1811, breezy Victorian near the beach and the Cliff Walk, $$$ CP; *Queen Anne Inn,* 16 Clarke Street, 846–5676, pleasant Victorian and a good value, $–$$ CP.) ● For a listing of smaller inns, write to *Guest House Association of Newport,* PO Box 981, Newport, RI 02840, 846–5444. Also see Bed-and-Breakfast registries on pages x–xii.

DINING   *La Petite Auberge,* 19 Charles Street, 849–6669, renowned French chef, $$–$$$ ● *Le Bistro,* 250 Thames Street, 849–7778, French café, one flight up, $$–$$$ ● *Clark Cooke House,* Bannister's Wharf, 849–2900, elegant eighteenth-century dining room, $$–$$$ ● *Black Pearl,* Bannister's Wharf, 846–3000, converted wharf warehouse, $–$$$ ● *White Horse Tavern,* Marlborough and Farewell streets, 849–3600, nation's oldest continuously operating tavern, the place to try Rhode Island jonnycakes, $$–$$$ ● *Gatsby's,* in the Bay Club, America's Cup Avenue and Thames Street, 849–9480, fun atmosphere, $$ ● For light and reasonable fare: Both the Black Pearl and Clark Cooke have café adjuncts; also try *Brick Alley Pub,* 140 Thames; *Cobblestone Restaurant,* 206 Thames; *Rhumbline,* 62 Bridge Street, and *The Ark,* 348 Thames. For brunch with a smashing view, *The Inn at Castle Hill* can't be beat.

SIGHTSEEING *Newport Mansions,* Preservation Society of Newport Country, 118 Mill Street, 847–1000. Hours for Marble House, the Elms, Château-sur-Mer: November to March, Saturday and Sunday 10 A.M. to 4 P.M. Hunter House open by appointment only. Other mansions open after April 1, 10 A.M. to 5 P.M.; later in summer. $4 to $4.50 at each house. Three houses: adults, $10; children, $4 ● *International Tennis Hall of Fame and Tennis Museum,* Newport Casino, Bellevue Avenue, 849–3990. Hours: November to April, daily 11 A.M. to 4 P.M.; rest of year, daily 10 A.M. to 5 P.M. Adults, $4; children 6–12, $2; families, $10 ● *Touro Synagogue,* 72 Touro Street, 847–4794. Hours: Sunday only through spring, 2 P.M. to 4 P.M. Rest of year, daily except Saturday, 10 A.M. to 5 P.M., 6 P.M. on Sunday. Free ● *Trinity Church,* Church and Spring streets, 846–0660. By appointment except in summer. Free ● *Newport Art Museum,* 76 Bellevue Avenue, 847–0179. Hours: Tuesday to Saturday 10 A.M. to 5 P.M.; Sunday from 1 P.M. Adults, $2; under 18 free; free to all on Friday ● *Belcourt Castle,* Bellevue Avenue, 846–0669. Hours: late November to early January, mid-February through March, 10 A.M. to 5 P.M.; April to mid-June and September to November, to 5 P.M.; mid-June to mid-September, daily 9 A.M. to 5 P.M.; weekends only in March. Adults, $4.50; children 6–12, $1.50; family, $10 ● *Hammersmith Farm,* Ocean Drive, 846–0420. Hours: daily April to mid-November, weekends March and November, 10 A.M. to 5 P.M.; to 7 P.M. in summer. Adults, $4.50; children 6–12, $1.50.

FOR FURTHER INFORMATION Contact the Newport Convention and Visitors' Bureau, PO Box 237, Newport, RI 02840, 847–1600.

Tapping the Maples in Stamford

The calendar says winter, but the crackling fires and the boiling syrup kettles tell you not for long. Maple-sugaring is the first sure sign we've made it through another winter, and it's a perfect reason for an early March Connecticut weekend not too far from home.

Though maple-sugaring is largely associated with the farms of Vermont, New Hampshire, and upstate New York, a pleasant sampling is available just 40 miles away at the Stamford Museum and Nature Center. The museum puts up its sugar shed as soon as the sap starts to rise and taps the sugar maple trees that dot its 100-acre grounds.

You'll spy the collection buckets on the trees as soon as you arrive, but you may be surprised to see that the sap running is as thin and clear as water. The filled buckets are taken to the shed, where the sap is emptied into an evaporator to simmer slowly over a wood fire until it thickens into golden, gooey delicious syrup. Staff members tending the fire are generous with free tastes and will allow you to chop a log or two for the fire if the outdoor spirit moves you.

Maple-sugaring is a time-honored occupation, and you'll also see demonstrations of how the Indians did it—in a hollowed tree trunk using heat from stones that had been baked in the fire—as well as the way the Colonists used to boil down their syrup in giant black kettles.

Maple-sugaring usually takes place the first two or three weekends in March, but the museum warns visitors to call ahead to be sure the sap is running and the weather cooperating before you plan to come. Since you are only an hour or so from New York, if the stars are shining Friday night you can also take advantage of the weekly open house at the Stamford Museum Observatory from 8 to 10 P.M. It's exciting to look through a professional telescope and discover that the stars are really round and that you can clearly see the rings around Saturn.

Stamford's emergence as a corporate headquarters center has created a boon for weekenders. The many new hotels that have gone up to serve visitors to more than 50 top corporations in the area are looking for customers when the business week is over, and all offer good value weekend packages, some as much as half off regular rates.

The hotels are quite cosmopolitan for a small town. My favorite is the new Sheraton, with a lobby as light and airy as a greenhouse and one of the best restaurants in town, Magnificent J's, named for the racing boat whose models adorn the spiffy nautical interior.

The Inn at Mill River is positively posh, and the Hyatt on the Greenwich-Stamford border has a four-story atrium and an indoor garden. The Marriott, the city's biggest, has a lively disco and revolving rooftop restaurant, and like its near-neighbor, the Holiday Inn Crown Plaza, is within walking distance of Stamford's Town Center, the ultimate in shopping centers. Not only will you find Macy's, Saks Fifth Avenue, and J.C. Penney stores here, but a wealth of upscale boutiques, from Williams Sonoma to Ralph Lauren, Brooks Brothers to Brookstone, all under one convenient roof.

If you prefer inn ambience, you best bet is the Homestead Inn in Greenwich, an elegantly refurbished Colonial home.

Come Saturday your first stop should be United Housewrecking Company, off exit 9 on the Connecticut Turnpike. It's hard to imagine anyone who wouldn't have fun at this one-of-a-kind emporium. As the name suggests the company began by selling off the contents of homes and buildings that had been torn down. It was a place where the locals came to browse outdoors among surplus phone booths, gasoline pumps, soda fountains, and church pews, or to search for bargains in secondhand storm windows, doors, fireplace tools, or furniture.

When it was discovered by decorators and out-of-town shoppers, the variety of wares grew even wackier to meet the new demands, and the company moved to new quarters, now mostly indoors. Today you might find a canopied wicker beach chair on wheels for $350 or an old New York City subway sign for $10. The surprises are part of the fun.

One of United Housewrecking's prime attractions is the possibility of finding old things to convert into nostalgic new ones. Some possibilities are ship's wheels, portholes, and hatch covers for tabletops; old-fashioned sewing machine heads for lamps; and wooden type cases whose many small compartments are ideal for showing off knickknacks and collections. Since the tourists started coming, many new versions of these old favorites are available and there are dozens of sizes and shapes of new wrought-iron pieces.

The scene changes dramatically when you drive into downtown Stamford, where you'll note all manner of futuristic architecture in the apartments, office buildings, corporate headquarters, and department stores that have transformed the city in recent years. The sloped sides of Landmark Plaza, the round glass buildings of St. Johns Towers, and the inverted pyramid of the GTE headquarters are some of the many unusual designs. Note that there is an outpost of the Whitney Museum in the Champion Paper headquarters.

One of the city's longtime architectural attractions is the First Presbyterian Church, a few blocks north of downtown on Bedford Street. Known as the Fish Church for its shingled contemporary shape, the building has extraordinary windows made of more than 20,000 pieces of inch-thick colored glass imported from Chartres, France. The glass is set in an abstract depiction of the Crucifixion and the Resurrection, and the panes are a glorious sight as the jewel-hued light varies with changes in the sun and clouds outside.

Continue north straight up Bedford Street until it becomes High Ridge Road, and you are on your way to the Stamford Museum. In addition to watching the maple-sugaring, you'll be able to see a reconstruction on the museum grounds of an old-fashioned Connecticut farm.

One of the last remaining eighteenth-century barns in the state was rescued, brought down from Cheshire, Connecticut, plank by weathered plank, and painstakingly reassembled here as the centerpiece of a model farm. Half a dozen kinds of seventeenth- and eighteenth-century fencing have been re-created by hand to enclose the fields, and an exhibit in a second barn shows how the early farmer accomplished so much with so little in the way of tools. The entire crop cycle is depicted, from plowing, harrowing, and sowing to cultivating, harvesting, and preserving, with displays of the authentic pre-machine-age implements that were used for each task.

Maple-sugaring is just one of the many seasonal demonstrations of farm activities here, such as apple cidering, ice-harvesting, and sheep shearing. All year round you'll see a barnyard full of the tamest and most appealing farm animals to be found anywhere outside of Mother Goose. They are longtime residents of the museum's Hecksher Farm for Children, which has been incorporated into the new display.

There is also a small zoo of native Connecticut wildlife, a pond inhabited by dozens of varieties of ducks and geese, miles of nature trails, and an imposing Tudor mansion up the hill, once the home of retail magnate Henri Bendel and now housing nature and art exhibits.

In the evening, you may find opera, ballet, concerts, or theater at the Stamford Center for the Arts and the Palace Theater, both on Atlantic Street.

Greenwich provides a variety of Sunday diversions for visitors. On pleasant days its Audubon Center offers 485 acres of beautiful woodland with many walking trails. The Bruce Museum has fine and decorative arts, as well as natural science and history exhibits and a salt-water aquarium. More unusual is the U.S. Tobacco Company Museum, which traces the history of tobacco on five continents in a collection of pipes, snuffboxes, and other tobacco-related artifacts. There are also a few cigar store Indians and advertising graphics around for nostalgia buffs.

Bush-Holley House in Cos Cob, home of the Greenwich Historical Society, traces another kind of history. It is a seventeenth-century saltbox home restored and authentically furnished, with impressive Jacobean fireplaces, as well as fine paneling and many rare early furniture pieces.

Greenwich, incidentally, is one of those towns like Southampton and Newport where you can pass a pleasant hour just driving and gazing wistfully at the mansions. Northbound roads like Lake Avenue,

North Street, and Round Hill Road and their environs offer ample opportunities for scenery- and estate-watching.

Finally, with or without the kids, you can detour on the way home to Rye, New York, for the Museum of Cartoon Art. It's crammed with original cartoon drawings from "The Yellow Kid," the first color comic, to "Peanuts." Though it may date you to admit that you remember, you can find some of the classic old-timers like "Buster Brown," "Oaky Doakes," and "The Katzenjammer Kids." Comic book heroes like Superman, Dr. Strange, and Captain Marvel are also part of the collection, along with political cartoons and satiric drawings, and animation strips.

There are continuous showings of old cartoons. Depending on what is being shown on the day you come, you may see some of the early silents, the first Disneys, vintage "Popeye" and "Betty Boop," the beginning of "Tom and Jerry" back in 1931, and the original "Tweetie Pie" from 1947.

It was interesting to see that grown-ups seem to outnumber the kids at the cartoon exhibits.

Connecticut Area Code: 203

DRIVING DIRECTIONS Take I-95, the New England Thruway, which becomes the Connecticut Turnpike. Greenwich exits are 3 to 5. Stamford exits are 6 to 9, just beyond. If you are going directly to the Stamford Museum, take the Hutchinson River Parkway to the Merritt Parkway, turn left at exit 35 (High Ridge Road), and proceed 1¼ miles. The museum is on the left.

Total distance: 40 miles.

ACCOMMODATIONS Rates listed are for weekdays; weekends are much less, but because packages change, are difficult to list. Ask for current packages at all ● *Sheraton Stamford,* First Stamford Place, Stamford, 967–2222, $$$$–$$$$$ ● *Inn at Mill River,* 26 Mill River Street, 325–1900, $$$$$ ● *Hyatt Regency,* 1800 East Putnam Avenue (Route 1), Old Greenwich (on the Stamford–Old Greenwich line), 323–6900, $$$$–$$$$$ ● *The Westin Hotel,* 2701 Summer Street, Stamford, 359–1300 (located between downtown and the museum), $$$$–$$$$$ ● *Marriott Hotel,* 2 Stamford Plaza (off exit 7), Stamford, 357–9555, indoor pool and game and exercise room, $$$$–$$$$$, weekend packages often available ● *Holiday Inn Crown Plaza,* 700 Main Street, Stamford, 358–8400, $$$$ ● *Homestead Inn,* 420 Field Point Road (off I-95, exit 3), Greenwich, 869–7500, $$$–$$$$.

DINING *Magnificent J's,* Sheraton Stamford (see above), grill specialities and seafood, excellent, $$–$$$ ● *Inn at Mill River* (see above), French, elegant, divided opinions—some say superb, others say overpriced, $$$–$$$$ ● *Le Mistral,* 781 Harbor Place, Stamford, 359–1890, contemporary French, $$$ ● *La Bretagne,* 2010 N. Main Street, Stamford, 324–9539, French, $$$ ● *Bourbon Street,* 20 Summer Street at the corner of Main Street, 356–1467, casual Creole and Cajun, $$ ● *Brock's,* High Ridge Road at Merritt Parkway exit 35, Stamford, 357–1679, steaks, burgers, terrific salad bar, $–$$ ● *Pellici's,* 98 Stillwater Avenue, Stamford, 323–2542, no atmosphere but reasonable and good Italian home cooking, $–$$ ● *Homestead Inn* (see above), $$$–$$$$ ● *Boodles,* 21 Field Point Road, Greenwich, 661–3553, varied menu, hanging plants, and whatnots, $$ ● *Greenstreet,* 253 Greenwich Avenue, Greenwich, 461–4459, varied menu, another "in" local spot, $$–$$$ ● *Tapestries,* 554 Old Post Road, Greenwich, 629–9204, nice nouvelle cuisine, $$$ ● *Jean Louis,* 61 Lewis Street, Greenwich, 622–8450, super French, super expensive, $$$$.

SIGHTSEEING *Stamford Museum and Nature Center,* 39 Scofieldtown Road, 322–1646. Hours: Monday to Saturday 9 A.M. to 5 P.M.; Sunday and holidays, 1 P.M. to 5 P.M. Admission for nonresidents: adults, $3; children and senior citizens, $2; admission not to exceed $10 per car. Observatory night: adults, $1.50; children, $.75 ● *United Housewrecking Company,* 535 Hope Street, Stamford (Connecticut Turnpike exit 9), 348–5371. Hours: Monday to Saturday 9:30 A.M. to 5:30 P.M. ● *First Presbyterian Church,* 1101 Bedford Street, Stamford, 324–9522. Hours: Monday to Saturday, 9 A.M. to 5 P.M., Sunday to 1 P.M. Donation ● *Whitney Museum of American Art,* 1 Champion Plaza, Stamford, 358–7630. Hours: Tuesday to Saturday 11 A.M. to 5 P.M. Free ● *Greenwich Audubon Center,* 613 Riversville Road, 869–5272. Hours: Tuesday to Sunday 9 A.M. to 5 P.M. Adults, $1; children, $.50 ● *Bruce Museum,* Museum Drive, Greenwich, 869–0376. Hours: Tuesday to Saturday 10 A.M. to 5 P.M.; Sunday 2 P.M. to 5 P.M. Adults, $2; children, $1 ● *Bush Holley House,* Strickland Road, Cos Cob, 869–6899. Hours: Tuesday to Saturday noon to 4 P.M.; Sunday 2 P.M. to 4 P.M. Adults, $2; children 12–16, $1; children under 12, $.50 ● *U.S. Tobacco Company Museum,* 96 West Putnam Avenue, Greenwich, 869–5531. Hours: Tuesday to Friday noon to 4:30 P.M., Sunday to 5 P.M. Free ● *Museum of Cartoon Art,* Comly Avenue, Rye, New York, (914) 939–0234. Hours: Tuesday to Friday 10 A.M. to 4 P.M.; Sunday 1 P.M. to 5 P.M. Adults, $1.50; children 12–18, $1; children under 12, $.75.

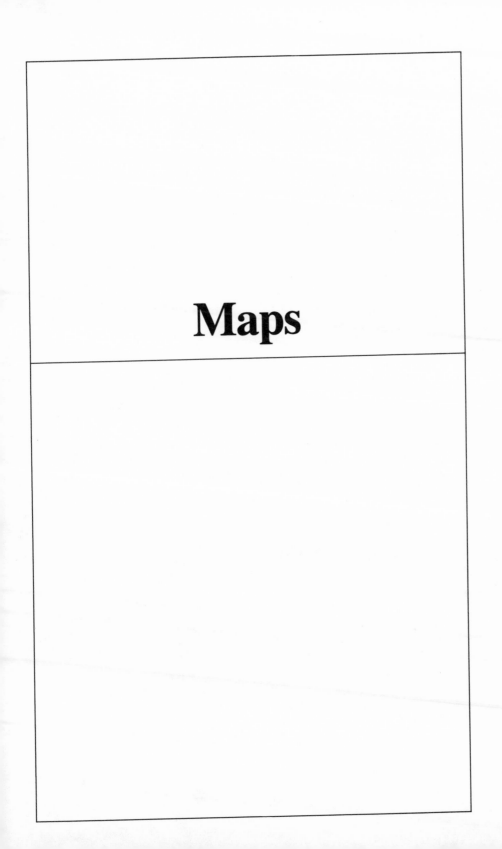

Maps

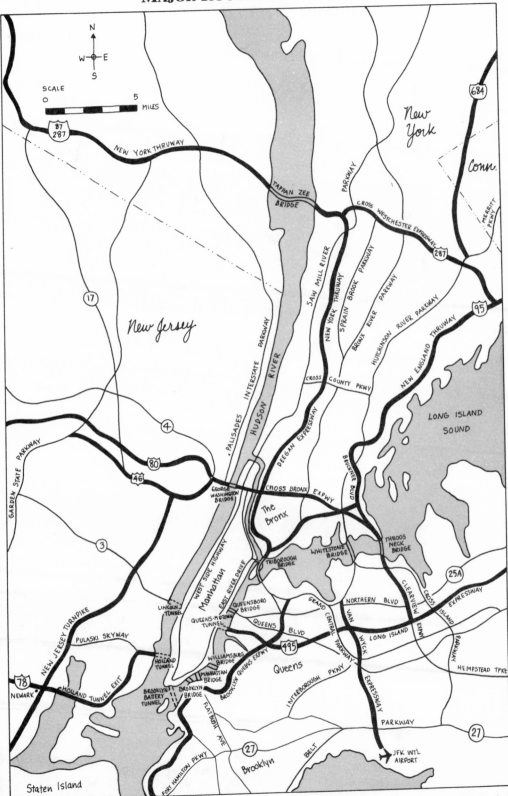

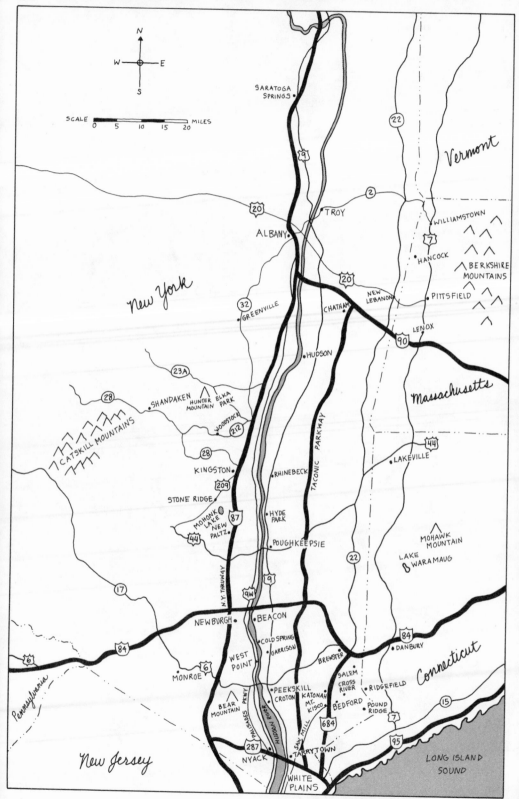

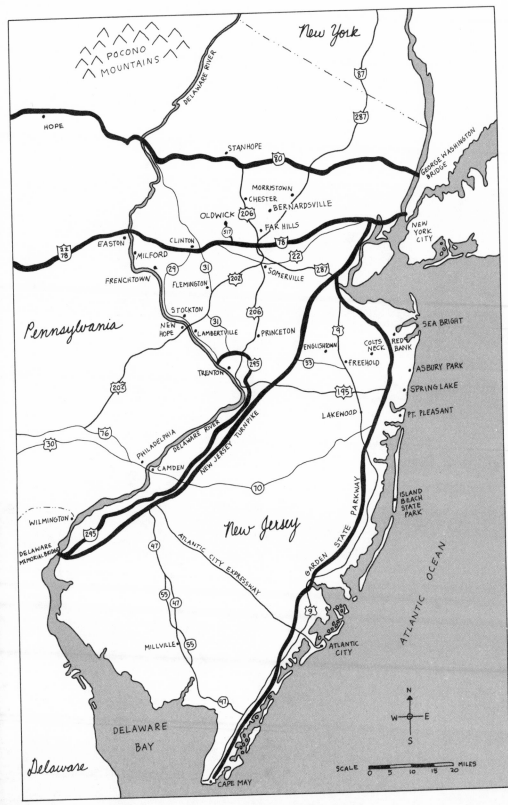

POCONO MOUNTAINS

New York

DELAWARE RIVER

HOPE

STANHOPE

80

87

287

GEORGE WASHINGTON BRIDGE

MORRISTOWN

CHESTER

BERNARDSVILLE

OLDWICK

206

FAR HILLS

NEW YORK CITY

EASTON

CLINTON

22
78

517

MILFORD

78

22

FRENCHTOWN

29

31

FLEMINGTON

202

SOMERVILLE

287

STOCKTON

206

Pennsylvania

31

NEW HOPE

LAMBERTVILLE

PRINCETON

9

ENGLISHTOWN

COLTS NECK

SEA BRIGHT

RED BANK

TRENTON

295

33

FREEHOLD

ASBURY PARK

SPRING LAKE

195

PT. PLEASANT

LAKEWOOD

202

76

DELAWARE RIVER

Philadelphia

30

NEW JERSEY TURNPIKE

CAMDEN

10

ISLAND BEACH STATE PARK

New Jersey

WILMINGTON

295

GARDEN STATE PARKWAY

ATLANTIC OCEAN

DELAWARE MEMORIAL BRIDGE

47

ATLANTIC CITY EXPRESSWAY

9

55

47

ATLANTIC CITY

MILLVILLE

55

DELAWARE BAY

N
W E
S

47

Delaware

SCALE
0 5 10 15 20 MILES

CAPE MAY

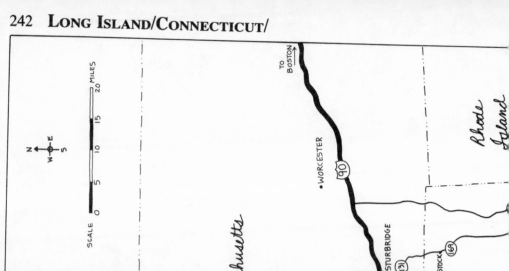

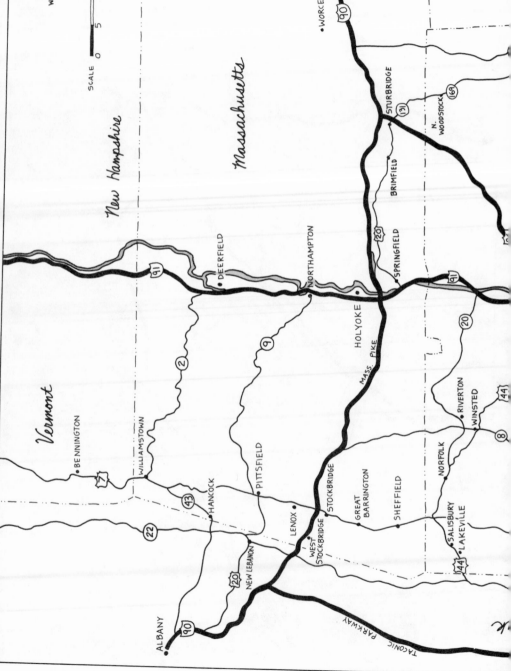

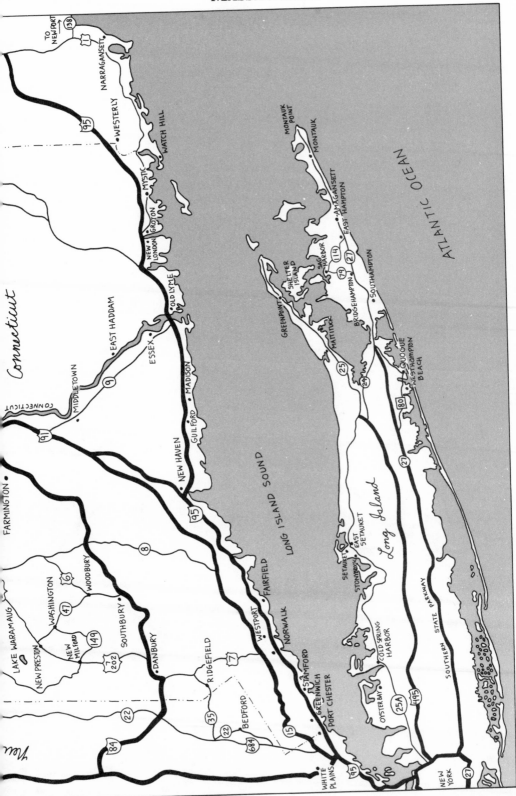

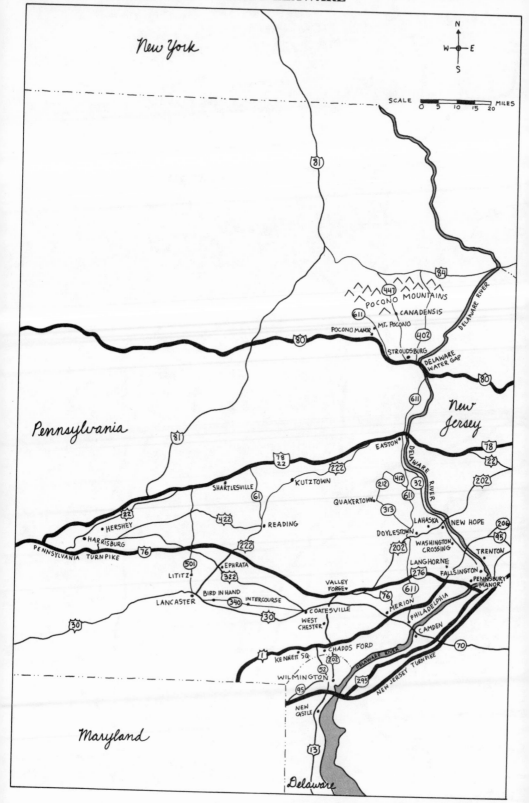

General Index

Category Index

Crafts and Fairs

Cultural Events

Historic Sites

Museums and Galleries

Nature

Shopping